PEACE MOVEMENTS IN ISLAM

PEACE MOVEMENTS IN ISLAM

History, Religion, and Politics

Edited by
Juan Cole

I.B. TAURIS
LONDON · NEW YORK · OXFORD · NEW DELHI · SYDNEY

I.B. TAURIS
Bloomsbury Publishing Plc
50 Bedford Square, London, WC1B 3DP, UK
1385 Broadway, New York, NY 10018, USA
29 Earlsfort Terrace, Dublin 2, Ireland

BLOOMSBURY, I.B. TAURIS and the I.B. Tauris logo are trademarks
of Bloomsbury Publishing Plc

First published in Great Britain 2022

Cover design by Charlotte Daniels
Cover image: *Dancing Dervishes*, Folio from a Divan of Hafiz ca. 1480.
Courtesy Metropolitan Museum of Art, Rogers Fund, 1917.

ISBN: HB: 978-0-7556-4317-2
          PB: 978-0-7556-4318-9
          ePDF: 978-0-7556-4319-6
          eBook: 978-0-7556-4320-2

Typeset by Integra Software Services Pvt. Ltd.
Printed and bound in Great Britain

To find out more about our authors and books visit www.bloomsbury.com
and sign up for our newsletters.

CONTENTS

Acknowledgments vii

Introduction *Juan Cole* 1

1 Between Compassion and Justice: Locating an Islamic Definition of Peace *A. Rashied Omar* 13

2 The Qur'an on Doing Good to Enemies *Juan Cole* 23

3 A Different Kind of Striving: Jihad as Peacemaking *Asma Afsaruddin* 47

4 Internal Peace versus Being in Society: Sufi Dilemmas *Alexander D. Knysh* 63

5 Principled Pacifism in Islamic West Africa *Rudolph Ware* 75

6 Rashid Rida and the 1919 Paris Peace Conference *Elizabeth F. Thompson* 89

7 Paradise Bound: Righteous Others in the Writings of Rashid Rida *Mohammad Hassan Khalil* 103

8 Abdul Ghaffar Khan: An Islamic Gandhi *James L. Rowell* 117

9 Islam and Peace: A Muslim Fundamentalist Perspective *Sherman A. Jackson* 133

10 Women, Religion, and Peace Leadership in Bosnia and Herzegovina   *Zilka Spahić Šiljak* 153

11 Muslim American Activism in the Age of Trump   *Grace Yukich* 171

Contributors 200
Subject Index 203

ACKNOWLEDGMENTS

The bulk of this book originated in two conferences of the Islamic Peace Studies Initiative supported by the Enterprise Fund of the International Institute at the University of Michigan and hosted by the Center for Middle Eastern and North African Studies. The Initiative was co-directed by Samer Ali and Juan Cole. The directors are grateful to the International Institute and Directors Pauline Jones and Mary Gallagher for this support. Thanks to Xiaoyue Li for help in formatting the manuscript.

I am grateful to Rory Gormley, my editor at Bloomsbury Academic, for his essential help in bringing this book to light.

For permission to reprint here the article of Zilka Spahić Šiljak, we are grateful to the author and to the Ecumenical Women's Initiative in Croatia. The chapter by James Rowell appears here by permission of the author and of Taylor and Francis. The work of Grace B. Yukich appears here by permission of the author and of Oxford University Press. Full bibliographical details are given with the chapters.

INTRODUCTION

Juan Cole

The chapters in this book treat themes in peace studies as they intersect with Islam and Muslim history. While some scholars have written on Islamic peace studies, this vast and exciting field has so far been all too little worked. Muslim thinkers on the nature of peace have contributed to many modern movements, including Sufism in West Africa, the Gandhist coalition in colonial India, anti-Apartheid activism in South Africa, and the 2011 youth revolts of the Arab Spring. European and North American journalists and academics have understandably given great attention to the dramatic events of September 11, the attacks on Paris in 2015, the brief ISIL mini-state in the Fertile Crescent, and movements such as the Taliban and Boko Haram. Too much concentration on such movements, however, has led to an imbalance in the field and a relentless focus on the intersection of Islam and violence. Some observers, moreover, have attributed small violent movements to some sort of Islamic essence, painting the whole religion with the brush of extremism. Further inexcusable is the Orientalist implicit contrast of Christians and Muslims in which the violence of the former is seen as contingent while the violence of the latter is configured as intrinsic to who they are. Religions do not have essences. They are sets of practices, traditions, ideas, and experiences, and are as diverse as their adherents. Just as it is not true that Islam is "a religion of peace" (at least it is no more true of Islam than any other religion), and it is not true that "Islam" means "peace" (it means something like "acceptance of the oneness of God"), it is also not true that Islam is a religion of violence. Along with all the other things Muslims do, they engage in diplomacy, peacemaking, nonviolent social action, and peaceful community building. The essays in this book are intended to explore this other, more eirenic dimension of the rich history of Islam, the religion of a fifth of humankind.

Peace Studies as a field has become well-established in academia. Over 150 colleges and universities in the United States offer courses in the area of Peace Studies, conceived broadly as everything from political philosophy to security studies and practical conflict resolution. Peace Studies thus straddles the humanities and social sciences as an analytical discipline on the one hand, and the policy world on the other. Refereed academic journals in the field include

The International Journal for Peace Studies housed at George Mason University and Sage's *The Journal of Peace Research*, among others. The religious dimension of peace studies has bulked large, with 46 percent of programs being in church-related colleges.[1] While Christian peace studies is a large sub-field, the scholarly literature on peace with regard to Islam is much smaller. This book is among a handful of works that seek to redress this imbalance.[2] Peace initiatives and peace movements are just as important (if not more so) as violent ones in human history, even if they are less dramatic. In modern times, it has been shown that peaceful social movements are twice as likely to achieve their objectives as violent ones.[3]

The history of the way Christian and European-heritage writers have put Islam and Muslims under the sign of violence is too long and complex to review here. It might be sufficient to note that a Google ngram search for "militant Islam" in American English (a count of the occurrences of the phrase in Google Books) shoots up from the late 1970s to a Himalayan peak in contemporary times. Despite the plentiful peaceful Muslim movements, some of which are discussed in this book, a search for "pacifist Islam" returns no ngram results.

This way of configuring the religion on the part of Christian writers goes back to the decades immediately after its founding, when some Christian monks alleged that the Muslim conquest of the Near East was sanguinary. In contrast, Professor Fred Donner of the University of Chicago has recently argued that if we base ourselves on the Qur'an itself and read the whole range of seventh-century Christian (and some later Muslim) accounts carefully, there is ample evidence that very early Islam was an ecumenical movement that involved an alliance of Muhammad's believers with some Christians and Jews.[4] I have provided further evidence for this thesis in my own biography of Muhammad.[5] See also my chapter in this book. Since this earliest Christian–Muslim encounter set a tone for subsequent polemics, it is worth discussing it further.

It is true that the Arab Muslims after the death of the Prophet Muhammad quickly established a world empire, and that war and conquest were part of their history. It is not clear at all, however, that they were different in this regard from the Byzantine Christian and Sasanian Zoroastrian empires in the same era, or from the expansionist Hindu Vardhana dynasty of Harsha (r. 606–47 CE) in North India. While it is sometimes alleged that Muslims were different because of the martial values enshrined in their scripture, the Qur'an, this argument fails on a number of grounds. The Bible contains much more violence than does the Qur'an, and Christians such as Augustine of Hippo lionized the biblical warrior David and saw him as an exemplar for Christian Roman Emperors in their wars. The sublime and spiritual Bhagavad-Gita, among the holy texts of Hinduism, presents itself as the discourse of Krishna, avatar of the god Vishnu, who argues that the Prince Arjuna must go to war despite his reluctance, because it is his duty (*dharma*) as a warrior.

The Abbasid caliphate from 750 forward established a great empire and fought many wars, and it was lucky in having many intellectuals to defend it. The same authors who shaped our image of classical Islam were often partisans of the Abbasid conquests and interpret Qur'an passages as authorizing them. These assertions are often anachronistic and tendentious, as Asma Afsaruddin points out in her chapter. Further, among medieval Muslim exegetes, some concentrated more than others on the scripture's peace verses. In our own day, scholars who would not dream of agreeing with Pope Urban II that the New Testament authorized the Crusades nevertheless routinely and uncritically allow late, imperial Muslim commentators to tell us how to read the Qur'an.

The initial Muslim Arab rule of the Near Eastern provinces of what had been the Eastern Roman Empire appears from the archeology to have been much more peaceful and tolerant than the Christian sources of the time alleged.[6] In the Transjordan during the years of the Muslim Arab conquest, archeologists have discovered Christians were allowed to go on building churches. The mosaic floors of the church in the town of Rihab dedicated to the Prophet Isaiah were finished in 635. At Khirbet al-Samra the mosaic floor in the church of St. George is dated 637, and that of the church of St. John the Baptist goes back to 639.[7] The famous battle at the Yarmouk River in the northern Transjordan in which the forces of the Muslim commander of the faithful, Omar, defeated the eastern Roman army of Emperor Herakleios occurred in 636. While war inevitably involves deaths and displacement, the scale of such phenomena in the newly Muslim-held Near East is so small that archeologists find virtually no trace of it. Many local Christians newly under Muslim rule clearly just carried on constructing their churches undisturbed, neither being attacked by the new rulers nor being dissuaded in any way from their pious building works.

Katia Cytryn-Silverman of the Hebrew University of Jerusalem, part of a team that has excavated seventh-century Tiberias, has concluded that under early Arab Muslim rule a small and unprepossessing mosque was built, but that churches and synagogues were left undisturbed, and the Byzantine cathedral went on dominating the cityscape as the largest edifice for over a century. She gave an interview in which she said that the archeology pointed to an age of coexistence in the city, adding

> You see that the beginning of the Islamic rule here respected very much the population that was the main population of the city: Christians, Jews, Samaritans ... They were not in a hurry to make their presence expressed into buildings. They were not destroying others' houses of prayers, but they were actually fitting themselves into the societies that they now were the leaders of.[8]

In the succeeding fourteen hundred years, of course, persons who happened to be Muslims were sometimes guilty of launching aggressive wars or of committing massacres. Again, it is not clear that they materially differed from adherents of other world religions in the frequency of their wars or in the severity of the casualties. My preliminary calculations suggest to me that in the twentieth-century world wars and colonial wars, persons of Christian heritage were responsible for nearly 100 million deaths, and that persons of Muslim heritage were responsible for on the order of 3 million deaths (mainly the death march of the Armenians under the Young Turks, the Iran–Iraq War, and the Afghanistan wars kicked off by the Soviet invasion; the Arab–Israeli wars racked up a much lower death toll than the others just mentioned).[9] This difference had nothing to do with scriptures or essences. Europeans industrialized warfare much earlier than did Muslims, and during the colonial era a majority of the world's Muslims were deprived of sovereignty and so were in no position to launch wars. Still, given these statistics, the firm conviction of some authors in Europe and the Americas that Muslims are mysteriously more violent than other peoples can only be seen as a form of self-serving amnesia. The history of violence by Christians has not impeded the study of Christian peace activism, and nor should the history of violence by Muslims pose any obstacle to studying Muslim thinking about peace and Muslim peace movements, as well as their efforts at diplomacy and reconciliation and work for social justice. Conflict and peace are a yin and a yang, and so far, too many journalists and scholars have concentrated on only half of the equation.

Let us turn to the contributions to this volume. Below, Rashied Omar surveys the intersection of Islamic Studies and Peace Studies, invoking the distinction made by Johan Galtung between negative peace and positive peace, and suggesting its salience for studies of peace in a Muslim context. Galtung filled the first academic chair in Peace Studies, established at Oslo University in 1955, and has been an important theorist of the field. He defines negative peace as the absence of war. In contrast, positive peace consists of efforts to forestall conflict.[10] For instance, if some conflict derives from class inequalities, then efforts to ensure that the poor have a safety net would fall under the rubric of positive peace. In keeping with the practical emphases often seen in Peace Studies, Omar offers four practical approaches to peace, basing his arguments in the Muslim theological and juridical tradition.

In my chapter, I treat verses in the Muslim scripture, the Qur'an, that instruct believers to avoid civil conflict with those who harass and persecute them, on the grounds that they lack any polity or authority. As one traces this sentiment through the Meccan period (c. 610–22 CE) of the Prophet Muhammad's ministry, the verses turn to instructing believers to return evil with good, a sentiment that can only evoke Jesus' instruction to turn the other cheek and his praise for peacemakers. I attempt to compare and contrast these Qur'an verses with similar ones in the New Testament and try to contextualize the Qur'an verses in what we know of late antique practices of peace, in time and space, of Arabic-speakers. I also argue that the turn of the Qur'an to permitting defensive war in the Medina period (622–32) has to do with the formation of a polity around the Prophet in that city, such that there is a duly constituted authority that can avoid mere individual vigilantism and can direct defensive operations. This development, I assert, does not abrogate the earlier verses on turning the other cheek (in contrast to what some medieval jurists suggested), since they have to do with individual behavior rather than with the state. I point out that this disjuncture is a commonplace of Christian late antiquity, since Church Fathers such as Augustine of Hippo and Ambrose of Milan upheld the need of the individual to live according to the Sermon on the Mount, but at the same time supported the wars and armies of Christian Rome and insisted on the duty of the Christian to protect the innocent by taking up arms against aggressors.[11] The verses on exercising forbearance in the face of provocations and on repelling evil deeds by doing good to persecutors typically have not been analyzed together for the Qur'an, and they form an important ethical imperative for peace and peacemaking.

Asma Afsaruddin examines the various meanings of the word "jihad" in Muslim texts, demonstrating that its contemporary demonization as a term always referring to warfare is not justified. Both in the Qur'an and in subsequent ethical texts, she argues, the term has a non-military meaning of spiritual struggle, and comprises the attitude of patience or forbearance (*sabr*). She reviews medieval ethicists and considers in detail the position of the great Sufi thinker Muhammad al-Ghazzali (d. 1111) on patient internal struggle, and also reviews the ideas of the contemporary Indian Muslim thinker, Wahid al-Din Khan (b. 1925), whom some have characterized as a pacifist.

Alexander D. Knysh also considers the interior dimension of peace in Islam, focusing on the Sufi tradition. He reviews magisterially the teachings of Sufi greats such as Abu Nasr al-Sarraj (d. 988), al-Ghazzali, and Muhyi al-Din Ibn al-`Arabi (d. 1240) on the internal life of peace. He argues that earlier thinkers especially focused on the progression of psychological states on the mystic path, but that in the thirteenth century we see a turn to engaging with mystical cognition. Knysh also attends to the issue raised by Max Weber's sociology of religion, regarding world-affirming and world-denying mystical movements. He finds that Muslim Sufism tends to advocate seclusion for beginners, but an engagement with the world for the mature mystic, which, he argues, allowed the ubiquitous and important Sufi orders to provide a basis for social order.

Rudolph Ware introduces us to key pacifist Sufi orders of Senegal, including the Murids and the Fayda Tijaniyya, and four prolific thinkers on peace. Ware adverts to the rise of this form of Muslim culture as a reaction against the machinations of European slave-traders in the eighteenth century (who often set petty principalities against one another in hopes they would take slaves for sale abroad), as well as in ruinous regional jihads of the nineteenth century, and finally in the colonial era of French domination where local arms were consistently overwhelmed by the foreigners' superior firepower. Ahmadu Bamba, the founder of the Muridiyya, thus looked to seventh-century Medina under the Prophet Muhammad as both a rupture and a model. He saw that episode as a historical rupture because he held that the jihad against militant attacking pagans waged by the Prophet at battles such as Badr (624) was a prophetic prerogative and that after Muhammad's passing, Muslims were to resolve conflicts peacefully. The way forward was suggested to him by the Constitution of Medina negotiated by the Prophet with Medina's non-Muslim inhabitants, including Jews, as a model for Muslim coexistence with other groups, such as Christians. This stance did not prevent him from denouncing colonialism and its avarice, but Ahmadu Bamba felt that the time for jihad had passed in ancient times, and attempts to revive it in the modern world were self-destructive. The four Senegalese Sufi figures on which Ware concentrates, he argues, all contributed to thinking about peace, but from different perspectives and with different emphases. Some, Ware says, concentrated on love and mercy, others on human liberty, and others still on the primacy and universality of truth.

Elizabeth F. Thompson addresses the 1919 peace conference at Versailles in the wake of the First World War. The literature on that conference often sees the punitive measures taken against a defeated Germany as having led to deep resentments and grievances that fueled nationalist mass politics in that country and contributed to the outbreak of yet another war. This Eurocentric view ignores the even greater injustices visited upon Africa and the Middle East, where populations eager to gain their freedom and to construct new states were instead placed in a supercilious manner under European tutelage as colonial "Mandates" for the foreseeable future. Thompson puts the Syro-Lebanese journalist and religious reformer Rashid Rida (d. 1935) in the context of movements for parliamentary rule in Ottoman Egypt in 1881–2 and in the Ottoman Empire in 1908. She shows how he swung around to support the Arab Revolt of Mecca's Sharif Hussein against the Ottomans, in hopes that from the ashes of the Ottoman state might rise the phoenix of a new Arabia. In his journalism, he warned the British against attempting to colonize Arabia, Iraq or Syria, and underlined that only an independent Arab state could bring peace in the aftermath of the Great War. Rida became an enthusiastic partisan of US President Woodrow Wilson's principle of self-determination for the peoples of the defeated empires and the latter's "Fourteen Points." At this point, just after the war, Rida seems to have seen Wilson's ideas as entirely compatible with Islamic thought. From Damascus, Rida championed the possibility of an independent Arab Syria and its relatively secular constitution, with Hussein's son Faisal as its proposed king. The British foreign ministry had, however, pledged Syria to France, and Paris insisted on receiving its promised bounty. The outcome of the peace conferences in Versailles and San Remo, with the imposition of European colonial rule on the Arabophone regions of the now-extinct Ottoman Empire, proved fateful for the attitudes of Arab Muslim intellectuals toward Western power throughout the twentieth century. Rida, Thompson argues, was pushed away from any flirtation with liberal internationalism. She does not say so, but there may be an analogy between him and the German thinker Carl Schmitt (d. 1985), who went from Weimar conservative in the 1920s to an adherent of National Socialism in the 1930s. Rida did not move as far right, but certainly his legacy was appropriated by the often anti-liberal Muslim Brotherhood. Thompson sees the grasping character of the victorious Powers in the age of high imperialism as having dealt a heavy blow to the ideals of early-twentieth-century Arab liberalism and to any hopes of a League of Nations guarantee of international peace and liberty.

Mohammad Hassan Khalil takes up a different dimension of Rida's thought on peace and tolerance, considering his theological views on the possibility of salvation for non-Muslims. If Thompson challenged the conventional view of Rida as an unsubtle fundamentalist with regard to ideas about the social order, Khalil similarly revises our view of him with regard to pluralism in matters of the afterlife. Khalil reviews medieval views like those of al-Ghazzali, who exempted from condemnation those non-Muslims who never received a fully fleshed out account of the Prophet Muhammad's mission or who only heard lies and anti-Muslim polemics. Only those who genuinely encountered Islam and rejected it, he held, would be punished in the next world. Still, even those so condemned, al-Ghazzali held, may ultimately be delivered out of hellfire, because of the cosmic reality of God's all-encompassing mercy on all things. Khalil then turns to Muhammad 'Abduh and Rashid Rida, exponents of early twentieth-century Muslim modernism. They held that non-Muslims such as Jews and Christians could attain paradise within the framework of their own traditions. He shows, however, that Rida was more an inclusivist (maintaining Islam's superiority while acknowledging legitimate and salvific spirituality in other traditions) rather than a pluralist (accepting that there are many equally valid paths to the truth). Still, he shows how Rida the reformist admitted that the traditionalist Islam he was striving to change was not particularly attractive to outsiders, and therefore he did not hold outsiders to account for a failure to convert. Further, Khalil sees evidence that Rida saw hell as a temporary condition and held out hopes of universal salvation, including for non-Muslims.

James L. Rowell discusses the life and thought of Abdul Ghaffar Khan (d. 1988), a major nonviolent freedom fighter in the struggle for independence from Britain in the first half of the twentieth century. Rowell depicts him as inspired above all by the Prophet Muhammad and Gandhi. He began by founding modern schools to educate other Pathans in what was then called the Northwest Frontier Province (now Khyber-Pukhtunkhwa) of British India. Ultimately, he became a Congress Party activist and a disciple of "Mahatma" Mohandas K. Gandhi. Abdul Ghaffar Khan embraced the precepts of nonviolent noncooperation wholeheartedly and believed they were entirely compatible with the Qur'an itself. He said that when he was imprisoned by the British for his activities as a freedom fighter, "in jail I had nothing to do except read the Koran. I read about the Prophet Muhammad in Mecca, about his patience, his suffering, his dedication. I had read it all before, as a child, but now I read it in the light of what I was hearing all around me about Gandhiji's struggle against the British Raj."

He differed in this regard from some other Muslims in Gandhi's circle, such as Abul Kalam Azad, who embraced nonviolent tactics as appropriate to that time and place but continued to believe that there were other circumstances where the Qur'an's war verses were applicable. Azad was not less a peace activist than Abdul Ghaffar Khan, and most adherents of peace movements are not utopian pacifists. Khan, however, saw no reason ever for violence or warfare. Rowell notes the irony of a Pathan pacifism, given the reputation of Pathans or Pukhtuns for martial prowess and for pursuing feuds. Abdul Ghaffar Khan deeply disapproved of feuding. Unlike the narrow-minded village clerics or mullahs of his home province, he loved the other religions around him and viewed all human beings as siblings. His Khudai Khidmatgar organization (servants of God), some 80,000–100,000 persons strong, played an important, peaceful political role in the Northwest Frontier Province.

Sherman A. Jackson tells the remarkable story of how a fundamentalist organization, Egypt's al-Gama`ah al-Islamiyya or Islamic Grouping, came to regret having developed a terrorist wing and having killed thousands. The Egyptian state in the 1990s resorted to mass incarceration in response to this threat, putting between 15,000 and 30,000 suspected members in prison. In the late 1990s, however, the leadership of the Islamic Grouping, in prison, met and decided to alter course, calling upon members to give up violence and turn to peaceful means of attaining their goals. The group issued a series of "repentance pamphlets" that confessed their previous errors and re-analyzed classic Islamic jurisprudence to come to the conclusion that violence was forbidden given the conditions that obtained in Egypt. In 2011, Islamic Grouping members participated in peaceful demonstrations and political meetings. Jackson lays out their arguments.

While it could be objected that the Islamic Grouping's turn to peace was pragmatic rather than principled, in fact they did appeal to principle in altering their course. Moreover, perhaps the majority of peace movements have chosen the tactics of peace out of pragmatic concerns, and unadorned pacifism is held by relatively few people anywhere. As noted above, the study of peace is not only a study of convinced pacifists but of all those who deploy peace for individual and social change, whatever the rationale. Peace movements in modern times have been estimated to be twice as successful as violent ones, which surely should commend this path to pragmatists.[12]

Zilka Spahić Šiljak, a Bosnian scholar and activist, shares with us the findings of her research on women peacebuilders working in the aftermath of the Bosnian War of 1992–5. Peace and reconciliation have been difficult tasks in the former Yugoslavia for the past twenty-five years, since the country is haunted by the specter of the brutal civil war promoted by Serbian hyper-nationalist Slobodan Milosevic. Despite the trope often found in the press, however, Croat Catholics, Bosnian Muslims, and Eastern Orthodox Serbs have not been possessed by "age-old hatreds" and have often lived quite peaceably with one another over long stretches of time. They speak three registers of a common language, and many, having lived decades under Communism, are not observant religiously, so that often very little divides them. Demagogues can teach people to hate in the blink of an eye, and that is what happened in the 1990s. When the multi-ethnic state of Bosnia and Herzegovina was recognized as independent in 1992 by the United States and the European Council, this development was rejected by the Serbian minority living there, which formed a paramilitary and brutally conquered, at one point, 70 percent of the new country. The Serbians in Bosnia were supported by the army of Serbia, which claimed to be the Yugoslav successor state, and which ultimately hoped to annex the country after the Muslims had been expelled. Likely over 100,000 persons, disproportionately Bosniak Muslims, were killed, and 2 million persons were displaced. This militant and sanguinary Serbian expansionism was halted by NATO intervention, and a fragile peace was negotiated at Dayton, Ohio. It had the advantage of ending the warfare, but it reified Bosnia and Herzegovina's ethnic divisions.

Šiljak analyzes the work of three women. Amra Pandžo is the founder of the Muslim, faith-based organization, "Small Steps," which promotes peace and conciliation. Although she is observant, she does not wear hijab, in accordance with the general Bosnian custom. Sehija Dedović leads a civil society ecumenical women's group, The Bee. Although its membership is predominantly Muslim, with both veiled and unveiled women participating, it is open as well to non-Muslims and most of its programs are not religiously specific. She includes in her three cases the story of Danka Zelić, a Catholic who runs a secular women's association not based on Christianity and which promotes dialogue across faiths. Women peace activists work with wartime rape survivors and those traumatized by other forms of gender-based violence, engage in peace education, provide humanitarian aid, and pursue conflict resolution, as well as supporting women who wish to enter the political sphere. The Muslim women studied here reported that they hold peace work to be indivisible from their religious identity, and they typically reject the word "leader" in describing themselves, since they see it as redolent of patriarchy and dictatorship.

Grace B. Yukich's chapter looks at Muslim American charitable and other activism in the United States in the Trump era. Although she does not explicitly frame her problematic in this way, I asked her to join us in this book because it seems to me that her writing addresses Muslim efforts in the arena of what Johan Galtung called "positive peace," that is, social action that has the effect ultimately of tamping down conflict before it spirals out of control. Muslim Americans faced a negative environment in the Trump years, with the president accusing "Islam" of hating America and imposing a ban on travel to the United States from a set of Muslim-majority countries (which cut Muslim American families off from relatives abroad). Yukich surveys ways in which Muslim Americans, who formed a little over 1 percent of the population, responded to that negative atmosphere, including advocating for forms of social change, building a progressive Muslim movement, strengthening interfaith bonds between Muslim communities and those of other faiths, advocating for Muslim rights, and attempting to educate others about Islam. Some cautioned against taking on the role of "defender of Islam," lest they fall into the rhetorical trap of Islamophobes who blamed all Muslims for anything any Muslim did. Some of their activities in this period were primarily directed at the Muslim community itself, including working to smooth over divisions between African-American Muslims and immigrant ones. She even found that a minority of Muslim Americans attempted to integrate into the US society of that time by supporting President Trump. (It should be noted, however, that before the wars launched by George W. Bush against Muslim-majority states in the early-twenty-first century, a plurality of Muslim Americans appears to have voted Republican, so that it would be difficult to disentangle Muslim American adherence to the GOP from any particular attachment to the one-term president.) Yukich shows that many Muslim American initiatives formed a part of larger trends in American religion in this era, for instance, the burgeoning of religious progressives, who have been too little studied.

This book explores various dimensions of Muslim peace work. Some of our authors attend to values and internal states of peace. Others have grappled with historical movements such as the Sufis of Senegal or the Muslim progressives of the contemporary United States. We examine verses of the Qur'an and chants of mystics, but also practical efforts at community-building and civil society efforts toward positive peace, as in post-war Bosnia or the early-twenty-first century United States. Our authors demonstrate that Islamic Peace Studies is potentially a rich and revealing field that highlights a crucial but neglected dimension of the everyday lives of the nearly 2 billion human beings.

Notes

1   Ian M. Harris, Larry J. Fisk, and Carol Rank, "A Portrait of University Peace Studies in North America and Western Europe at the end of the Millennium," *The International Journal of Peace Studies* 3, no. 1 (January 1998). http://www.gmu.edu/programs/icar/ijps/vol3_1/Harris.htm

2   See inter alia Juan Cole, *Muhammad: Prophet of Peace amid the Clash of Empires* (New York: Nation Books, 2018); Lamin Sanneh, *Beyond Jihad: The Pacifist Tradition in West African Islam* (Oxford: Oxford University Press, 2016); Irfan A. Omar, "Jihad and Nonviolence in the Islamic Tradition," in *Peacemaking and the Challenge of Violence in World Religions*, ed. Irfan A. Omar and Michael K. Duffey (Chichester,

West Sussex: John Wiley & Sons, 2015), 9–41; Ramin Jehanbegloo, "Peace and Nonviolence in Islam," in *The Routledge Handbook of Pacifism and Nonviolence*, ed. Andrew Fiala (London: Routledge, 2018), 54–63; Rudolph T. Ware, *The Walking Qur'an: Islamic Education, Embodied Knowledge and History in West Africa* (Chapel Hill: University of North Carolina Press, 2014); Zayn Kassam, "Islam, Gender, and Peace," in *Terrorism, Religion, and Global Peace: From Concepts to* Praxis, ed. Karikottuchira Kuriakose (Piscataway, NJ: Gorgias Press, 2012), 33–52; Amitabh Pal, *"Islam" Means Peace: Understanding the Muslim Principle of Nonviolence Today* (Santa Barbara, CA: Praeger, 2011); Qamar-ul Huda, ed., *Crescent and Dove: Peace and Conflict Resolution in Islam* (Washington, DC: US Institute of Peace, 2010); James L. Rowell, "Abdul Ghaffar Khan: An Islamic Gandhi," *Political Theology* 10, no. 4 (2009): 591–606; Aida Othman, "'An Amicable Settlement is Best': Sulh and Dispute Resolution in Islamic Law," *Arab Law Quarterly* 21, no. 1 (2007): 64–90; Fred Donner, "Fight for God—but Do So with Kindness: Reflections on War, Peace, and Communal Identity in Early Islam," in *War and Peace in the Ancient World*, ed. Kurt Raaflaub (Oxford: Blackwell, 2006), 297–311; Irfan A. Omar, "Peace," in *The Qur'an: An Encyclopedia*, ed. Oliver Leaman (London: Taylor and Francis, 2005), 489–91; Mohammed Abu-Nimr, *Nonviolence and Peace Building in Islam: Theory and Practice* (Gainesville: University Press of Florida, 2003).

3   Maria J. Stephan and Erica Chenoweth, " Why Civil Resistance Works: The Strategic Logic of Nonviolent Conflict," *International Security* 33, no. 1 (2008): 7–44.

4   Fred Donner, *Muhammad and the Believers: At the Origins of Islam* (Cambridge, MA: Harvard University Press, 2010).

5   Cole, *Muhammad*.

6   Michael Philip Penn, *Envisioning Islam: Syriac Christians and the Early Muslim World* (Philadelphia: University of Pennsylvania Press, 2015).

7   Robert Schick, "Archaeological Sources for the History of Palestine: Palestine in the Early Islamic Period: Luxuriant Legacy," *Near Eastern Archaeology* 61, no. 2 (1998): 74–108.

8   Ilan Ben Zion, "By Sea of Galilee, Archaeologists Find Ruins of Early Mosque," *Associated Press*, January 28, 2021.

9   Juan Cole, "Terrorism and the other Religions," *Informed Comment*, April 23, 2013, https://www.juancole.com/2013/04/terrorism-other-religions.html

10   J. Galtung and D. Fischer, "Positive and Negative Peace," in *SpringerBriefs on Pioneers in Science and Practice*, vol. 5, ed. Johan Galtung (Berlin: Springer, 2013), https://doi.org/10.1007/978-3-642-32481-9_17

11   Louis J. Swift, "Early Christian Views on Violence, War, and Peace," in *War and Peace in the Ancient World*, ed. Kurt Raaflaub (Oxford: Blackwell , 2006), 279–96.

12   Stephan and Chenoweth, " Why Civil Resistance Work."

1 BETWEEN COMPASSION AND JUSTICE: LOCATING AN ISLAMIC DEFINITION OF PEACE

A. Rashied Omar

In the contemporary period, Islam is frequently depicted as predisposed to conflict and violence. The intractable Middle East conflicts, the attacks on the United States in September 2001, and the subsequent events during the first quarter of the twenty-first century in which Muslim extremists have been implicated in acts of terror have served only to reinforce this widespread perception. Even conventional academic perspectives regard Islam as having a predilection for violence.[1]

As a direct consequence of this toxic contemporary context, Muslims are currently living through one of *the* most challenging periods in their history. Islamophobia and hate crimes are at an all-time high.[2] Never before in recent history has the Muslim commitment to a more peaceful and human world being challenged as it is at this time.

Against this backdrop, locating the Islamic definition of and role of Muslims in peace is critical. It is a task that I and an increasing number of other Muslim scholars and activists have undertaken and continue to undertake with great passion and commitment, since it counterbalances the current preoccupation with Islam and violence.[3]

A number of key questions undergird my research on the role of Islam in Peacebuilding:

1) What are the complex causes of the erosion of peace in contemporary Muslim societies?

2) How consonant or disparate is the Islamic definition of peace from that of the leading perspectives?

3) How should the core Islamic values of Compassion and Justice be configured in an Islamic theology of peace?

4) What concrete strategies and practices could Muslim peace activists adopt in pursuit of a more just and humane world?

This chapter addresses the above four questions and concludes with four modest proposals that may create the conditions for the recovery of the Islamic principles of peace and making them part of the fabric of contemporary Muslim culture. I argue that the complex justice struggles in which many Muslim social movements have been engaged during the past century and a half have led to the erosion of the core Islamic value of compassion, and consequently, the loss of peace. It might be expedient to begin with a definition of peace.

The Peace Studies Definition of Peace and Peacebuilding

Like the end state itself, a consensus definition of "peace" is elusive. A number of contending interpretations of peace exist in the literature.[4] The disparate definitions of peace can be plotted on a horizontal graph, with one axis called negative peace and the other positive peace. Negative peace has also been described as a minimalist definition of peace and positive peace as a maximalist definition. Negative peace is simply the absence of war.

The Islamic perspective is perhaps best compared to that of scholars in the field of international peace studies, which has broadened and deepened the conventional understanding of peace defined simply as the absence of war (negative peace), into recognizing that the underlying conditions of a society, even absent overt violence, predicate the presence of deadly conflict.[5] This idea, known as positive peace, originated in the work of the Norwegian peace scholar, Johan Galtung, and stresses the recognition of a more indirect, frequently hidden, and insidious form of violence, called structural violence. This form of violence is less dramatic and often works slowly, eroding human values and eventually, human lives. Violence, it is argued, can be built into the very structure of the socio-political, economic, and cultural institutions of a society and has the effect of denying people important rights such as economic opportunity, social and political equality, and human dignity. When children die of starvation or malnutrition, a kind of violence is taking place. Similarly, when human beings suffer from preventable diseases, when they are denied a basic education, housing, the right to freely practice their religion, an opportunity to raise a family, or to participate in their own governance, a kind of violence is taking place even when no blood is shed.[6]

The quintessential example of structural violence is apartheid South Africa. This vicious system institutionalized the oppression and dehumanization of people of color. It legalized racial discrimination, socio-political oppression, and economic exploitation. Writing in support of such a view, David Chidester (1997) contends that under the apartheid system, "violence was everywhere. It was an integral part of the discourses, practices and social formations through which human beings struggled to be human."[7]

This nuanced understanding of peace as a substantive value has been increasingly embraced among scholars, religious leaders, civil society, state actors, and the United Nations. With this understanding, the practice of peacebuilding extends beyond the laying down of arms to include addressing and transforming the underlying conditions of structural violence and social cleavages, to foster social integration at every level of society, with roles played by actors among the grassroots, civil society, government, and international organizations. The sought-after end state is best described by John Paul Lederach and R. Scott Appleby (2010) as *just peace*:

The dynamic state of affairs in which the reduction and management of violence and the achievement of social and economic justice are undertaken as mutual, reinforcing dimensions of constructive change. Sustainable transformation of conflict requires more than the (necessary) problem solving associated with mediation, negotiated settlements, and other elements of conflict resolution; it requires the redress of legitimate grievances and the establishment of new relations characterized by equality and fairness according to the dictates of human dignity and the common good.[8]

Positive Peace, Compassion, and Justice in Islam

An examination of the Islamic concept of peace reveals that it is closer to that of positive peace. This is underscored by the strong emphasis the primary source of Islamic guidance, the Qur'an, places on justice as a substantive value.

The Qur'an uses two terms interchangeably to refer to justice: *qist* and *'adl*, meaning—"to give someone his or her full portion."[9] In fact, the Qur'an regards "actions for justice as being the closest thing to piety" (Q5:6). The Qur'anic verses pertaining to justice are often specific about those areas of social affairs wherein lapses are most likely to occur, such as the trusts and legacies of orphans and adopted children (Q4:3; Q33:5), matrimonial relations (Q4:3; Q49:9), contractual and business dealings (Q2:282), judicial matters (Q5:42; Q4:56), interreligious relations (Q60:8), economic relations (Q11:65), and dealing with one's adversaries (Q5:8). The strong emphasis on justice in the Qur'an has led some Muslim jurists, like the renowned Ibn Qayyim al-Jawziyyah (d. 1350), to argue that justice is the *raison d'etre* of the establishment of religion:

God has sent His Messengers and revealed His Books so that people may establish *qist* (justice), upon which the heavens and the earth stand. And when the signs of justice appear in any manner, then that is a reflection of the *shari'ah* and the religion of God.[10]

The Islamic concept of peace is integrally related to the struggle for justice. Moreover, Muslims are not alone in this twinning of the two. This focus resonates well with the exhortation from Pope Paul V1 in 1972 that "if you want peace work for justice."[11] It is a clarion call to the redress of legitimate grievances. The numerous struggles for social justice—starting with the anti-colonial movements of the first half of the twentieth century and the continuing struggles against narrow, autocratic elites in the post-colonial period that have been waged in parts of the world with Muslim majority populations—have inevitably led justice to be the central hermeneutical key through which most contemporary Muslims view Islam.

Yet, as important as justice may be in the comprehensive matrix of Islamic values, it is not the preeminent one. Rather, al-Rahman, or the Compassionate One, is undoubtedly the most important attribute of God in Islam. It is the equivalent of the Christian preeminent understanding of God as Love. One of the most well-known Qur'anic verses with which Muslims commence every action is *bismillahir rahmanir rahim*, translated as, "in the name of God, the Most Compassionate, and the Dispenser of Grace." Compassion is so central to God's existence that it embraces all that exists in the universe (Q40:7). The Qur'an describes the Prophet Muhammad's central mission as *rahmatan lil 'alamin*, a source of compassion and mercy to the world (21:107).

Moreover, the Arabic word *rahma* (compassion, mercy, and tenderness) and its various derivatives occur more than 326 times. According to Imam al-Raghib al-Isfahani (d. 1108/9) in his famous lexicography, *Mufradat al-Qur'an* ("Vocabulary of the Qur'an), the term *rahma* means "softening of the heart towards one who deserves our mercy and induces us to do good to him/her." It is interesting to note that the womb of mother is also called *rahm*. A mother is always very soft and gentle toward her children (*raqiq*); she showers love and affection on them.[12]

It is this understanding of Islam that has allowed Muslim mystics, Sufis, to develop the doctrine of what is called *sulh-i-Kull*, that is, peace with all, which means no violence and no aggressiveness.[13] In mystical (Sufi) traditions of Islam the greatest form of jihad, personal jihad is to purify the soul and refine the disposition. This is regarded as the far more urgent and momentous struggle and it is based on a prophetic tradition (*hadith*). Prophet Muhammad is reported to have advised his companions as they return after a battle, "We are returning from the lesser jihad [physical fighting] to the greater *jihad al-nafs* [disciplining the self]." Sufis have traditionally understood this greater form of jihad to be the spiritual struggle to discipline the lower impulses and base instincts in human nature. The renowned thirteenth-century Sufi teacher, Jalal al-Din Rumi (d. 1273), articulated such an understanding of jihad when he wrote: "The prophets and saints do not avoid spiritual struggle. The first spiritual struggle they undertake is the killing of the ego and the abandonment of personal wishes and sensual desires. This is the greater jihad."[14]

I have thus far argued for an Islamic concept of peace that navigates between two core values in Islam, namely justice and compassion. I have also argued that whenever these two core values of Islam come into tension with each other, compassion trumps justice. In my view, therefore, a struggle for justice (*jihad*) that claims Islamic legitimacy must locate itself within an ethos of compassion. How then does one balance between the two critical concepts of justice and compassion in constructing a viable project of Muslim peacebuilding?

The numerous struggles for social justice—starting with the anti-colonial wars of the first half of the twentieth century, the watershed Afghan war against the Soviet invasion in the 1980s, and the continuing struggles against secular elites in the post-colonial period that have engaged many parts of the world with Muslim majority populations—have inevitably led justice to be the central hermeneutical key through which Muslims view Islam.

This obsession with justice has in turn led to an erosion and exclusion of the central Islamic concept of compassion. The kind of wanton violence into which some Muslim struggles for justice have degenerated can in large measure be attributed to the phenomenon of struggling for justice without compassion. Without compassion, struggles for justice invariably end up mimicking the oppressive orders against which they revolt. And compassion without justice likely leads only to more of the status quo of political, cultural, and social upheaval and pervasive overt and structural violence against Muslims by despotic regimes.

Ironically, it is precisely here that the crisis of contemporary Muslims is located and consequently where the challenge of a credible project on Muslim peacebuilding resides. How can the central Islamic concept of compassion be recovered and reinvigorated such that it once again becomes part of the fabric of contemporary Muslim culture? This is indeed the critical challenge facing contemporary Muslims.

Proposals for Muslim Peacebuilding

I suggest four modest proposals that may create the conditions out of which a credible Muslim role in peacebuilding could be spawned. My suggestions emerge primarily from my own assessment of the current geo-political realities and the corresponding Muslim crisis of extremism.

First, Muslims themselves must not become weary from stating again and again both loudly and unequivocally, that acts of wanton violence and barbarism are contrary to the teachings of Islam. And the news media must do more to make sure their voices are heard. In Islamic ethics, the end does not justify the means. Religious extremism has no virtue in Islam and has been unequivocally condemned by the Prophet Muhammad. He is reported in *hadith* to have declared thrice "the extremists shall perish."[15] For contemporary Muslims this condemnation requires the acknowledgment, no matter how painful it is, that they do have extremists (*mutatarrifun*) in their ranks. This is, of course, not unique to Islam; what is peculiar to Islam is that extremists appear disproportionately within their ranks, not least because of the proclivity of the media for sensationalism and spectacle (a proclivity upon which extremists have capitalized). Muslim leaders have an especially onerous challenge of condemning violent overreactions while still peacefully acknowledging, refuting, and struggling against the injustices that spawned such violence. This challenge is eased, however, by the overwhelming presence of compassion at the heart of Islamic tradition, but they must seize it and speak of it.

Second, despite growing attention from both Muslim and non-Muslim scholars, there is dire need for more rigorous academic studies of the potentially fertile sources of nonviolence and peacebuilding in Islam and Muslim societies. Regrettably, a search on the Library of Congress subject catalogue for resources on "Islam, Nonviolence and Peace" produces fewer than a dozen items. A similar search for items on "Islam and Violence," by contrast, produces a plethora of materials. It is palpable that Islam and Muslim societies are a rather neglected area of peace studies and peace research. Reflecting on this bias in the current peace research agenda, Mohamed Abu-Nimer, in a pioneering book in the field *Nonviolence and Peacebuilding Islam* (2003), argues that by shifting the emphasis from war and violence to peace and conflict transformation in the study of Islam and Muslim societies, it can contribute significantly to buttressing and reinvigorating courageous peace initiatives that are already currently in progress in many different Muslim settings. Abu-Nimer's ground-breaking book establishes a theoretical framework for peacebuilding and nonviolence in Islam and deals comprehensively with almost all the major academic contributions to this field.[16]

Not surprisingly, despite the paucity of publications directly on this topic, the field is rich and includes leading Muslim scholars from diverse countries and cultures, such as Abdul Aziz Sachedina (United States), Jawdat Sa'id (Syria), Mawlana Wahiduddin Khan (India), Asghar Ali Engineer (India), Chandra Muzaffar (Malaysia), Chiawat Satha-Anand (Thailand), Farid Esack (South Africa), and Rabia Terri Harris (United States).[17] Notwithstanding the sterling efforts of these courageous scholars, the field of Islamic peace studies and conflict transformation remains inchoate and urgently needs much more attention.

Resources such as quantitative and qualitative research will provide empiric support for strengthening the tenants of justice and compassion in Islam and model successes for Muslim peacebuilders to learn and adapt at every level of society. Ideally, such research may be used to inform and alter the actions of powerful nations, whose foreign policy is a central factor in the violence experienced in many Muslim majority countries.

Third, there is an urgent need for the nurturing and training of a new critically minded class of *'ulama* (Muslim religious scholars). The established Muslim religious leaders in countries such as Saudi Arabia, Egypt, and Pakistan have abandoned their role as the moral conscience of their societies by refusing to speak out coherently on the human rights violations and injustices that permeate their countries. Many of them, while speaking out apologetically against certain forms of injustices against Muslims, are providing religious legitimacy to despotic and oppressive regimes. Moreover, nonviolent civil resistance campaigns are not tolerated in most Muslim countries and progressive religious leaders are either incarcerated or exiled.

Drawing on the theoretical insights gleaned from the recent deluge of studies on the causes and prevention of religious conflict, the conclusion is unmistakable: religion does not spawn violence independently of predisposing social, economic, and political conditions, as well as the subjective roles of belligerent leaders.[18] Moreover, because sacred text traditions may be interpreted in the service of peace as well as violence, the role of religious leaders is decisive, whether as advocates for sustainable peace or violence or as agents of willful ignorance.

The studies of two historians of religion, Bruce Lincoln and Scott Appleby, have offered similar but independent arguments in support of this theoretical assertion. Appleby has for example proposed that because of the ambivalent nature of the sacred (that it can be interpreted in the service of peace as well as violence), the role of religious leaders is decisive.[19] He contends: "Corrupt, craven or merely indecisive religious leadership invites interlopers, claimants who would associate the energies and purposes of religion with their own."[20]

In light of this finding, as well as the existing crisis in Muslim religious leadership, it is critical to support the emergence of a new generation of scholars who are well versed in both the traditional Islamic sciences and the modern social sciences. Peace education and conflict transformation skills grounded within the key Islamic principles of compassion and justice must form an integral and essential part of this formation and training for future Imams. A useful starting point might be to offer training programs and scholarships to enhance the knowledge horizons of existing Imams, especially the younger ones. Fortunately, a few such programs have begun, although their numbers and ranks need great expansion. Another key undertaking is fostering exchange programs between existing students from Muslim, Christian, and Jewish seminaries. Fortunately, a few religious seminaries have already begun working on such an initiative.

Lastly, peace advocates need to support the call for a public debate concerning the most effective means to counteract Muslim and other forms of extremism. A number of scholars have already pointed this out. For example, the renowned scholar of Islam John Esposito has ominously warned in his book, *Unholy War: Terror in the Name of Islam* (2002), that, "if foreign policy issues are not addressed effectively, they will continue to be breeding ground for hatred and radicalism, the rise of extremist movements, and recruits for the bin Laden's of the world."[21]

In line with this analysis, interreligious peace activists from all faiths need to attend to the many voices all over the world that are questioning the wisdom of the current strategy pursued in the "war on terrorism," and the injustices it has wrought. They also need to back the call for a serious reassessment concerning the controversial US foreign policy that abets authoritarian Muslim regimes in the Middle East, and elsewhere, as well as its uncritical and too often unilateral support for the present policies of the State of Israel. The current political environment is not seeking to address or ameliorate the root causes of violence experienced among Muslims. On the contrary, it generates the very conditions that favor extremism.[22] More importantly, such an unequivocal call for a *just peace* in the Middle East and elsewhere coming from Jewish, Christian, Hindu, and Buddhist institutions will help rebuild trust and confidence in the beleaguered initiatives of Muslim peacebuilders and their support bases.

Assessment

Returning to the initial question of how to account for the elusive nature of peace in many Muslim societies, my simple answer is as follows: the contemporary global order is not by any stretch of the imagination a just one. Islam places a strong emphasis on social justice as an integral part of its concept of peace. Muslim legitimization of violence does not occur in a socio-historical vacuum, but rather within concrete human settings in which power dynamics are paramount. Against this backdrop, the Muslim pre-occupation with justice has led to an erosion of the core Islamic value of compassion. Extremists have a disproportionate influence within the ranks of Muslims, and the global communications media have inadvertently become their ally. Our primary strategy toward combating Muslim and all other forms of violence and terrorism should be that of ameliorating the root causes that provide a fertile ground on which extremism can thrive.

This chapter has offered four concrete proposals that can make a modest contribution toward creating the conditions necessary for a more positive peace role for Islam to counterbalance the disproportionate yet awesome power of Muslim extremists. There exists a dire need for the followers of Judaism, Christianity, and Islam, as well as all other religious traditions, and of none, to retrieve our common humanity and to end the horrific dehumanization that is currently taking place on such a wide scale. The challenge of peace for Muslims in particular is to develop a theology of healing and embrace (*ta'aruf*) so eloquently described in the following verse of the Qur'an:

> O Humankind! We have created you into a male and female and fashioned you into nations and tribes, so that you may come to know each other (not despise one another). The most honored of you in the sight of God, is those who display the best conduct. And God is All-Knowing, All-Aware.

> (Q 49:13)

Notes

1   The stereotype of a bellicose and inherently violent Islam, so pervasive in the media, has wide currency among Western policymakers. For two of the most popular academic accounts that depict Islam as inherently violent, see Bernard Lewis, *What Went Wrong?: The Clash Between Islam and Modernity in the Middle East* (New York: Oxford University Press, 2002) and Samuel P. Huntington, *The Clash of Civilizations and the Remaking of World Order* (New York: Simon & Schuster, 1996). There has also been an alarming amount of anti-Islamic propaganda published in the wake of the attacks of September 11, 2001. Two particularly sinister works that attempt to demonize all politically active Muslim individuals or organizations are: Steven Emerson, *American Jihad: The Terrorists among Us* (New York: Simon & Schuster, 2002) and Daniel Pipes, *Militant Islam Reaches America* (New York: W. W. Norton & Company, 2002). Both of these works brand all American Muslims who are critical of Israeli policies as potential terrorist threats, and they incite suspicion against American Muslims by claiming that many of those Muslims are taking part in a secret conspiracy to promote terrorism in America.

2   For a definition and development of Islamophobia, see Omar, A. Rashied, "Overcoming Islamophobia." In *Dharma World,* October–December 2012.

3   In August 2000, I temporarily left my post as a full-time Imam of a local mosque in Cape Town, South Africa, and joined the Joan B. Kroc Institute for International Peace Studies at the University of Notre Dame to deepen my own understanding of the causes of religiously motivated violence, and more importantly to identify resources for peacebuilding within Islam and Muslim societies.

4   For a useful introduction to the contending definitions of peace in the literature, see David Barash, *Introduction to Peace Studies* (Seattle: University of Washington, 1991), 5–30. For a deeper reflection on the meaning and sources of peace, see Kenneth Boulding, *Stable Peace* (Austin: University of Texas Press, 1978).

5   For a deeper reflection on the meaning and sources of peace, see Boulding, *Stable Peace*. I am indebted to a former Peace Studies teacher of mine, Professor Siobhan McEvoy-Levy, for first introducing me to the contending definitions of peace in the literature.

6   For a further exploration of the new understandings of peace, see Johan Galtung. "Violence, Peace and Peace Research," *Journal of Peace Research* 6, no. 3 (1969): 167–91. For a related idea due to the Galtung distinction between direct violence (children are murdered), structural violence (children die through poverty), and cultural violence (whatever blinds us to this or seeks to justify it), see Hugh Miall, Oliver Ramsbothan, and Tom Woodhouse, "Introduction to Conflict Resolution," in *Contemporary Conflict Resolution* (Cambridge: Polity/Blackwell, 1999), 5–22.

7   David Chidester, "Comprehending Political Violence," in *Dealing with Diversity: Keywords for a New South Africa*, eds. Emile Boonzaier and John Sharp (Cape Town: David Phillip, 1997).

8   John Paul Lederach and R. Scott Appleby, "Strategic Peacebuilding: An Overview," in *Strategies of Peace: Transforming Conflict in a Violent World*, eds. Daniel Philpott and Gerard F. Powers (New York: Oxford University Press, 2010), 24.

9   See E. W. Lane, *Lane's Arabic-English Lexicon* (Beirut: Librairie du Liban, 1980) q-s-t.

10 Ibn Qayyim al-Jawziyya, *Al-Turuq al-Hakimiyyah fi al-Siyat al-Shar'iyyah* (Cairo, 1953), 14–16. R. Scott Appleby, *Ambivalence of the Sacred: Religion, Violence, and Reconciliation* (Boulder, CO: Rowman & Littlefield Publishers, Inc), 54–6.

11 "Message of His Holiness Pope Paul VI for the Celebration of the Day of Peace,"
    http://www.vatican.va/content/paul-vi/en/messages/peace/documents/hf_p-vi_
    mes_19711208_v-world-day-for-peace.html
12 For a useful discussion of the concept of compassion in Islam, see Asghar Ali
    Engineer; http://newark.rutgers.edu/~rtavakol/engineer/compassion.htm
13 Ibid.
14 Chittick William, trans. *The Sufi Path of Love: The Spiritual Teachings of Rumi*
    (Albany: State University of New York Press, 1983).
15 This prophetic tradition is found in the famous compilation of Sahih Muslim;
    translated into English by Abdul Hamid Siddiqui.
16 Mohammed Abu-Nimer, *Nonviolence and Peace Building in Islam* (Gainesville:
    University Press of Florida, 2003).
17 For a useful list of publications on Islam and Peacebuilding, see Mohammed Abu-
    Nimer's bibliography in *Nonviolence and Peacebuilding in Islam*, 213–28. An outdated
    but comprehensive bibliography on Islam-Peace-Nonviolence was also compiled by
    Karim Douglas Crow and can be found online at: http://www.members.tripod.com/
    nviusa/islam.htm. Accessed November 1, 2017.
18 See Carnegie Commission on Preventing Deadly Conflict, *Preventing Deadly
    Conflict: Final Report with Executive Summary*, Carnegie Corporation of New York,
    December 1997.
19 R. Scott Appleby, *Ambivalence of the Sacred: Religion, Violence, and Reconciliation*
    (Boulder, CO: Rowman & Littlefield Publishers, Inc), 54–6.
20 It was a privilege for me to represent the Kroc Institute at the Global Dialogue
    Institute's "25th" International Scholars Annual Trialogue in Skopje, Macedonia,
    from May 10–May 14, 2002. The trilateral dialogue was co-sponsored by a wide range
    of international organizations including the Macedonian Center for International
    Cooperation, the World Conference on Religion and Peace, and partially funded
    by the United States Institute of Peace. One of the most exciting dimensions of the
    trialogue was the sessions held at the Orthodox and Islamic theological seminaries. A
    bold proposal was made for exploring creative ways of interreligious collaboration in
    the theological formation and education of the students at these two seminaries.
21 John Esposito, *Unholy War: Terror in the Name of Islam* (New York: Oxford
    University Press, 2002), 157.
22 Support for this view is presented in Graham E. Fuller (2002). "The Future of
    Political Islam," in *Foreign Affairs* March/April 2002, Council on Foreign Relations,
    New York, 60.

2 THE QUR'AN ON DOING GOOD TO ENEMIES

Juan Cole

The Qur'an contains numerous passages urging forgiveness of enemies and returning their evil deeds with good works, although they have not been studied analytically as a coherent ensemble.[1] These scattered counterparts of the Sermon on the Mount raise questions similar to those over which New Testament scholars have puzzled, of the social setting in which they arose and their social implications. In approaching them, it will be useful to remember the dictum of New Testament scholar Gerd Theissen that "it is impossible to determine what love of enemies and nonviolence meant apart from the social situation in which these demands are made and practiced."[2] Here, I will survey the relevant Qur'an verses and compare and contrast them, where appropriate, to New Testament passages of similar import, as well as considering the arguments of Theissen and other scholars about the importance of social setting. I will take the Qur'an as our primary source, and will prefer it to dependence on the much later, often anachronistic and unreliable Abbasid biographical materials.

In the Meccan period (610–32) of the Prophet's ministry, the Qur'an was preached in a small shrine city to itinerant merchants and peddlers as well as to townspeople.[3] Some verses complain of the hardheartedness of the rich toward the poor in the town. The city is portrayed as dominated by wealthy and powerful pagans, many of whom opposed Muhammad's preaching of monotheism.[4] It is to their taunts and ridicule that believers are urged to reply, first with gentle withdrawal, and ultimately with doing good to those who do evil. What is the social meaning of these practices in the shrine city, and are they in any way related to Christian belief, exemplified in Jesus' Sermon on the Mount?

The turn in the Medina period to a "just war" doctrine in the Qur'an, in response to military attacks, has obscured the verses, both in Mecca and Medina, regarding love of the civil enemy. While a few verses of the Medina period urge the prosecution of defensive war, moreover, peace, love, and reconciliation remain

Thanks to Asma Afsaruddin for her helpful comments on this chapter.

important themes in the suras or chapters of this period. Although a comparison of the Qur'an to the New Testament may seem outlandish to those who read the latter as consistently advocating nonviolence, the scholarly literature does not find that Jesus and his movement were always pacifist, though the notion, popular in some quarters in the 1960s, that he was a Zealot revolutionary has largely been rejected by scholars.[5] Likewise, seeing the Qur'an only under the sign of militancy is a distortion of a complex work. If we look beyond the New Testament to late antique Christianity, interpersonal nonviolence and state-led warfare coexisted in the thought of Church Fathers, and the same is true of the Qur'an. The precise contexts in which pacifist approaches to enemies were prescribed as opposed to taking up arms in self-defense will be explored below.

Withdrawing Graciously

In the Qur'an, there are two grounds on which powerful pagans are castigated. One is that although they are wealthy, they are also miserly and refuse to help the indigent.[6] *The City* 90:1-20 lays out some of these conflicts:

> I swear by this city—and you are a citizen of this city—and by parents and their children! We created humans for hardship. Does he think that no one will ever overcome him? He says, "I have squandered fortune!" Does he think that no one has seen him? Did we not make for him two eyes, and a tongue, and two lips? Did we not guide him on the two pathways? But he never attempted the steep path. How to explain to you the steep path? It is freeing a slave or feeding, during a famine, an orphan related to you, or a grubby vagrant. Then he would be one of the believers who counseled patience and compassion. They are the companions of the right hand. But those who disavow our verses are companions of the left hand. They will be trapped in walls of fire.

The affluent individual here critiqued appears to question Muhammad's standing in Mecca, such that the prophet is defended as being *hill* or legitimate. In addition, this individual glories in being a wastrel (a way for the wealthy to demonstrate high status) and refuses to help the needy. *The Clot* 96:9-12 contains a further complaint against such elites, which is their hostility to the new faith: "Have you seen the one who forbids a worshipper to pray? Have you noticed whether he is guided or enjoins piety?"

The opposition of wealthy and powerful pagans created the need for a response on the part of the Prophet and his followers. It was a very different response than that common in the Old Arabic Safaitic inscriptions that recorded the culture of pastoralists. One such inscription speaks of Habad, who made camp the year that siege was laid to one of the clans of Dayf. He scratched out on the stone his grief and mourning for Hay, who was killed, and cried out, "O Allat, vengeance on whosoever committed [this act]!"[7] Another says, "By Sny son of Sny ... and he was distraught with grief for Sh'r. So O Allah [grant] vengeance [*nqmt*]."[8] Such requests to the gods for retribution are common in the inscriptions, which speak of a culture of raiding and occasional bloodshed.

In an early chapter, the Qur'an (*Enwrapped* 73:10-12) speaks of Muhammad having his integrity impugned by the affluent (*al-mukadhdhibin uli al-ni`ma*), but the advice is given, "Be patient with what they say and take your leave of them graciously. Leave to me the affluent who impugn your integrity, giving them a short reprieve, for we possess shackles and a searing abyss." Here, he is advised to deal with this oral harassment at the hands of the rich and powerful by showing patience (*isbir*) with them and simply withdrawing (*uhjurhum*) from the company of the abusers. Muhammad is advised, however, to leave the group "graciously" or, literally, "beautifully" (*jamilan*). The Abbasid-era exegete Muhammad ibn Jarir Tabari (d. 923) interpreted "withdrawal" in a spiritual, almost Sufi sense, as "emigrating in the essence of God" (*al-hijr fi dhat Allah*), a turn to inward communing with the divine.[9] Even Ibn Kathir (1300–73), the conservative exegete of Mamluk Syria, explained that God was "ordering the Messenger to be patient with the lies of the foolish among his people and to withdraw from them graciously, which is to say, without rebuke (*la `itab*)."[10] Patience and graciousness are the key terms here for reacting to humiliation at the hands of Mecca's elite. Asma Afsaruddin has argued that "patience" (*al-sabr*) is a keyword in the Qur'an's discussion of peaceful and tolerant responses to persecution.[11] Clearly, Muhammad is being counseled against the opposite, i.e., impatience and coarseness. The voice of God next commands him to "leave me with those who impugn your integrity," and his opponents are menaced with hellfire. The verb *kadhdhaba* is often translated as "to deny," but it is an intensive and it implies calling someone a liar rather than simply denying the facticity of what they say, which is why I suggest the rendering "to impugn the integrity of." Muhammad is then (73:15-16) compared to Moses, and the wealthy Meccan elite implicitly are likened to Pharaoh. It is implied that Muhammad need take no action, other than to absent himself courteously from that gathering, because God is responsible for chastising them.[12] This motif, of what Gerd Theissen called an "eschatological postponement of violence," also occurs in the epistles of Paul, as with Rom. 12:19, "Beloved, never avenge yourselves, but leave room for the wrath of God; for it is written, 'Vengeance is mine, I will repay, says the Lord.'"[13]

The themes of oral harassment by pagans and divine punishment of the latter are common in the early chapters of the Qur'an. *The Swindlers* 83:29-36 complains,

Surely, the miscreants used to laugh at those who believed, and when they passed by them would wink archly at one another, and after they went home, they would return poking fun, observing whenever they saw them, 'They've gone astray.' They were not, however, sent to be their custodians. Today, the ones laughing at the pagans are the believers as they lounge on adorned couches, gazing. And have the pagans been rewarded for what they were doing?

This passage describes the way the pagans made fun of the believers, with cutting remarks and jokes at their expense. It is underlined, however, that the believers had to allow this behavior, since they were not dispatched as the "custodians (hafizin)" of the pagans. Then the timescale is shifted to the perspective of eternity as the believers, rewarded in paradise with sumptuous couches, are shown gazing down into the depths of hell and laughing at the fate of their tormenters.

This verse is an example of what Theissen calls the eschatological punishment model. It paints a picture of the condign punishment awaiting the smirking wicked in the next life, recalling Lk. 6:25, "Woe to you who are full now, for you will be hungry. Woe to you who are laughing now, for you will mourn and weep." Likewise, in Mt. 10:14-15 Jesus urges detachment from the destiny of the obstinate and issues a dire prediction concerning them: "If anyone will not welcome you or listen to your words, shake off the dust from your feet as you leave that house or town. Truly I tell you, it will be more tolerable for the land of Sodom and Gomorrah on the day of judgment than for that town." Theissen classed this verse of Matthew with "fantasies of vengeance."[14]

That Muhammad should not attempt to impose himself but rather should simply preach and leave the outcome to God is underlined in *The Enveloper* 88:21-24: "Then remind (fa-dhakkir), for you are only a reminder. You are not a ruler (musaytir) over them. Those who turn their backs and blaspheme, however, God will chastise them with the most severe affliction." It is this status of the Prophet as a reminder but not a ruler that allows him to withdraw graciously from any confrontation and to leave the fate of obstinate pagans to God. That Muhammad's followers had no position of authority over their pagan adversaries is reaffirmed in *The Rangers* 37:29-30, where they are described as telling the pagans in the afterlife, "you were never believers and we never had any authority (min sultanin) over you. Rather, you were a tyrannical (taghin) people."

Another relatively early Meccan passage, *The Scatterers* 51:52-60, says,

Never did a messenger come to their predecessors except that they excoriated him as a wizard or a madman. Did they bequeath this calumny? Indeed, they are a lawless people. So, turn away from them. No blame attaches to you. Be mindful, for the remembrance benefits the believers. We only created *jinn* and human beings for worship. "I wish no sustenance from them and do not want them to feed me. Instead, it is God who is the nourisher, and he is the possessor of power, the invincible. The wrongdoers will have their share, like the share of their companions, so let them not hurry it. Unfortunate are the pagans in the day they were promised."

Muhammad is instructed, in the face of obstinate insults and calumnies, to "turn away from them (*tawalla 'anhum*)" and is assured that no blame will attach to him for so doing. His duty to preach is not absolute, and he is absolved when the level of abuse on the tongues of his audience reaches a crescendo. The passage then switches from the voice of God to the autobiographical voice of the Prophet, who assures his interlocutors that he makes no claim on them for material support. This sentiment is repeated in *Consultation* 42:23, "Those are the glad tidings of God to his servants, who believed and carried out exemplary works. I solicit no remuneration from you for it save the loving-kindness owed to relatives. God will enhance goodness for those who accomplish good works. He is forgiving and appreciative." This independence recalls Luke 6:35, "but love your enemies, do good, and lend, expecting nothing in return." In *The Scatterers* (51), Muhammad's independence of his audience is the flip side of the coin of his lack of authority over them. He seeks neither to regiment them nor to exploit them. They are free to accept or reject the teaching. If they go beyond merely declining the invitation and their behavior becomes too outrageous, however, they thereby relieve the Prophet of any obligation to continue to counsel them and he can turn away from them without risking divine opprobrium, leaving them to their doom in the afterlife.

The theme that the Prophet has no worldly authority is repeated in *Qaf* 50:39-45,

Be forbearing in the face of their taunts and recite the praises of your lord before sunrise and before sunset, and some of the night, magnifying him, and after you prostrate yourselves. Listen for the day on which the crier will call out from on nigh, the day on which they hear the cry in truth, for that is the Resurrection Day.

Verse 50:44 describes, "The day on which the earth is riven asunder as they rush about—an ingathering that we arrange effortlessly." In *Qaf* 50:45, God is depicted as addressing Muhammad, "We know best the things they say. You are not a despot over them. Remind, by means of the Qur'an, those who fear my threats." As in *Enwrapped* 70:10, Muhammad is counseled to be patient or forebear (*isbir*) in the face of "what they say" (which implies that they were taunting and insulting him). He and his community should simply go on with their worship and late-night prayers, and await the Resurrection Day, when their persecutors will be fleeing in apprehension. Muhammad is again prompted that his obligation is "to remind by means of the Qur'an" (*dhakkir bi al-Qur'an*), but that he is not to be overbearing toward his audience (*ma anta 'alayhim bi jabbarin*). Later in the Qur'an (*The Table*

5:22), the Canaanites who forestalled Moses' entry into the Holy Land are called *jabbar*, implying tyranny and oppression. Muhammad's lack of oversight over the pagans, which frees him from any obligation to do more than to preach them, is a constant theme. *Consultation* 42:6 says, "Those who adopt patrons other than God nevertheless have God as their guardian (*hafiz*), but you are not their manager (*wakil*)."

The quranic advice to "withdraw" or "turn away" from abusive pagans does not imply bearing them any ill will in this world. *Hobbling* 45:14 says, "Say to the believers: Let them forgive the ones who do not anticipate the days of God, so that he may be the one who gives a people the wages of their deeds." Muhammad's followers are to forgive (*ighfir*) their tormenters, who deny the Resurrection Day. This forgiveness is portrayed as an act of humility, since it relinquishes to God the imposition of the penalty for wicked deeds. Not only does the Prophet pardon the pagans, he wishes them well and would, if he could, shower them with good things. In *Ornaments* 43:33-35, Muhammad appears to speak in his own voice with these sentiments:

> If it would not have caused all people to observe a single communal path (*an yakun ummatan wahida*) we would have bestowed roofs of silver and staircases for their houses on those who reject the All-Merciful, and would have furnished their homes with fine doors and couches on which to recline, and gilded ornaments. But all that is merely for the enjoyment of the life of this world, whereas the hereafter is for the God-fearing.

That is, Muhammad would have been willing to be munificent in this life toward the militant pagans, but is forestalled from doing so by the divine plan for the universe in which paganism is to be discouraged. Without punishments both in this world and the next, people might all follow the polytheist way, and there would be no incentive for pagans to become part of the monotheistic nation instead.

Later in the same chapter, with regard to a "people who do not believe," verse 89 contains the command, "pardon them, and say, 'Peace!' Soon they will know." The verb "to pardon" (*safaha*) can also mean to "turn away from." But in this verse, it is coupled with an order to wish them peace and security, which is more compatible with forgiveness than it is with turning one's back on someone. In *The Cow* 2:109, the believers are instructed concerning the People of the Book (Jews and Christians) who wish they would just go back to being pagans rather than espousing a new monotheistic religion, "then forgive (*u`fu*) and pardon (*isfahu*) until God comes with his decree." The use of the two verbs as a parallelism here sheds light on their similar meaning. In *Ornament*, Muhammad can "pardon" the pagans because their fate is God's to determine, not his. He cannot, however, be as generous toward them as he would like lest he misguide them into thinking that their prosperity made their polytheism acceptable.

Quranic "Beatitudes"

Some of the middle Mecca period chapters elaborate directly and at some length on the principle of replying to harassment with wishes for the peace and wellbeing of one's tormenters. *The Criterion* 25:63-76 contains a series of statements analogous to the Beatitudes of Jesus (Matt. 5:3-12) in the Sermon on the Mount:

> The servants of the All-Merciful are those who walk humbly upon the earth—
> and when the unruly address them, they reply, "Peace!"
> And those who spend the night bowing down and rising again to their Lord;
> those who say, "Lord, divert the desolation of Gehenna from us, for its anguish is unrelenting, and it is a horrid clime in which to dwell;"
> and those who, when they spend, are neither reckless nor miserly, but keep to the middle of these extremes;
> and those who do not supplicate any other deity than God,
> who do not take the life of a person whose killing God has forbidden, except where they are in the right;
> nor commit fornication, for those who behave that way will receive a punishment; indeed, their torment will be doubled on the Resurrection Day, and they will persist, abject, for eternity therein, save for those who repent, believe, and do good works—God will transform their evil actions into good deeds, for God is forgiving and merciful;
> those who repent and perform good works turn wholly unto God,
> those who close their eyes to falsehood, and who, if they pass by some impiety, proceed on with dignity;
> those who, when they are admonished by the verses of their Lord, do not fall down, deaf and blind.
> And those who say, "Lord, grant to us wives and children who will be the apple of our eye; and make us exemplars for the God-fearing"
> they will be rewarded with a celestial chamber for their patience, wherein they will receive salutations and the greeting of "Peace!"—reposing in it forever—how beautiful an abode in which to reside.

This passage enumerates the characteristics of servants of the All-Merciful: (1) they walk humbly (*hawnan*) on the earth; (2) they reply to the words of the unruly (*al-jahilun*) by responding with wishes of "peace;" (3) they stay up late praying and prostrating; (4) they pray to be spared hellfire; (5) they spend in moderation; (6) they do not call on divinities other than God; (7) they do not take life, save, in accordance with the *lex talionis*, that of a murderer who killed one of their own (and in later chapters they are counseled even against that); (8) they are faithful to their spouses, or if they stray, they repent wholeheartedly; (9) they repent and do good; (10) they are not tempted by falsehood or impiety and determinedly walk by such displays; (11) they accept the admonishment of God's verses; and (12) they pray to be good family members and moral models.

Humility, praying for peace and security for their enemies, and eschewing violence in response to verbal harassment are prominent among these twelve attributes of the servants of the All-Merciful. Tabari glosses *Criterion* 25:63 as saying that they walk the earth "with an even-tempered character, with divine calm (*sakina*), and dignity, not arrogant or bullying, nor committing disorder (*fasad*) or rebellion against God." He says that the commentators differed as to whether *hawnan* meant "with dignity and calm" or "with humility." As for 25:64, he says it means that "when those ignorant of God address them with words they are loathe to hear, the believers respond to them with kindly discourse and upright speech."[15] Humility is a sign of belief in the Qur'an, whereas it has been argued that one of the primary attributes of the pagan is haughtiness.[16] Verses 25:63-64 became a favorite of later Sufi commentators, who elaborated on the principle of wishing peace and security toward and showing love toward enemies, actions they thought were enabled by the mystic's immersion in the attribute of God's mercy and compassion, citing "the servants of the All-Merciful"[17] (see Rashied Omar's essay in this volume).

The late Meccan chapter *Consultation* 42:36-38 restates these quranic "beatitudes" briefly:

> Whatever things you have been given are only the enjoyment of this world, but what is with God is superior and more enduring for those who have believed and put their trust in their lord, and those who avoid mortal sins and adultery, and who, when they are angered, forgive, and who respond to their lord, perform their prayers, run their affairs by consultation among themselves, and who expend in charity from the provisions we bestow on them.

The ideal believers as described here put aside their anger, and instead forgive those who provoked it.

Lex Talionis

Consultation 42:39-43 both affirms the principle of an eye for an eye and yet softens it:

> The retribution for a tort is a similar injury, but those who forgive and make peace will be rewarded by God. He does not love wrongdoers. Those who exact satisfaction after having been wronged are not in turn liable to any reprisal. Those subject to reprisal are only those who commit wrongs against people and

exercise tyranny in the land without any right, and for them awaits a painful chastisement. But whoever shows patience (*sabara*) and forgives (*ghafara*), that is true steadfastness (*la-min 'azm al-umur*).

By urging forbearance and forgiveness rather than revenge, this passage seeks to move away from the *lex talionis* in a way that resembles Jesus' Sermon on the Mount Mt. 5:38-41:

You have heard that it was said, 'An eye for an eye and a tooth for a tooth.' But I say to you, Do not resist an evildoer. But if anyone strikes you on the right cheek, turn the other also; and if anyone wants to sue you and take your coat, give your cloak as well; and if anyone forces you to go one mile, go also the second mile.

To be fair, the examples given here are of injuries (a humiliating slap, confiscation of a garment, a lawsuit, a Roman conscription of transport animals) that fell well short in seriousness of the murder of a loved one, for which the Qur'an had authorized the demanding of tribal justice in *Criterion* 25:68.

A very late passage of the Qur'an (*The Table* 5:45) in the Medina period refers to the Hebrew Bible and paraphrases Deuteronomy 19:21. Arberry[18] translates it this way:

And therein We prescribed for them: 'A life for a life, an eye for an eye, a nose for a nose, an ear for an ear, a tooth for a tooth, and for wounds retaliation'; but whosoever forgoes it as a freewill offering (*tasaddaqa bi*), that shall be for him an expiation (*kaffara*). Whoso judges not according to what God has sent down-they are the evildoers.

Taking the last phrase first, I think the Qur'an is here warning against a disproportionate response. It should be remembered that the principle of "an eye for an eye" was an attempt to limit the extent of retaliation. The second part of the verse encourages the believers not to demand even this satisfaction for torts, however, but to forgo vengeance as a form of charity and also as a means of obtaining forgiveness for their own sins. Ashraf Dockrat interprets it as describing "pardon as a non-compulsory but preferable elective leading in an immediate way to expiation (i.e., remittance of own sins)."[19]

As for Jesus, scholars have argued vigorously about whether he meant to abrogate Deuteronomy 19:21, "Show no pity: life for life, eye for eye, tooth for tooth, hand for hand, foot for foot." That he was not bringing a new law was at least asserted in Matthew 5:17-18, "Do not think that I have come to abolish the law or the prophets; I have come not to abolish but to fulfill. For truly I tell you, until heaven and earth pass away, not one letter, not one stroke of a letter, will pass from the law until all is accomplished." Benno Przybylski argued that Jesus may have been deploying a rabbinical, Tannaitic, form of argumentation about the law, which the rabbis referred to as "fencing it in." That is, believers were urged to stay well clear of the limits of the law, lest they transgress it. Matthew 5:21 has this form: "You have heard that it was said to those of ancient times, 'You shall not murder'; and 'whoever murders shall be liable to judgment.' But I say to you that if you are angry with a brother or sister, you will be liable to judgment."[20] In the Qur'an, too, there appears to be an attempt to "fence in" the *lex talionis*, permitting a proportional response to a tort but urging that believers instead forgive their enemies.

Repelling Evil with Good

Late in the middle Meccan period, *The Believers* 23:91, 96 puts forward an even more challenging response to persecution, of replying to it by doing favors for the persecutors.

> God has never taken unto Himself any offspring, and there is no other deity with Him—for then each god would have taken away what he created, and some of them would have been ranged against others. Glory be to God above how they describe Him ... Repel the evil deed with what is better [or best, *bi allati hiya ahsan*]. We know best how they describe [the divine].

Tabari glossed this as "He says, exalted my he be, in reminding his prophet, 'Repel, Muhammad, the defect with what is better.' That is overlooking and forgiving the undisciplined pagans, and patience with the harm they do."[21]

The chapter of *The Believers* 21:110-111 goes on to praise the believers for their patience or forbearance. God addresses the pagans who mistreated the believers, "You, however, mocked the latter, until preoccupation with them caused you to forget to remember me, while you were making fun of them. I will reward them on that day for having been longsuffering (*sabirin*). They are the ones who won out."

In chapters that fall in Theodor Nöldeke's third Meccan period (618–22?), this general principle is presented in a more elaborate manner. After a stock scene in which the pagans are consigned to hellfire and angels bestow blessings on the believers in paradise, *Distinguished* 41:33-35 observes,

> Whose discourse is more beautiful than one who calls others to God and performs good works and proclaims, 'I am among those who have acquiesced in the monotheist tradition (*min al-muslimin*)'? The good deed (*al-hasana*) and the evil deed (*al-sayyi'a*) are not equal. Repel (*idfa'*) the latter with what is

better (*ahsan*) and behold, it will be as though the one, with whom you have a mutual enmity (ʿ*adawa*), is a devoted patron (*wali hamim*). Yet to none is this granted save the patient (*alladhina sabaru*), and to none is it granted save the supremely fortunate (*dhu hazzin azim*).

This remarkable verse goes beyond counseling gracious withdrawal from and forgiveness of foes to urging doing good toward them and returning their evil deeds with good ones, which over time has the prospect of winning them over and making them patrons rather than enemies. The elative *ahsan* wielded in that cause may here be a superlative even though it is indefinite, so that the phrase means "that which is best" or "the greatest good" because it is elliptical, leaving out the rest of the sentence. That is, it is implied that the action is better ... "than any other deed" (just as "*Allahu Akbar*" implies that God is most great, i.e., that he is greater than everything else, not merely that he is "greater"). Doing "the best" by evildoers is implicitly contrasted not only with "the evil deed" (*al-sayyiʾa*) but also with the mere "good deed" (*al-hasana*). It is by performing this implicitly superlative deed that is "better" (than any other) for evildoers that one can transform them from inveterate enemies into patrons and supporters. This accomplishment, however, depends on the believer having a vast store of forbearance and being extremely fortunate. It is marked as no ordinary spiritual achievement, to do the supreme good for those who have done evil to you. Tabari gave a saying he had ultimately from Ibn ʿAbbas in interpretation of the verse, "Repel the latter with what is better:" He said, "God commanded the believers to meet anger with patience and an even temper (*hilm*), and to meet mistreatment with forgiveness. If they do this, he safeguards them from Satan, and their enemies will yield to them, as though a devoted patron."[22] Others, Tabari said, interpret it to mean, "Push back with peace (*al-salam*) against the abuse of someone who mistreats you."[23] The verse only mentions acting in an exemplary way, but Tabari gives many quotes from exegetes who concur that it is the proffer of peace that is being spoken of when "the better" or "best" is commanded.

This quranic assertion that doing good to hostile others can over time have a transformative effect on them addresses one critique of the Christian form of this principle, which is that "love your enemies" is one-sided rather than dialogical. In this formula, *Distinguished* 41:33-35 resembles the *Didache*, the early Christian teaching manual. This work instructs Gentile converts to Christianity,

Speak well of the ones speaking badly of you, and pray for your enemies, (and) fast for the ones persecuting you; For what merit [is there] if you love the ones loving you? Do not even the gentiles do the same thing? You, on the other hand, love the ones hating you (τους μισούντας), and you will not have an enemy (ἐχθρόν).

"You will not have an enemy" is very close to the Qur'an's "it will be as though the one, between whom and you exists enmity, is a devoted patron."

Thus far, these Qur'an passages have covered the proper attitude of the early community of the believers toward the persecution mounted by pagans. In *Stories* 28:52-55 it appears that local Christians are addressed. They appear to be sympathizers with Muhammad's movement or to be converts, since their acceptance of the Qur'an is spoken of:

> As for those to whom we granted scripture beforehand, they believed in it, and when it was recited to them, they said, "We have believed in it; it is the truth from our Lord. Even before it, we had acquiesced in the monotheistic tradition (*muslimin*)." They will be given their recompense twice over, inasmuch as they have been patient (*sabaru*), and they repel (*yadra'una*) evil with good, and donate to charity from the provisions we bestowed on them. When they hear nonsense, they turn away from it and say, "To us are our works and to you are yours. Peace be upon you, we do not seek out the unruly."

This group, despite belonging to a pre-quranic religious tradition, exemplifies the same virtues as the believers in the forgoing accounts.[24] They are open to the truth of the Qur'an, though it is not clear whether they necessarily forsook their own tradition for it, or simply expressed a pluralist appreciation of it. Fred Donner has argued that Muhammad's movement was initially ecumenical.[25] These Christians are praised for giving charity to the poor, for exercising forbearance, for responding to evil deeds with good works, and for replying to oral harassment by wishing their opponents "peace." Their repaying of evil with good and dedication to peace with their enemies will earn them a reward in heaven twice over. Tabari quotes 'Abd al-Rahman Ibn Zayd as saying that the group had been "*muslimin* following the religion of Jesus," which shows awareness that "*muslim*" in the Qur'an means something like "monotheist" rather than referring solely to followers of Muhammad.[26]

It is likely that this passage of the Qur'an, praising ecumenically minded Christians for these virtues, was intended to evoke the Sermon on the Mount. In wishing peace on their unruly neighbors, they resemble the "peacemakers" (εἰρηνοποιοί) who are blessed in Mt. 5:9. By declining to tangle with them and by returning good for evil, they are turning the other cheek (Mt. 5:39). In Jesus' first-century Jewish context, being slapped was a form of humiliation, whereas in seventh-century Mecca the Qur'an mainly contains mentions of oral insults.[27] These people of the Book exemplify the principle, "Love your enemies and pray for those who persecute you" (Mt. 5:44), since wishing "peace" for someone has the form of a prayer. The praise for their charity recalls Mt. 59:42, "Give to everyone who begs from you, and do not refuse anyone who wants to borrow from you." If the passage in *Stories* is speaking of Christians and obliquely referring to the Sermon on the Mount, it is remarkable how similar the description of their nonviolence and goodwill toward their enemies is to that given in *Al-Furqan* 25:63-76 of Muhammad's own believers.

One of the Christian communities that cultivated commentaries on and aphorisms drawn from the Sermon on the Mount was the monks. Muhammad's younger contemporary, Maximos the Confessor (c. 580–662), penned the *Four Centuries on Love* in 626.[28] There he says,

> Has someone vilified (εβλασφημήσε) you? Do not hate him; hate the vilification and the demon which induced him to utter it. If you hate the vilifier, you have hated a man and so broken the commandment. What he has done in word you do in action. To keep the commandment, show the qualities of love and help him in any way you can, so that you may deliver (απαλλάξης) him from evil.[29]

Likely this sort of Christian sentiment was praised in *Stories* 28:52-55. This context also underlines that the community of Muhammad's believers in the Mecca period resembled a lay order, giving themselves over to praying much of the night and other spiritual practices, and adopting the discipline of returning good for evil.

Pagan Parents and Relatives: Accompanying with Kindness

Stories 28:56-57 contains an address to Muhammad by God:

> You are unable to guide those whom you love, but God guides whomever he will, and he knows better who will be guided. They say, 'If we were to follow the guidance along with you, we would be kidnapped (*nutakhattaf*) away from our land.' Have we not, however, guaranteed to them a safe sanctuary (*haraman*) to which are brought all sorts of fruit as nourishment from us? But most of them do not know.

The relatives of Muhammad are implicitly contrasted with the Christians. Whereas the Prophet was able to reach the latter, despite their being distant from him socially, he failed to guide his own kin. The Banu Hashim and Banu Muttalib are portrayed as fearing to convert because of the danger that they would be apprehended by the militant pagans and exiled. They are reminded in this passage, however, that Mecca, the site of the shrine to the Lord, is a sanctuary in which no violence is permitted, with the implication that their fears are unfounded. This portrayal of Mecca sheds light on the commitment to nonviolence and to doing good to one's enemies of the Meccan chapters of the Qur'an, since the believers were not facing violent persecution there. The challenge they faced was being taunted and humiliated, which they were encouraged to deal with by praying for the peace and security of their tormentors.

Ethical advice attributed in the Qur'an to the sage Luqman (likely a reference to the ancient Greek philosopher Alcmaeon of Croton, b. 510 BC) further takes up the issue of pagan relatives and their treatment by believers. *Luqman* 31:15 is a counsel regarding polytheist parents in the voice of God:

> But if they strive to get you (*jahadaka*) to associate with me those [gods] about whom you have no knowledge, do not obey them. Still, accompany them in this world with kindness (*sahibhuma fi al-dunya ma'rufan*), but follow the path of those who turn in repentance to me. You will return to me, and I will inform you about your past deeds.

The distinction is made explicitly that in this world, the believers are to associate socially with and do good toward polytheist relatives. There is no conception here of shunning pagans or behaving militantly toward them. Rather, believing children of pagan parents are to mingle with them, and behave well toward them. The term *ma'ruf* in the Qur'an implies acts of kindness, and acts that are honorable, right and fair, as opposed to acts that are censured (*al-munkar*).

This passage can be contrasted with Mt. 10:34-39,

> Do not think that I have come to bring peace to the earth; I have not come to bring peace, but a sword. For I have come to set a man against his father, and a daughter against her mother, and a daughter-in-law against her mother-in-law and one's foes will be members of one's own household. Whoever loves father or mother more than me is not worthy of me; and whoever loves son or daughter more than me is not worthy of me; and whoever does not take up the cross and follow me is not worthy of me.

Both the New Testament and the Qur'an contain an expectation that the novel religious teachings of a new prophet will provoke familial conflict. In the Qur'an, believers are instructed not to obey parents who "strive" (*jahada*) to impose paganism on their children, and Jesus' saying rebukes believers who defer to their parents in forsaking their faith. Matthew 10:34, however, emphasizes the prospect of conflict ("the sword"), whereas in *Luqman* 31:15 reconciliation is stressed. Despite the paganism of their parents and the vigorous opposition of the latter to Muhammad's teachings, his believers are urged to continue closely to associate with those parents, and to treat them honorably and with kindness.

Controversies have raged for two millennia about the meaning of the "sword" (μάχαιρα) invoked by Jesus. The parallel verse in Luke 12:54 says, "Do you think that I have come to bring peace to the earth? No, I tell you, but rather division (διαμερισμός)!" The church fathers tended to interpret the "sword" as allegorical, and to see the passage as a prediction that relatives would persecute Christian converts rather than as an indication that Christians would take up the sword against them. Some twentieth-century exegetes influenced by anti-colonial revolutions saw the passage as a sign that Jesus was no pacifist but was willing to deploy revolutionary violence, a position, however, that has been largely rejected by the academy.[30] Still, the New Testament authors portrayed Jesus' disciples as walking around armed with swords, and showed Jesus as willing to deploy violence on occasion, as when he went into the temple in Jerusalem to inflict stripes on moneylenders and livestock brokers with a bullwhip that he had sat and carefully constructed for the purpose (Jn 2:13-16). John Dominic Crossan saw Jesus' comments on "hating" one's mother and father (Lk 14:26) and his prediction of familial conflict as the challenge of a younger generation to an older patriarchal family establishment.[31] Likewise, *Luqman* 31:15 implies a generational struggle of young monotheists against powerful pagan elders (with whom many of them would have continued to live in extended family households), but with more optimism than in the New Testament.

The early community of believers was a missionary community, but they are told in the Qur'an to pursue that vocation in ways that did not injure the feelings of their interlocutors. Even in the course of the dramatic story of the confrontation of Moses with Pharaoh, in chapter *Taha* 20:44, God is said to have told Moses and Aaron, "Speak gently (*qawlan layyinan*) with him, in hopes that he may take a lesson and be struck with fear." Surely such an instruction is intended to model for Muhammad's believers the ideal sort of interaction with their pagan associates. With regard to Jews and Christians as well, the believers are urged to eirenic methods of mission and dialogue, as in *The Spider* 29:46: "Debate (*tujadilu*) the scriptural communities only in the best of ways, except for those who do wrong. Say 'We believe in the revelation sent down to us, and the revelation sent down to you; our God and your God is one, and to him we have submitted.'" The believers are also counseled to this course of action in *The Bee* 16:125, with regard to Jews with whom they had a dispute over the Sabbath: "Call to the way of your lord with wisdom and good counsel (*wa al-maw'izati al-hasanati*). Debate them in the best of ways (*bi allati hiya ahsan*). For your lord knows best who has strayed from his path, and he knows best who is guided."

Medina

In 622, according to Muslim tradition, Muhammad and his believers emigrated to nearby Yathrib, which became known as Medina "the city" (for the city of the Prophet).[32] The Qur'an contains accounts of Meccan pagan attacks on the small community and briefly describes two major battles, a siege (mentioning Yathrib by name), and some smaller skirmishes. Much attention has been paid to the last eleven years of the Prophet's life and to the permission given in the Qur'an for the believers to mount campaigns of what are portrayed in that book as self-defense. In the sanctuary city of Mecca, with its shrine to the Lord, where fighting was by custom forbidden, the earliest community of believers had been more or less pacifist under most circumstances, though members were permitted to insist on tribal justice for one who murdered their own. In Medina, they turned instead to a doctrine of just war. It has been pointed out that Church Fathers such as Augustine of Hippo supported imperial Christian Roman warfare, or "just war," in terms difficult to distinguish from those of the Qur'an, even if scholars have for the most part called the struggles urged in the latter not "just war" but "holy war" (a misnomer, since no such phrase or conception occurs in the Muslim scripture).[33] Even in the era of hostilities, however, hopes are expressed in the Qur'an for reconciliation between the warring parties. A verse in the chapter *al-Baqara* 2:190 says, "Fight in the path of God those who enter into combat against you, but do not commit aggression. God does not love aggressors." *Al-Anfal* 8:38 and 8:61, which later authorities attribute to the year 624 in the wake of the Battle of Badr, contain these sentiments: "Say to the pagans that if they desist they will be forgiven for what went before. But if they backslide, the way of the ancients has already passed" and "if they incline toward peace, you must incline toward it. Trust in God—he is all-hearing and omniscient." The much later Abbasid era writers differed from the Qur'an, depicting Muhammad and his followers as Arabian raiders virtually in the way of the pre-Islamic poetry of battle days, but the Qur'an mentions no caravan raids and urges peacemaking even in the midst of war. Any successful grappling with peace as a theme in the life of the Prophet must begin with the quranic primary source, which contradicts the biographers of a century and a half and more later.

The just war policies of the Medinan Qur'an are not necessarily in contradiction with the pacifist policies of the Meccan period, since the two situations were not comparable. Mecca was a peaceful shrine city where believers were at most ridiculed and ostracized. Medina was a statelet with a written constitution, which was under military attack and the innocents of which were in danger. Thinkers in late antiquity recognized that there is a distinction between personal ethical interactions with others in peacetime and the ethics of soldiers who have been sent to the front by a political authority. The Christian monk Athanasios of Alexandria (d. 373) wrote,

> For even in the case of the other actions in life we will find that there are differences based upon the circumstances in which they are done. For example, it is not permitted to commit murder, but in wars it is both lawful and praiseworthy to destroy one's enemies, so much so that those who displayed

valor in war are deemed worthy of the highest honors, and monuments to them are erected to proclaim their achievements. And so, the same action is not permitted in certain circumstance and at certain times, but is allowed and excused in different circumstances and at the right time.[34]

There are continuities between the two periods in quranic prescriptions, for instance, in a willingness to forgive enemies and let bygones be bygones. The late chapter, *The Woman Tested* 60:7-8, says, "Perhaps God will create love (*mawaddatan*) between you and those among whom were your enemies. God does not forbid you, with regard to those who have not fought you over religion nor expelled you from your homes, from being righteous and just toward them, for God loves those who are just." That is, the general population of Mecca and its allies had given moral support to the pagan campaigns against Medina, but only a small number of warriors had practically speaking committed crimes against the believers, and the latter are discouraged from holding a grudge or pursuing vendettas against the passively hostile. Hope is even held out that the believers will be led by God to "love" the enemy population that had rooted for its demise.

Apart from hopes for peace and reconciliation at the front, the Qur'an in the Medina period contains verses urging kindly treatment of others in a civilian context. *The Chambers* 49:11-12 says,

> Believers, let not one people ridicule another, for the latter may be better than they; nor should women ridicule other women, for the latter may be better than they. Do not insult each other, or call each other names. Using an obscene name is a miserable thing after faith. Whoever will not repent, those are wrongdoers. Believers, avoid too much suspicion, for some suspicion is sin. Do not spy on others nor should some of you backbite others. Would any of you like to eat the flesh of your dead brethren? Fear God, for God is forgiving and merciful.

Not only have the believers been urged to reply to oral abuse and harassment with wishes of peace and with good deeds toward their tormenters, they are here prohibited from engaging in verbal abuse themselves. Negative gossip is so excoriated as to be compared to cannibalism.

The putting aside of old enmities is celebrated in *The Family of Amram* 3:103:

> Hold fast, all of you, to the cord of God, and do not divide into factions. Remember God's favor to you, inasmuch as you were enemies, but he united your hearts—so that by his blessing you became siblings. You were on the brink of a pit of fire, and he delivered you from it. In this way does God make clear his signs to you, so that you might be guided.

This plea for unity concerns the internal divisions in the community, probably of a clan sort.

Universal such sentiments are also found in the Medinan Qur'an. *The Chambers* 49:13 says, "People, we have created you male and female and made you nations and tribes so that you may come to know one another. The noblest of you in the sight of God is the most pious of you. God is knowing and aware." The implication is that gender and ethnic diversity should be viewed as a positive, since it creates distinctive subcultures that carry valuable knowledge that can then be acquired by outsiders. A further implication is that high birth is in and of itself no qualification, and piety is the determining factor in deciding a person's station in society. A similar validation of difference, this time religious difference, is in chapter *The Table* 5:48: "We have prescribed to each of you a law and a tradition. If God had desired, he could have made you a single community. Instead, he is testing you with regard to the revelations you received. So, compete in doing good. You will all return to God, and he will inform you then concerning those things about which you argued." The response to another monotheistic religious tradition, then, should be to establish a friendly competition to see who can do the most charity and perform the best works in society, rather than which hierarchy can issue the most stinging anathemas.

The Social Setting of Meccan Nonviolence

Theissen suggested that only roaming holy men could afford to have a consistent policy of turning the other cheek, since if settled burghers routinely let people take advantage of them, it would encourage their tormenters to go further and further.[35] He posits that Jesus had been such a charismatic wanderer and that the logia in Q urging this policy derived from that milieu, such that he was replying to harassment from Romans. He compares this ethic of nonviolence and non-resistance to that of the mobile Cynics who espoused Stoic philosophy. Theissen argues that the later, settled, Christian communities received Jesus' *logia* on turning the other cheek and doing good to one's enemies in two main ways. The Matthew tradition, he argues, was that of a Jewish Christian milieu who saw themselves as righteous "sons of God" who, by being magnanimous, were imitating God himself. They had been defeated by the Romans in 70, and asserted themselves as spiritually victorious and inwardly sovereign by their divine magnanimity toward Gentile imperial forces. Melavic rejects this interpretation, arguing along with John Dominic Crossan that the main context for the Matthew verses about turning the other cheek and loving one's enemies is the extended Jewish family, within which young Christians would have faced constant harassment from elders. The youth are instructed to respond lovingly and with self-abnegation while upholding their new faith.[36] The majority of scholars have, however, seen a Roman context for at least some of the passages in Matthew on acquiescing to opponents' unreasonable demands.

Theissen said that the Lucan reception of these logia reflected instead the concerns of Gentile converts with a Hellenistic outlook. This community tended to universalize these precepts. They exhibited anxiety about conflict between the wealthy and the poor and about commercial disputes between moneylenders and borrowers within the Gentile community.

The *Sitz-im-Leben* of the quranic prescriptions for forgiving and doing good toward enemies was very different from that of the New Testament, though mobility may have been a common context between the life of Jesus and the early career of Muhammad. The merchants and peddlers of the Hijaz in West Arabia, including Muhammad and his initial circle, may have been relatively mobile, traveling among small towns for trade fairs, and so may not have had to deal consistently with the same elites. Many of the believers are portrayed in the Qur'an as merchants and peddlers.[37] For what it is worth, some Abbasid-era accounts also suggest such mobility.[38]

Even those who mainly resided in Mecca, however, benefited from social control mechanisms that discouraged a ratcheting up of advantage-taking on the part of their detractors. One was the convention of sanctuary, whereby raiding and violence were prohibited around shrines such as the Kaaba in Mecca. Those who broke this convention suffered reputational damage, which often served as a deterrent. Photios reported the impressions of a sixth-century Roman ambassador to Arabia, Nonnosos:

> He tells us that most of the Saracens, those who live in Phoenicon as well as beyond it and the Taurenian mountains, have a sacred meeting-place consecrated to one of the gods, where they assemble twice a year. One of these meetings lasts a whole month, almost to the middle of spring, when the sun enters Taurus; the other lasts two months and is held after the summer solstice. During these meetings complete peace prevails, not only amongst themselves, but also with all the natives; even the animals are at peace both with themselves and human beings.[39]

Apart from this regulation of vendettas by sacred time, we know that in the Near East sacred stones and sanctuaries were erected as inviolable, where peace was mandated.[40] In the Qur'an, Mecca is described as such a sanctuary, and, as we have seen, pagan relatives of the Prophet were assured for this very reason that they need not fear reprisals by polytheists if they converted to the new religion (*Stories* 28:56-57). The social setting for quranic injunctions to make peace, forgive enemies, and reconcile rather than pursue vendettas was the shrine-city or sanctuary of Mecca.

Conclusion

The Qur'an depicts Muhammad's believers and their pagan foes as having the same ethnicity, so that the Jewish-Gentile dynamics Theissen discerned in Matthew did not arise. The Melavic-Crossan interpretation of Matthew as having to do with intra-Jewish generational divisions, or the Lucan concern with wealth inequality, is closer to the situation described in the Qur'an. The constitution of the Mecca community as a sort of lay order, devoted to supererogatory prayers and strict morality, may be a further context for the ethic of repelling evil with good, so that it is no accident that some of these Qur'an verses somewhat resemble sentiments of monks such as Maximos the Confessor in the same era.

Some passages of the Qur'an, praising ethnic and gender diversity as a good of which the inquisitive should take advantage to increase their knowledge, display a more Lucan universalist emphasis. Like Luke, the Qur'an exhibits a concern with smoothing out conflicts between the wealthy and the poor. One reason given for doing good to enemies was that Muhammad's early community possessed no authority over the pagans and so had no choice but to bear their rude behavior graciously and to leave the punishment of these polytheists to God. This rationale resembles the "postponed eschatological punishment" motif in Rom. 12:19. Another reason given was that such high ethics have a transformational effect and might lead the persecutors to repent and become supporters. This rationale resembles the one mentioned in the first-century Christian *Didache* and its later, more elaborate version, the *Didascalia Apostolorum*, where it is asserted that loving one's enemies will mean, over time, that one has no enemies.

An important difference between the milieu of Jesus of Nazareth and that of Muhammad was the absence of the state in the latter. Issues in law and order were not the purview of the individual in Roman Palestine. In a frontier such as the early-seventh-century Hijaz, power was diffuse and embedded in a tribal segmentary lineage system. The threat to commerce of longstanding feuds among clans was severe. Mercantile clans like some of the ones in Mecca would have gone out of their way to attempt to defuse budding vendettas. In the absence of a central state, moreover, tribal mechanisms for the adjudication of torts operated according to the *lex talionis*. Thus, Muhammad's followers are instructed to avoid violence and murder, though they may demand, it is implied, a life for a life where one of their own has been murdered. They were encouraged to forgo even that deterrence. But that reluctance would not prevent the pagan kinsmen of Muhammad's believers from making such a demand on clan grounds, and so for the more militant pagan Meccans to go to extremes would remain a risky move.

The change in emphasis, from something close to pacifism to an acceptance of just war, in the Medina period had to do with a new and radically different social context. Unlike Mecca, it was not recognized as a shrine city or sanctuary, and so militant pagans suffered no reputational damage from attacking it. The early believers, shielded from being physically attacked or murdered in Mecca, were now vulnerable to having their blood shed at will. A polity also formed in Medina, with legitimate authority. The Meccan verses urging avoidance of violent responses to harassment often made the point that Muhammad and his followers had no authority or sovereignty. Now that the believers formed a people (*umma*) in Medina, with Jewish, and likely, Christian allies, they were authorized to wage just war as a means of restoring peace, as long as they did not commit aggression. There is no evidence that these new rules for the battlefield changed the ethical obligation of individuals to do good in return for the evil deeds of their opponents with regard to actions less serious than a murderous attack. This distinction between civilian behavior under ordinary circumstances and the exigencies of warfare in defense of innocents was one widely drawn by Christian authorities in late antiquity, including by Athanasios, Augustine, and Ambrose.[41] If we return to Theissen's location of ethical imperatives in particular social settings, we might conclude that advocacy of just war as an adjunct to the civilian practice of turning the other cheek is a feature of the bishopric. While Muhammad was a prophet and not a bishop, his role as guide and authority for a city-wide, large community in Medina differed from the one he had played in Mecca, of leading something like a small lay order of devotees.[42] It was with his more expansive role in Medina that just war thinking was added to the ethical repertoire of his community.

Notes

1   See, however, comments in Juan Cole, *Muhammad: Prophet of Peace amid the Clash of Empires* (New York: The Nation Books, 2018), chapters 2, 3. This chapter is an extended consideration of some points first made there, though I consider many more apposite Qur'an verses here and suggest an analytical framework for considering them. In what follows, unless otherwise noted, translations of the Qur'an are my own.

2   Gerd Theissen, *Social Reality and the Early Christians* (Minneapolis, MN: Fortress Press, 1992), 130.

3   Fred Donner, *Muhammad and the Believers: At the Origins of Islam* (Cambridge, MA: Harvard University Press, 2010), chapter 2; Aziz al-Azmeh, *The Emergence of Islam in Late Antiquity: Allah and His People* (Cambridge: Cambridge University Press, 2014); F. E. Peters, *Muhammad and the Origins of Islam* (Albany: State University of New York Press, 1994), chapter 6.

4   Juan Cole, "Infidel or Paganus? The Polysemy of kafara in the Quran," *Journal of the American Oriental Society* 140, no. 3 (2020): 615–35.

5 Michel Desjardins, *Peace, Violence and the New Testament* (Sheffield: Sheffield Academic Press, 1997).

6 W. Montgomery Watt, *Muhammad's Mecca: History in the Quran* (Edinburgh: Edinburgh University Press, 1988), 82–5.

7 In OCIANA, http://krc.orient.ox.ac.uk, Siglum C 777; M.C.A. Macdonald, M. Al Mu'azzin, and L. Nehmé, "Les inscriptions safaïtiques de Syrie, cent quarante ans après leur découverte," *Comptes rendus des séances de l'Académie des Inscriptions & Belles-Lettres* (1996): 435–94 at 462.

8 http://krc.orient.ox.ac.uk/ociana/corpus/pages/OCIANA_0038662.html

9 Tabari, *Tafsir: Jami' al-bayan 'an tawil ay al-Qur'an*, ed. 'Abd Allah ibn 'Abd al-Muhsin al-Turk, 26 vols (Cairo: Dar Hijr, 2001), 23: 380. Tabari notes the opinion of Qatada that this verse was abrogated by the later verses about just war in the Medina period, but Tabari clearly does not agree.

10 Abu al-Fida Isma'il Ibn Kathir, *Tafsir al-Qur'an al-Karim* (Beirut: Dar Ibn Hazm, 2000), 1932.

11 Asma Afsaruddin, "Recovering the Early Semantic Purview of Jihad and Martyrdom: Challenging Statist-Military Perspectives," in *Crescent and Dove: Peace and Conflict Resolution in Islam*, ed. Qamar-ul Huda (Washington, DC: US Institute for Peace, 2010), 39–62. See also her chapter in this book.

12 *Enwrapped* 73:20 is an interpolated Medinan-era verse that need not detain us here, since we are beginning with the Meccan chapters.

13 Theissen, *Social Reality and the Early Christians*, 126–7. Bible verses are quoted from the New Revised Standard Version, copyright 1989 by the National Council of Churches and used by permission.

14 Theissen, *Social Reality and the Early Christians*, 127.

15 Tabari, *Tafsir*, 17:489.

16 Toshihiko Izutsu, *Ethico-Religious Concepts in the Qur'an* (Montreal: McGill University Press, 2002 [1959]), 142–4.

17 Abu 'Abd al-Raḥman al-Sulami, *Ḥaqa'iq al-Tafsir*, ed. Sayyid 'Umran, 2 vols. (Beirut: Dar al-Kutub al-'Ilmiyya, 2001), 2: 66–7; 'Abd al-Karim al-Qushayri, *Laṭa'if al-Isharat*, ed. 'A. 'Abd al- Rahman 3 vols. (Beirut: Dar al-Kutub al-'Ilmiyya, 2nd edn. 2007), 2: 392–3; 'Abdallah al-Ansari, *Kitab Manazil al-Sa'irin* (Beirut: Dar al-Kutub al-'Ilmiyya, 1988), 60–61.

18 A. J. Arberry, *The Koran Interpreted* 2 vols. (New York: Macmillan, 1950 [1973]), 1: 135.

19 M. A. E. (Ashraf) Dockrat, "Retaliation and Pardon as Expressed in Chapter 5: 45 with Reference to Matthew 5: 38–42," *Journal for Semitics* 26, no. 1 (November 2017): 275–93, at 291–2.

20 Benno Pryzybylski, *Righteousness in Matthew and His World of Thought* (Cambridge: Cambridge University Press, 1980), 81–4, 149 n47; Francois P. Viljoen, "Jesus' halakhic Argumentation on the True Intention of the Law in Matthew 5: 21–48," *Verbum et ecclesia* 34, no. 1 (2013): 5.

21 Tabari, *Tafsir,* 17:104. He added, "That was his instruction to him before he ordered him to go to war with him." But this Abbasid positioning of the verse as abrogated by subsequent events is not substantiated by the Medinan chapters of the Qur'an themselves, which clearly speak of having good relations with non-belligerent pagans. See, e.g., *al-Nisa'* 4:94, which requires that the believers accept the greeting "peace" from friendly pagans, instead of automatically treating them as hostiles. The technique of "abrogation" (*naskh*) is ahistorical and not based on anything in the

Qur'an itself, and is not relevant to this article, which is centered in the early seventh century, not on later Muslim understanding of the Qur'an. Moreover, scholars differed widely in their application of it. Tabari did not abrogate as many of the peace and reconciliation verses as some more hard line scholars, as demonstrated by Asma Afsaruddin, "Jihad and Martyrdom in Islamic Thought and History," *Oxford Research Encyclopedia of Religion* (online), 2016, https://oxfordre.com/religion/view/10.1093/acrefore/9780199340378.001.0001/acrefore-9780199340378-e-46?rskey=yw0w1g&result=7. The use of abrogation or naskh to contradict quranic pluralism is also discussed in Asma Afsaruddin, "The Hermeneutics of Inter-Faith Relations: Retrieving Moderation and Pluralism as Universal Principles in Qur'anic Exegeses," *Journal of Religious Ethics* 37, no. 2 (June 2009): 331–54 at 348–9.

22   Tabari, *Tafsir*, 20:432.

23   Ibid., 20:433. It is remarkable that in commenting on this verse, he and the other exegetes he quotes do not bring up the abrogation issue and that they interpret the verse in a straightforward way.

24   For the Qur'anic view of previous monotheist communities such as Christianity, see Juan Cole, "Paradosis and Monotheism: A Late Antique Approach to the Meaning of Islām in the Quran," *Bulletin of the School of Oriental and African Studies* 82, no. 3 (2019): 405–25.

25   Donner, *Muhammad and the Believers*, 69–70.

26   Tabari, *Tafsir*, 18:281; Cole, "Paradosis," 405–25.

27   John Granger Cook, "Matthew 5.39 and 26.67: Slapping Another's Cheek in Ancient Mediterranean Culture," *Journal of Greco-Roman Christianity and Judaism* 10 (2014): 68–89.

28   Marek Jankowiak and Phil Booth, "A New Date-List of the Works of Maximus the Confessor," in *The Oxford Handbook of Maximus the Confessor*, ed. Pauline Allen and Bronwen Neil (Oxford: Oxford University Press, 2015), online: DOI:10.1093/oxfordhb/9780199673834.013.2. For his life, see the essay of Pauline Allen in the same volume.

29   Maximus, De Char. 4.83, in *Patrologiae cursus completus, Series græca*, ed. Jacques-Paul Migne (Imprimerie Catholique: Paris, 1865), 90: 1067; quoted from St. Maximus the Confessor, "Four Hundred Texts on Love," in G. E. H. Palmer, Philip Sherrard, and Kallistos Ware, trans. and ed., *The Philokalia*, 2 vols (New York: Farrar, Straus and Giroux, 1981), 111 (4.83).

30   N. Clayton Croy, "Sword Handling: The Early Christian Reception of Matthew 10:34," *Journal of the Bible and Its Reception*, 6, no. 1 (2019): 135–62.

31   John Dominic Crossan, *Jesus: A Revolutionary Biography* (San Francisco, CA: HarperCollins, 2009), 66–7.

32   Al-Azmeh, *The Emergence of Islam*, chapters 6–7; Harry Munt, *The Holy City of Medina: Sacred Space in Early Islamic Arabia* (Cambridge: Cambridge University Press, 2014), chapter 2; Michael Lecker, *Muslims, Jews and Pagans: Studies on Early Islamic Medina* (Leiden: Brill, 1995).

33   Khalid Yahya Blankinship, "Parity of Muslim and Western Concepts of Just War," *Muslim World* 101, no. 3 (2011): 412–26; Philip Wynn, *Augustine on War and Military Service* (Minneapolis, MN: Augsburg Fortress, 2013); Cole, *Muhammad*, chapter 5. For the Roman Christian context of some Qur'an verses about punishing pagan rebels, see Juan Cole, "Muhammad and Justinian: Roman Legal Traditions and the Qur'ān," *Journal of Near Eastern Studies* 79, no. 2 (2020): 183–96.

34 Athanasius, "Letter to Amoun," trans. Mark DelCogliano, in Ellen Muehlberger, ed., *The Cambridge Edition of Early Christian Writings*, vol. 2 (Cambridge: Cambridge University Press, 2017), 66–7; Louis J. Swift, "Early Christian Views on Violence, War, and Peace," in *War and Peace in the Ancient World*, ed. Kurt Raaflaub (Oxford: Blackwell, 2006), 286.

35 Theissen, *Social Reality and the Early Christians*, 149; Aaron Milavec, "The Social Setting of 'Turning the Other Cheek' and 'Loving One's Enemies' in Light of the Didache," *Biblical Theology Bulletin: Journal of Bible Culture* 25, no. 3 (1995): 131–43.

36 Milavec, "The Social Setting of 'Turning the Other Cheek'," 136–41; Crossan, *Jesus*, 66–7.

37 Patricia Crone, "How Did the Quranic Pagans Make a Living?" *Bulletin of the School of Oriental and African Studies* 68, no. 3 (2005): 387–99; Crone incorrectly wanted to displace the Qur'an from Mecca to the north, but her study of the language used about occupations remains valuable.

38 Aziz Al-Azmeh, *The Emergence of Islam in Late Antiquity*, 194–7.

39 Karl Gottfried Müller et al., *Fragmenta historicum graecorum*, 4 vols. (Paris: Didot Frères, 1853), 4: 179–180; Nonnosus in Photius, *The Library of Photius*, trans. J. H. Freese (New York: Macmillan, 1920), 18–19.

40 M. Gawlikowski, "The Sacred Space in Ancient Arab Religions," in *Studies in the History and Archeology of Jordan*, ed. Adnan Hadidi (Amman: Department of Antiquities, Hashemite Kingdom of Jordan, 1982), 301–3; Hans J. W. Drijvers, "Sanctuaries and Social Safety: The Iconography of Divine Peace in Hellenistic Syria," in *Commemorative Figures: Papers Presented to Dr. Th. P. van Baaren* (Brill: Leiden, 1982), 66–73.

41 Swift, "Early Christian Views on Violence, War, and Peace," 279–96.

42 Nicolai Sinai, "Muḥammad as an Episcopal Figure," *Arabica* 65, no. 1–2 (2018): 1–30.

3 A DIFFERENT KIND OF STRIVING: JIHAD AS PEACEMAKING

Asma Afsaruddin

The word jihad, especially as deployed in the Western media, immediately conjures up images of violence perpetrated by zealots claiming to act in the name of Islam against all those who stand in their way—Muslim and non-Muslim. And since these zealots often cite verses from the Qur'an to justify their acts, the average consumer of Western media may be forgiven for thinking that such violence is indeed sanctioned by Islam. Adding fuel to fire, the writings of certain Western academics, known as Orientalists, similarly convey the image that jihad—misleadingly glossed by them as "holy war"—inevitably means aggressive warfare waged by adult male Muslims against non-Muslims *qua* non-Muslims in fulfillment of a supposedly fundamental religious duty imposed on them by the Qur'an.[1]

The Qur'an does allow fighting (*qital*) against intractable enemies but under highly circumscribed conditions. Fighting is primarily in self-defense against the enemy who has attacked first (Qur'an 22:39; 2:190; 9:13) and only actual combatants may be targeted (Qur'an 2:190). While the military dimension of jihad has received and continues to receive overwhelming attention from scholars and non-scholars alike, another very important component and non-combative dimension of the overall enterprise known as *al-jihad fi sabil allah* ("striving in the path of God") is overlooked. This dimension is encapsulated by the Qur'anic term *sabr*, translated here as "patient forbearance." In Qur'anic discourse, *sabr* is the constant, defining attribute of the believer in any and every circumstance, which aids him or her in carrying out the simplest to the most arduous quotidian and exceptional tasks in obedience to God—in other words, carrying out jihad in the broadest sense. Generous posthumous rewards are promised in the Qur'an to believers for the conscious inculcation of patience and forbearance.

To understand the full extent of what is implied by the concept of "striving in the path of God," we therefore have to take into account how *sabr*, as a component of *jihad*, finds reflection in key Islamic texts. Such texts include the Qur'an, the commentaries written on it, and certain non-legal writings of Muslim scholars and thinkers concerned with issues of morality and practical ethics. If *sabr* is understood mainly as the non-combative and internal dimension of *jihad*, then it is not surprising that we find inadequate or no reflection of it in standard juridical works. In such works the treatment of *jihad* is primarily in the context of external relations with non-Muslim polities and thus their focus is inevitably military and political in nature. Discourses on the merits of inculcating and practicing *sabr* as an internal moral and psychological attribute of the pious believer belong more appropriately to the realm of religious ethics and social conduct (broadly *akhlaq* and *adab* in Arabic), not to the hard-headed realms of international law and Realpolitik. *Sabr*, after all, could be neither legislatively mandated nor enforced by the state. But moral and ethical treatises composed by scholars of various stripes praised this essential trait in the believer and pointed to its priority in both Qur'anic and sunnaic (referring to the Prophet Muhammad's *sunna* or "customs" and "practices") discourses.

The first part of this chapter discusses a significant verse—Qur'an 39:10—that underscores the importance of *sabr* within the moral vocabulary of Islam. This importance is amplified in the exegetical works composed by well-known pre-modern commentators, as evident below. *Sabr* is also praised as a normative attribute of the pious in a specific literary genre called the "excellences of patient forbearance" (*fada'il al-sabr*). I highlight this point by focusing on the content of a notable treatise belonging to this genre that was composed by the ninth-century pietist scholar Ibn Abi al-Dunya. An essay by the celebrated late-eleventh-century moral theologian and philosopher Abu Hamid al-Ghazali (d. 1111) also constitutes a notable example of such a literary composition and is discussed next. In the final section of this chapter, I provide an overview of the thought of two modern Muslim thinkers and activists, Abdul Ghaffar Khan and Wahiduddin Khan, who emphasize the peaceful and spiritual dimensions of jihad by highlighting the importance of *sabr* within the Qur'anic milieu and in the ethical worldview of the believer.

A. The Recompense of Patient Forbearance: Exegeses of Qur'an 39:10

Qur'an 39:10 unambiguously makes clear that *sabr* is an essential virtue for the Muslim (and humanity in general) whose assiduous cultivation wins divine approval. The verse states, "O my servants who believe—fear your Lord! For those who do good in this world is goodness and God's earth is wide. Indeed the patiently forbearing ones will be given their reward without measure" (*innama yuwaffa al-sabirun ajrahum bi-ghayr hisab*).

The importance of the cultivation of this virtue is recognized and emphasized by prominent Qur'an commentators. For example, the early-eighth-century exegete

Muqatil ibn Sulayman (d. 767) briefly comments that the first part of this verse means that believers who perform good deeds (al-'amal) will be given paradise (al-janna). The last part of the verse indicates, comments Muqatil, that the reward of the sabirun is "paradise and their [unlimited] provisions within it."[2]

In the late ninth century, the celebrated exegete Muhammad ibn Jarir al-Tabari (d. 923) says the verse commands the Prophet to say to the believers that if they obey God and avoid disobeying Him they will reap al-hasana, which is variously understood to refer to paradise by a majority of scholars or goodness in this world, such as health (al-sihha) and vigor (al-'afiya). Like Muqatil, al-Tabari says that the last part of this verse promises that "the people of patient forbearance" (ahl al-sabr) will be given their reward without measure in the hereafter for what they endured in this world. He refers to an early authority, Qatada b. Di'ama (d. 736), who had understood the verse to make clear that there would be no "weighing and apportioning" of the reward due to the people of patient forbearance.[3] Both Muqatil and al-Tabari therefore understand "patience" or "patient forbearance" to be a general, necessary attribute practiced by righteous believers in the midst of life's tribulations.

The late-twelfth-century exegete al-Razi (d. 1210) understands al-sabirun to refer specifically to those who were patient during their exile from their homeland and their relatives and who steadfastly endured the anguish and tribulations visited upon them as they strove to obey God (that is to say, in emigrating from Mecca to Medina). On account of this, they have earned "reward without measure" which means "reward without limit." Such limitless reward, he remarks, confers the entirety of benefits (manafi' kamila) upon the faithful, the essence of which the human intellect cannot comprehend. Thus the Prophet had said, "There is in paradise what no eye has seen, no ear has heard, and what no heart has perceived." Such reward exceeds what a human can imagine and expect; this is the probable meaning of "reward without measure," says al-Razi.[4]

This kind of reward that is beyond assessment by means of weights and scales is reserved primarily for "the people of tribulation" (ahl al-bala'), continues al-Razi. He refers to the earlier exegete al-Zamakhshari (d. 1144) who had said that in contrast to the people given to much prayer and alms-giving and who are rewarded in exact measure, the people who had undergone much tribulations will receive their reward without measure, so much so that people who had enjoyed more favorable circumstances on earth would be envious of their greater reward.[5]

As this brief survey shows,[6] a number of the most prominent pre-modern commentators generally understand the sabirun to be those who struggle to obey God in adverse circumstances and bear life's tribulations with fortitude. They also specifically connect this verse to emigration to Medina (known in Islamic history as hijra) because of the unusual hardship and the pain of separation from loved ones that it entailed. It is worthy of note that in this Meccan verse, fighting is not yet understood to be one of life's tribulations and therefore sabr is not specifically yoked to it, as it is later in some of the Medinan revelations. "Reward without measure" clearly trumps all other kinds of rewards in the Qur'an and is earmarked solely for the *sabirun*, who, in the context of this verse, stand head and shoulders above other righteous Muslims for having borne with fortitude the fierce persecution and severe afflictions heaped upon them in Mecca for their faith alone, and later for braving the hardships of the perilous journey to Medina.

Ibn Abi al-Dunya and the Merits of Patient Forbearance

An early treatise available to us on the merits of patience and forbearance is the ninth-century work of "Abd Allah b. Muhammad Ibn Abi al-Dunya (d. 894), called *al-Sabr wa-"l-thawab 'alayhi* ("Patience and the Rewards for It"). Renowned for his piety and abstemiousness, Ibn Abi al-Dunya was a popular teacher and became the tutor of several 'Abbasid princes. He was the author of over 100 works, only roughly twenty of which have survived. He lived and died in Baghdad.[7]

Most of Ibn Abi al-Dunya's works, like the current one under discussion, deal with ethics and the cultivation of exemplary virtues, such as patience, humility, trust in God, and charity. *Al-Sabr wa-'l-thawab 'alayhi* is remarkable for having preserved from a relatively early period *hadith*s, Companion reports, and various anecdotes, which eulogize the attribute of *sabr* as superior to other qualities and give assurance of bounteous rewards in the hereafter for those who possess and manifest this attribute. In this work, patience above all is defined as an essential aspect of faith (*al-iman*). The author cites the fourth caliph 'Ali b. Abi Talib (d. 661), also Muhammad's cousin and son-in-law, who described patience as occupying the position of the head to the body in relation to faith, with the implication that faith itself would be gravely impaired if patience were to be severed from it. Subsequently, 'Ali went even further and proclaimed that whoever lacks patience lacks faith.[8]

Other scholars described the trait of *sabr* as being essentially non-aggressive and non-retaliatory. Thus the famous eighth-century pious scholar al-Hasan al-Basri (d. 728) is said to have declared, "O humankind, do not cause harm; if you are harmed, be patiently forbearing!"[9] Al-Hasan also considered those who suppressed their anger as commendably self-restrained and greatly forbearing (*al-kazim al-sabur*).[10] According to the Kufan pietist Muhammad b. Suqa,[11] patiently awaiting deliverance (*al-faraj*) from a trial is an act of worship.[12]

This perspective is affirmed in *hadith*s and other kinds of reports and anecdotes which point to the greater moral excellence of those who possess *sabr*. In one such *hadith* recorded by Ibn Abi al-Dunya, Muhammad states, "Whoever is patient (*yasbir*), God will grant him solace (*yusabbiruhu*), and no one has been granted anything better or more abundant than patience."[13] Another *hadith* quotes the Prophet thus,

> When God will gather together creation [on the Day of Judgment] a caller will cry out, "Where are the people of patient forbearance" (*ahl al-sabr*)? A group of people, few in number, will rise and hasten towards paradise. The angels will meet them and inquire, "We see you rushing towards paradise—who are you?" They will reply, "We are the people of patient forbearance." They [sc. angels] will ask, "What did your patience consist of?" They will respond, "We used to patiently persevere in obeying God and were steadfast in not disobeying Him." Then it will be said to them, "Enter paradise—the best of recompense for those who have acted [well]."[14]

Other reports explicitly proclaim that those practicing the virtues of veracity and patience are equivalent in moral status to the military martyr. Ibn Abi al-Dunya records a statement attributed to the pious Khurasanian scholar 'Abd al-'Aziz b. Abi Rawwad (d. 775), who related, "A statement affirming the truth (*al-qawl bi -'l-haqq*) and patience in abiding by it is equivalent to the deeds of the martyrs."[15] Another report goes further and establishes the moral superiority of the patient, forbearing individual over all others, including the military martyr. It states,

The Messenger of God, peace and blessings be upon him, wept and we asked him, "What has caused you to weep, O Messenger of God?" He replied,

> "I reflected on the last of my community and the tribulations they
> will face. But the patient from among them who arrives will be given the reward
> of two martyrs (*shahidayn*)."[16]

This report categorically challenges other, better-known reports which assign the greatest merit to military martyrs and posits instead a different, non-martial, and nonviolent understanding of virtuous self-sacrifice. The affirmation of a greater reward for patiently forbearing individuals in the next world is also a validation of their higher moral status in *this* world.[17]

Many of the *fada'il al-sabr* (virtues of patience) reports contained in Ibn Abi al-Dunya's work testify in fact to the existence of competitive discourses on the constitutive aspects of piety by his time. These reports typically emphasize the superiority of patience and forbearance over all other traits and activities. One such report is attributed to Abu 'Imran al-Juni[18] who stated, "After faith, the believer (*'abd*) has not been given anything more meritorious (*afdal*) than patience with the exception of gratitude, but it (sc. patience) is more meritorious of the two and the fastest of the two to reap recompense (*thawab*) [for the believer]."[19] A similar report attributed to the early pietist scholar Sufyan b. 'Uyayna (d. ca. 811) says, "The believers have not been given anything better or more meritorious than patience, by means of which they enter heaven."[20] These reports are at odds with other, more frequently quoted reports which claim that falling on the battlefield brings swift and immeasurable heavenly rewards to the military martyr. One of the best-known reports on the issue of compensation in the hereafter for the military martyr is recorded by Muslim (d. 875) and Ibn Maja (d. 887) in their two authoritative *hadith* collections, which states that all his sins will be forgiven except for his debt.[21]

Jihad as Nonviolent, Spiritual Struggle in the Pre-Modern and Modern Periods

A. The Pre-modern Period

In Western academic literature, *sabr* is not understood to have any connection with jihad. The Qur'anic *sabr* is, however, firmly linked by a number of Muslim authors in the pre-modern period to peaceful, spiritual struggle and described as the more arduous and constant aspect of jihad. *Sabr* was the term used throughout the early and late medieval periods to describe what in later Arabic usage became known as *jihad al-nafs* ("spiritual struggle") or *al-jihad al-akbar* ("the greater struggle") while *qital* was renamed *jihad al-sayf* ("struggle with the sword") or *al-jihad al-asghar* ("the lesser struggle"). The absence of these specific terms in the earliest literature, therefore, does not mean that the concept of the greater, spiritual struggle was non-existent in the earliest layers of Islamic moral thought. The late provenance of the Arabic terms *al-jihad al-akbar* and *jihad al-nafs* has led a number of Orientalists to mistakenly assert, sometimes in a highly polemical vein, that jihad in its earliest incarnation connoted primarily aggression and violence and the concept of the spiritual struggle was a later post-Qur'anic development.[22] When exactly this typology of jihad became predominant, we cannot be sure without undertaking a systematic analysis of relevant literature. Since the well-known jurist Ibn Qayyim al-Jawziyya (d. 1350) still uses *sabr* to describe the internal, spiritual jihad in one of his works,[23] we may assume that at least through the fourteenth century, this Qur'anic term still held sway over other related terms.

A. The Pre-modern Period

One of the most eloquent essays written on the virtues of patient forbearance in the pre-modern period is contained in the celebrated scholar al-Ghazali's magnum opus *Ihya ulum al-din* ("The Revival of the Religious Sciences"). In this chapter, al-Ghazali stresses that over seventy verses in the Qur'an refer to *sabr*, its merits, and the reward earned by the believer for cultivating this attribute. He adduces several of these Qur'anic verses as proof-texts to establish the excellence of patience (*fadilat al-sabr*), as selectively referred to below. Verses which affirm that patient forbearance leads to positive consequences in this world and the next include Qur'an 32:24[24]; 7:137[25]; 28:54[26]; and 39:10.[27] This last verse, al-Ghazali explains, stresses that unlike other deeds and attributes which are rewarded according to a certain measure, patience and forbearance are not subjected to such limitations (as already discussed above).[28]

The superiority of patience is established in various *hadith*s and other reports, continues al-Ghazali. Thus the Prophet asserted, "Patience is half of faith." According to another *hadith* narrated by Ibn 'Abbas, when Muhammad came into the presence of the Ansar ("the Helpers," referring to the Muslims of Medina), he asked them, "Are you believers (*mu'minun*)?" When they remained silent, 'Umar spoke up, "Yes, O Messenger of God." He asked, "And what is an indication of your faith?" They said, "We give thanks during times of ease and are patient during times of hardship and we are content with what befalls us." The Prophet exclaimed, "By the Lord of the Ka'ba, [these are] believers!"[29]

Using well-established Sufi terminology, al-Ghazali describes patience as one of the way-stations (*maqam*) of religion, and a stop among the many stops for the traveler (on the path to God). He says all the way-stations (*maqamat*) of religion are fashioned from three things: knowledge (*ma'arif*), states (*ahwal*), and deeds (*a'mal*). Knowledge is the basis which generates states which in turn generate deeds. He adds lyrically, "Knowledge is like the trees, states like the branches, and deeds like the fruit. This is a constant [dynamic] in all the stops along the way for the traveler to God."[30] Faith sometimes has to do specifically with knowledge and at other times with all of the three. Thus, patience, as an essential component of faith, is contingent upon one's prior knowledge and current state.[31]

Patience is specifically a human attribute (*khassiyat al-ins*), continues al-Ghazali, denied to the animals on account of their deficient nature and to the angels on account of their perfection. Humans in their youth are like animals in that there is a preponderance of animal instincts in them at this stage and they lack patience. Through God's infinite mercy, two angels are sent to the human at the onset of puberty, "one of which guides him and the other strengthens him," thereby elevating the human from the level of animals. Then ensues a fierce struggle in the human soul between the "army" (*jund*) championing base, animal instincts on one side and the army fighting on behalf of religious piety on the other. Patience, our author asserts, is required in the successful waging of "war" by the "troops" of religiosity over those of base desires.[32]

The explicitly martial imagery invoked by al-Ghazali in his description of this primal spiritual battle in the human soul is quite vivid and dramatic and underscores his conscious appropriation of militant vocabulary in order to subvert its conventional meanings. Thus he remarks,

Patience is an expression of the perseverance of the religious impulse in its confrontation with the impulses present in the lower self. If it [the religious impulse] perseveres until it overcomes and prevails over the opposed baser instincts, then the party of God has triumphed and becomes affiliated with the patient ones (al-sabirin). If it should flag and weaken so that the baser instincts vanquish it and it does not resolutely repel it, then it becomes affiliated with the followers of devils.[33]

The external cosmic battle between the forces of good and evil which will persist until the last times has been completely internalized by al-Ghazali and transferred to the "battle-ground" of the human heart. To rephrase this, the external military *jihad* of the jurists and theologians which theoretically has to be waged against the enemies of God until the end of time has become transmuted into a relentless spiritual struggle in al-Ghazali's exposition of the basic human duty to strive in the path of God.

Al-Ghazali maintains that no one can persist in patience through difficult and easy times except through strenuous struggle (*illa bi-juhd jahid*) and indefatigable effort; this persistence is called *tasabbur*. *Tasabbur*, wedded to reverence for God (*al-taqwa*) and a firm conviction in the positive consequences resulting from it, ultimately leads to the effortless inculcation of patience in the human soul. This has been promised by God in Qur'an 92:5-8, which states, "As for those who give [alms], are God-fearing, and believe in the good, we will facilitate ease for them." The strong man, after all, easily vanquishes the weaker one with little effort. This is how the battle between the religious and the base impulses within the human soul is conducted, representing the battle between the troops of the angels and the devils, comments al-Ghazali. Constant cultivation of patience leads to satisfaction or contentment (*al-rida*), which is a higher stage or way-station (*maqam*) than patience. This is what the Prophet indicated when he said, "Know that much good inheres in patient forbearance of what you dislike."[34]

Sabr is particularly needed in carrying out obligatory and supererogatory religious duties (*al-tā'at*). Three of such duties are mentioned in Qur'an 16:90, which says, "Indeed God has enjoined justice and kindness (*ihsan*) and the giving [of alms] to kinsfolk." Justice is mandatory (*fard*), says al-Ghazali, *ihsan* is supererogatory, while the giving of alms to relatives is a manifestation of one's noble character (*al-muru'a*) and familial loyalty. The performance of all these duties requires patience and forbearance.[35]

But greater patience is required in abstaining from all those matters expressly forbidden by God (*al-ma'asi*), to which we are urged by the lower self. As mentioned in Qur'an 16:90, "He forbids lewdness (*al-fahsha'*), reprehensible behavior (*al-munkar*), and injustice/rebellion (*al-baghy*)." The merits of such patient abstinence are evident in the *hadith* in which Muhammad says, "The emigrant (*al-muhajir*) is one who emigrates from what God has forbidden and the striver (al-mujahid) is one who strives against his self."[36]

Al-Ghazali singles out patient endurance of the harm inflicted by other people as "one of the highest levels of patience." He quotes from the Gospel (al-Injil) as follows:

Jesus, the son of Mary, upon him be peace, said, 'It was said to you before—a tooth for a tooth, a nose for a nose, but I say to you, do not return evil with evil but rather to the one who strikes your right cheek turn to him the left cheek, and whoever takes your cloak, give him your shawl.

This statement, al-Ghazali comments, enjoins patient forbearance in the face of injury by others. Such forbearance is deemed great because it is exercised in the face of religious and base impulses along with anger which are incited on such occasions.[37]

In al-Ghazali's exposition of sabr in the Ihya', jihad is thus unequivocally conflated with sabr and revives thereby one of the principal Qur'anic significations of the term. Moreover, the principal site for staging jihad shifts from the earthly battleground to within the human heart and/or soul, already a powerful imagery for the Muslim faithful by al-Ghazali's time. Such a transformation would strike a highly emotional chord within Islamic realms and practically universal receptivity to it would become codified in the much-quoted hadith dividing jihad into greater (physical/combative) and lesser (spiritual/non-combative) ones. Sabr, as an irreducible component and product of faith, is the main defense against the forces of evil. Without sabr, no other attribute or deed is meaningful and may in fact become contaminated by hubris and other base motivations. The highly evocative language employed by al-Ghazali in this discussion of sabr is meant to convey to us that compared to the military warrior, the "militantly" patient and forbearing individual is engaged in a more arduous, and therefore, more meritorious, battle against even more trenchant enemies—the passions and base desires of the soul.

B. The Modern Period

There are several modern scholars who have focused in their written works on the peaceful activism they understand to be the predominant meaning of jihad. A number of such scholars and thinkers typically emphasize the virtue of patient forbearance as the most important aspect of jihad, and, therefore, of nonviolent resistance to wrongdoing and the problem of evil. This modern emphasis on nonviolent public activism as the best manifestation of jihad has been espoused by a number of well-known and less well-known figures.[38] Below, I broadly sketch the thought of two prominent Muslim scholars who advocated/advocate nonviolent struggle against oppression and injustice as the most important aspect of jihad.

They are the Pashtun leader Syed 'Abd al-Ghaffar Khan (d. 1988) who organized a peaceful resistance movement called the Khudai Khidmatgars ("the Servants of God") against the British colonizers of India and the Indian Muslim scholar and activist, Wahiduddin Khan, who is one of the best-known contemporary writers on the topic of nonviolence in Islam. Some of the key points of their thinking are now presented below.

Abdul Ghaffar Khan

Syed Abd al-Ghaffar Khan (d. 1988), also known as Badshah Khan, attained legendary status during his lifetime for his principled nonviolent opposition to British colonial occupation of his homeland in the early twentieth century (see also Chapter 8). Khan was ethnically a Pashtun from Utmanzai in the Northwest Frontier province of what is today Pakistan. He was born in 1890 when the Indian subcontinent was already under British colonial rule. As part of its brutal policy of repression against the local inhabitants, the British would frequently send armed expeditions to the Northwest Frontier Province to attempt to "pacify" it—beating, jailing, and killing Pashtuns in order to achieve their goals. The Pashtuns, fabled for their martial prowess, fought back resolutely and frequently repelled the British invaders successfully. They kept up their armed resistance to the foreign occupiers for more than eighty years.

Abdul Ghaffar Khan grew up in this environment and developed a strong inclination to improve the condition of his people through education and social reform. This desire was nurtured by his religious upbringing as a Muslim and by what he felt was a personal call to serve God in his youth. In 1910 he established the first non-British school in his region and embarked on a campaign to establish more schools for males and females. He launched a campaign to dig wells and latrines for the common people and teach hygiene to them. Social reform led to a desire to effect political reform as well; the goal was to achieve self-governance for the Pashtuns. This was of course a highly risky venture under colonial occupation. Khan faced imprisonment and degrading treatment at the hands of the British as a result of his social and political activism. Undaunted, he established a group in 1929 that he named Khudai Khidmatgars—meaning "the Servants of God"— that would resist British occupation and seek to liberate the Pashtuns through nonviolent tactics.

Not surprisingly, Abdul Ghaffar Khan stressed the Quranic principle of sabr and drew his inspiration from Quranic verses such as 42:39 which states: "He who forgives and is reconciled, his reward is with God." He also taught his followers that nonviolence (which Khan termed 'adam tashaddud) was the "weapon of the Prophet" and that it characterized the greater part of his prophetic career before he received divine revelations to defend his community militarily. He also emphasized, based on Muhammad's teachings, that no Muslim can hurt any human being by word or deed. Khan stressed that he understood the Islamic way of life to consist of deeds, faith, and love. It is noteworthy that Khan articulated his principle of nonviolent resistance to oppression and injustice before he came into contact with Mohandas Gandhi, a contemporary, who would achieve world renown for a similar principled adherence to nonviolence (known in Hindi as *satyagraha*).

Membership in the Khudai Khidmatgars was open to both men and women as well as to Muslims, Hindus, and Sikhs. Those who joined had to take the following ten-point pledge:

1. I put forth my name in honesty and truthfulness to become a true Servant of God.
2. I will sacrifice my wealth, life, and comfort for the liberty of my nation and people.
3. I will never be a party to factions, hatred, or jealousies with my people, and will side with the oppressed against the oppressor.
4. I will not become a member of any other rival organization, nor will I stand in an army.
5. I will faithfully obey all legitimate orders of all my officers all the time.
6. I will live in accordance with the principles of nonviolence.
7. I will serve all God's creatures alike, and my object shall be the attainment of the freedom of my country and my religion.
8. I will always see to it that I do what is right and good.
9. I will never desire any reward whatever for my service.
10. All my efforts shall be to please God and not for any show or gain.

Despite the fact that Khan was repeatedly harassed, intimidated, and jailed by the British, he continued his nonviolent movement and continued to attract recruits until the end of British rule in 1947. Abdul Ghaffar Khan died in an independent Pakistan, where he faced resistance to his ideas. In recent years, his thought and movement have enjoyed somewhat of a comeback, attracting the attention of some international proponents of nonviolent activism, who take heart from the example he had set in very adverse circumstances.[39]

Wahiduddin Khan

A younger contemporary of Abdul Ghaffar Khan is the Indian Muslim scholar and activist Wahiduddin Khan (no relation), who was born in 1925. Like Abdul Ghaffar Khan, Wahiduddin Khan was born under the British occupation of his homeland.

A number of his family members were engaged in the independence struggle against the British. The campaign against political oppression and social injustice had a profound influence on him and would provide the impetus for his religious and social activism. When Abul Alaa Mawdudi in 1941 established the political party called Jamaat-i Islami (The Islamic Association) in India, Khan became a member of it. Khan, however, broke with Mawdudi after fifteen years because of fundamental disagreements concerning the relation between Islam and politics. Khan emphasized, in contrast to Mawdudi, that belief in monotheism and peaceful submission to God was at the heart of all things Islamic. Political and economic reform was at best a secondary consideration and not the primary motivation for one's commitment to Islam. In 1970, Khan established the Islamic Centre in New Delhi which has published over 200 of his books, a number of which have been translated from the original Urdu into English, Arabic, and other languages.

In his book *The True Jihad: The Concept of Peace, Tolerance and Non-Violence*[40] written in the aftermath of September 11, Khan stresses that the main purpose of Islam was the peaceful propagation of the faith (*da'wa*) and that political and social reforms were at best secondary concerns which would inevitably result from the spiritual reformation of Muslims. He begins this short treatise by pointing to Qur'an 22:78 which exhorts the believer to "strive for the cause of God as it behooves you to strive for it." *Jihad*, derived from the Arabic root *jhd*, points to this earnest struggle for the sake of God, a term which eventually came to be applied to the early battles in Islam as well, since they were part of this overall struggle. Strictly speaking, the term for fighting is *qital*, and not *jihad* per se. On the basis of the *Musnad* of Ahmad b. Hanbal, he identifies the *mujahid* as "one who struggles with himself for the sake of God"; as "one who exerts himself for the cause of God"; and as "one who struggles with his self in submission to the will of God." *Jihad*, therefore, should be rightly understood as essentially a peaceful struggle against one's ego and against wrongdoing in general.[41]

Khan proceeds to establish the peaceful essence of *jihad* by invoking the following proof-texts. He refers to Qur'an 25:52 ("Do not yield to the unbelievers, but fight them strenuously with it [the Qur'an]"), which establishes that *jihad* is essentially a peaceful, nonviolent struggle to establish the truth since no military activity is referred to in this verse. A *hadith* narrated by the Prophet's widow, 'A'isha (recorded in the famed hadith collection of al-Bukhari [d. 870]), quotes Muhammad as expressing a preference for the easier of any two options. Since war is a hardship, this *hadith* encodes the superiority of the peaceful struggle for truth. The Prophet's biography reveals that he never initiated hostilities and that he went to great lengths to avoid it. Examples from his life which support this interpretation are as follows: (1) in the Meccan period, Muhammad was primarily concerned with challenging polytheism through peaceful, verbal means; (2) even when during the thirteen-year Meccan period the Quraysh became his arch-enemy and prominent members of the tribe conspired to kill him, he avoided any physical confrontation and resorted instead to migration to Medina at the end; (3) the battle of the Trench is a stellar example of avoiding unnecessary violence; as is (4) the Treaty of al-Hudaybiyya which the Prophet signed with the pagan Meccans in order to avoid the shedding of blood; and (5) the peaceful conquest of Mecca at a time when the Muslims were militarily strong testifies to the preference for nonviolent methods over violent ones to promote truth and justice. These examples provide testimony, states Khan, that "the position of peace in Islam is sacrosanct, while war in Islam is allowed only in exceptional cases when it cannot be avoided."[42]

Islam is fundamentally a religion which teaches nonviolence, he asserts. The Qur'an states that God does not love *fasad*, which Khan glosses as "violence." Qur'an 2:205 clearly indicates, he comments, that "*fasad* is that action which results in disruption of the social system, causing huge losses in terms of lives and property." God loves nonviolence, and He promises in Qur'an 16:5 that "those who seek to please God will be guided by Him to 'the paths of peace.'" As a consequence of this high valorization of nonviolence, the Qur'an eulogizes patience (*sabr*) as a human virtue, promising reward for it that is beyond measure (Qur'an 39:10). *Sabr* is the equivalent of nonviolence as understood in the modern period. The absolute higher valuation of nonviolence over violence is further indicated in a *hadith* in which the Prophet remarks, "God grants to *rifq* (gentleness) what he does not grant to '*unf* (violence)."[43]

Nonviolent activism is particularly relevant for Muslims in the contemporary period and is the most important aspect of *jihad* for them today, affirms Khan. Peaceful interactions between Muslims and non-Muslims will allow for serious dialogue to emerge between them and expose Muslims to the kind of intellectual stimulation they are badly in need of "if they are to tread the path of progress."[44] Adopting the path of nonviolence, continues our author, will be tantamount to "reviving the sunnah of Hudaybiyya;" an event the Qur'an (48:26) had referred to as "a clear victory."[45] Ideally, peace should be accompanied by justice. But so strong is the imperative toward nonviolence in Islam, asserts Khan, that one may settle for peace first even if it falls short of justice, as was exemplified by the Prophet's agreement to the terms of al-Hudaybiyya, which were unfavorable toward Muslims. This acceptance of a lopsided peace treaty did however lead to the establishment of justice and made unnecessary the waging of war to attain it. He reminds that "God calls to the Abode of Peace" (Qur'an 10:25) and there is no other way to realize God's will.[46]

Conclusion

Any project which wishes to reconstruct more holistically the range of perspectives on what constitutes *al-jihad fi sabil allah* and who most efficaciously strives in the path of God must also include discussions of the attribute of *sabr* as an essential ingredient of jihad. As recognized by pre-modern and modern Muslim authors, *sabr* is the constant attribute of the righteous individual who strives to fulfill God's will in the minutiae of daily life, particularly in purifying one's soul of base desires and promoting what is good and preventing what is wrong— the overarching moral imperative in Islam, and the principal objective of jihad. The foregrounding of *sabr* as the guiding principle for promoting nonviolence and peacemaking in the modern world by several influential Muslim thinkers constitutes a robust recognition of the continued centrality of this concept in the lexicon of contemporary Islam—from both an ethical and praxis-based perspective. The imperative to establish a just and moral society—now more than ever on a global scale—through peaceful means is just as relevant for twenty-first-century Muslims as it was for their seventh-century predecessors. The voices of Muslim peacemakers, however, struggle to gain recognition on the global stage, overshadowed as they are by more strident, militant ones that are wrongly amplified in the Western media at their expense. The existence of these tenacious voices is nevertheless indisputable and their potential to bring about a sea change in an inequitable world order—provided such opportunities are afforded them—is undeniable.

Notes

1   For a critique of these Orientalist views still pervasive in the Western academy, see Asma Afsaruddin, "Jihad and the Qur'an: Classical and Modern Interpretations," in the *Oxford Handbook of Qur'anic Studies*, ed. Muhammad Abdel Haleem and Mustafa Shah (Oxford: Oxford University Press, 2020), 512–26.

2   Muqatil b. Sulayman, *Tafsir Muqatil b. Sulayman* (Cairo: Mu'assasat al-halabi wa-shuraka'uh, 1969), 3: 672.

3   Al-Tabari, *Jami' al-bayan fi ta'wil al-qur'an* (Beirut: Dar al-kutub al-'ilmiyya, 1997), 10: 622.

4   Al-Razi, *Al-Tafsir al-kabir* (Beirut: Dar ihya' al-turath al-'arabi, 1999), 9: 430–1.

5   Ibid., 9:431.

6   For more commentaries on this verse, see Asma Afsaruddin, *Striving in the Path of God: Jihad and Martyrdom in Islamic Thought* (Oxford: Oxford University Press, 2013), 181–3.

7   Cf. art. "Ibn Abi 'l-Dunya," *Encyclopaedia of Islam*, new edition, ed. C.E. Bosworth et al. (Leiden: E.J. Brill, 1980), 3: 684.

8   Ibn Abi al-Dunya, *Al-Sabr wa-'l-thawab 'alayhi* (Beirut: Dar Ibn Hazm, 1997), 24.

9   Ibid., 26.

10 Ibid., 86.

11 For whom see Ibn Hajar, *Tahdhib al-tahdhib*, ed. Khalil Ma'mun Shiha et al. (Beirut: Dar al-ma'rifa, 1996), 5: 126–7; generally regarded as a *thiqa* ("a trustworthy scholar").

12 Ibn Abi al-Dunya, *Sabr*, 87. The literary genre known as *al-Faraj ba'd al-shidda* emphasizes this point.

13 Ibid., 17.
14 Ibid., 23.
15 Ibid., 116.
16 Ibid., 84–5.
17 Reports such as this belie Reuven Firestone's statement to the effect that there is virtually no evidence of dissenting traditions challenging the predominantly militaristic interpretation of *jihad* by the ninth century; see his *Jihad: the Origin of Holy War in Islam* (Oxford: Oxford University Press, 2002), 100.
18 This is very likely 'Abd al-Malik b. Habib al-Azdi (d. 123/740), also known as Abu 'Imran al-Juni, a scholar from Basra, who was generally regarded as a reliable transmitter of hadiths; cf. Ibn Hajar, *Tahdhib*, 3:468.
19 Ibn Abi al-Dunya, *Sabr*, 85.
20 Ibid., 51.
21 See A. J. Wensinck, *Concordance et indices de la traditions musulmane* (Leiden: E.J. Brill, 1988), 2: 165.
22 For example, see David Cook, *Understanding Jihad* (Berkeley: University of California Press, 2015), 35 ff, where he launches a diatribe against modern scholars who discuss the spiritual aspects of jihad in their writings.
23 This work is titled *'Uddat al-sabirin wa-dhakhirat al-shakirin* ("The Preparation of the Patiently Forbearing Ones and Treasures of the Grateful Ones"). For an extended discussion of this work, see Afsaruddin, *Striving*, 199–204.
24 This verse states, "We appointed from among them leaders who guide according to our command when they were patiently enduring."
25 This verse states, "Your Lord's fair word was fulfilled for the Children of Israel for what they had borne in patience and we brought to nought all that the Pharaoh and his people had done."
26 This verse states, "These will be given their reward twice over because they endure patiently and ward off evil with good and spend from what we provide for them."
27 This verse states, "Those who are patient will be given their reward without measure."
28 Al-Ghazali, *Ihya' 'ulum al-din*, ed. 'Abd Allah al-Khalidi (Beirut: Dar al-arqam, n.d.), 4: 84.
29 Al-Ghazali, *Ihya'*, 4:84–5.
30 Ibid., 4:86.
31 Ibid.
32 Ibid.
33 Ibid., 4:87.
34 Ibid., 4:94–5. As al-Khalidi, editor of the *Ihya'*, points out, this *hadith* related by the famous Companion Ibn 'Abbas is recorded by the prominent hadith scholars Ahmad b. Hanbal and al-Tirmidhi.
35 Ibid., 4:98.
36 According to al-Khalidi, the foremost hadith scholar al-Bukhari records the following *hadith* from 'Abd Allah b. 'Umar, "The Muslim is one from whose tongue and hand [other] Muslims are safe, and the Emigrant is one who has emigrated from what God has forbidden." Variants are given in other standard collections. Ahmad b. Hanbal records a *hadith* in which the Prophet says, "The striver (*al-mujahid*) is the one who fights his self for [the sake of] God or speaks [the truth] concerning God the Exalted." A variant is given by al-Tirmidhi.
37 Al-Ghazali, *Ihya'*, 4:100.

38 For further discussion of this strand of peaceful activism, see Afsaruddin, *Striving*, 256–64.

39 For detailed studies of Abdul Ghaffar Khan's movement, see Robert C. Johansen, "Radical Islam and Nonviolence: A Case Study of Religious Empowerment and Constraint among Pashtuns," *Journal of Peace Research* 34 (1997): 53–71; Eknath Easwaran, *A Man to Match His Mountains: Badshah Khan Nonviolent Soldier of Islam* (Petaluma, CA: Nilgiri Press, 1984), and James Rowell's chapter in this volume.

40 Published by Goodword Books, New Delhi, 2002.

41 Khan, *True Jihad*, 13 16.

42 Ibid., 16–23.

43 Ibid., 46–8.

44 Ibid., 94.

45 Ibid., 95.

46 Ibid., 105–8.

4 INTERNAL PEACE VERSUS BEING IN SOCIETY: SUFI DILEMMAS

Alexander D. Knysh

Preamble

Writing in the middle of the twentieth century the renowned German Islamologist Hellmut Ritter (1892–1971) averred:

> The medieval Islamic outlook on life is to a great extent dominated by the basic attitude that it is not worthwhile to engage very actively in this world, to enter into psychic or material commitments in it, because death all too quickly brings an end to everything … Everything on this earth is transitory, joy as well as sorrow … [And] the whole surface of the earth is one great cemetery.[1]

Ritter's statement is based on his painstaking study of medieval Sufi literature, which indicates that devaluation of life in this world and involvement in its transient affairs are particularly prominent in the ascetic-mystical stream of Islam or Sufism (from the Arabic *tasawwuf*, "putting on a woolen garment").[2] Indeed, numerous other Western scholars of Sufism confirm that its adherents are devoted primarily, if not exclusively to the cultivation of their internal, spiritual life, paying scant attention to economic concerns and social transactions.[3] According to early Sufi theorists, the goal of the Sufi's self-disciple or struggle (*riyada*; *mujahada*) is to render the human soul (*nafs*) immune to the fleeting and treacherous enticements of this world that they depict as an abode of sin and trials.[4] In the words of an eminent early Sufi teacher al-Harith al-Muhasibi (d. 857),[5] one has to abandon the false trappings of this world and commerce with its sinful inhabitants for the sake of the fabulous otherworldly rewards that he describes in exquisite detail in his imaginary journey to paradise.[6] As we shall see, the perception of Sufism as being both inwardly and otherworldly oriented is accurate in principle, but does not reflect the complexity of relations between its followers and their social environments.

The overriding significance that the Sufis attribute to the life of the human spirit finds support in the amount of time and effort that they devote to contemplating God, serving him, engaging in intimate conversations with him (*munajat*), and avoiding any action or thought that might provoke his displeasure.[7] Sufi manuals from the pre-modern and modern age are replete with sophisticated descriptions of the emotional and mental phenomena that individual Sufis experience as they progress along the Sufi path to God (*tariq* or *tariqa*) perceived as the True or Ultimate Reality (*al-haqiqa* or *al-haqq*) of existence.[8] Sufi teachers (*masha'ikh*; sing. *shaykh*) describe the ascetic-mystic's progress on this path as being punctuated by "stations" (*maqamat*; sing. *maqam*) that he is required to reach and "conquer" in order to move on to the next one. In the process, the Sufi traveler experiences various spiritual "states" (*ahwal*; sing. *hal*) that are also described in detail in classical Sufi manuals.[9]

Swimming in the Ocean of the Soul

In what follows I will discuss the Sufi concepts that have to do with the internal peace, equilibrium, and quietude that come as result of the Sufi's putting his trust fully and exclusively in God (*tawakkul*) and being satisfied (*rida*) with his external circumstances, no matter how adverse and uncomfortable they might be. Some Sufi teachers treat these spiritual phenomena as "stations" of the Sufi path, while others consider them to be "states."[10] I would like to begin my conversation by quoting a description of the spiritual state (*hal*) of "tranquility" (*itmi'nan*) provided by the Persian Sufi Abu Nasr al-Sarraj al-Tusi (d. 988). Born in the city of Tus (near today's Mashhad in Iran), he spent most of his life in Iraq (Basra and Baghdad), where he distinguished himself as an early formulator, advocate, and promoter of "Sufi science" (*"ilm al-tasawwuf*). His partiality to Sufism is evident from the fact that in his "Book of the Essentials of Sufism" (*Kitab al-luma' fi 'l-tasawwuf*) al-Sarraj places Sufi teachers above the two other categories of the religious authorities of his age, namely, the collectors of prophetic sayings (*ahl al-hadith*) and experts on Muslim legal theory (*fuqaha*").[11] Before analyzing al-Sarraj's definition of tranquility, mention should be made of a cluster of related Sufi concepts, namely, (a) satisfaction (with God) and divine decree (*rida*); (b) contentment [with one's personal state and state of affairs in the world] (*qana'a*); (c) certainty in the veracity of one's faith and knowledge of God (*yaqin*), (d) and trust in God and reliance exclusively on him and his mercy (*tawakkul*). In Sufi lore, these states and stations of the mystical path are intimately associated with the concept of tranquility (*itmi'nan*) and complement one another. The semantic interconnectedness of these notions is obvious from the way in which they are discussed by Muhammad al-Ghazali (d. 1111) in his seminal work "The Revivification of Religious Disciplines" (*Ihya' 'ulum al-din*).[12] This highly influential medieval Sunni theologian, who at some point in his life embraced Sufism's ascetic and mystical discipline, examines closely various aspects of what we would call "equanimity" or "serenity," especially in the face of adversity, distraction, or disquiet. Numerous details aside, the ultimate meaning and practical implications of all the aforementioned concepts can be summarized as follows: you should remain steadfast and quiet in the face of the inscrutable workings of the divine predestination or decree until you reach the stage at which sufferings and afflictions not only do not undermine your trust in God's mercy and kindness, but also strengthen your faith and certitude even further.[13] Reliance on or recourse to anyone or anything other than God is a case of misplaced certitude (*yaqin*) or trust (*iman*) that may lead you to forgetfulness of God and, as a consequence, to perdition in the hereafter.[14]

If, argues al-Ghazali, your social environment is morally corrupt, disturbing and thus unconducive to spiritual quietude and tranquility (the city of Baghdad is mentioned specifically as a negative example), then you should leave it as soon as possible. At the same time, al-Ghazali seems to imply that surrendering oneself to the inscrutable workings of the divine will even in such an unfavorable milieu is still preferable for God's faithful servant than fleeing for it. It is, after all, up to God to either keep you in the condition of disquiet or to rescue you from it. If you actively seek to escape from it, you are unwittingly violating the principle of entrusting God with your fate and wellbeing (*tawakkul*).[15]

After you have experienced the states or stations of tranquility and internal peace, your external condition, be it pleasure or suffering, wealth or poverty, physical comfort or discomfort, no longer matters in your eyes. Completely absorbed into a contemplation of God and quest for intimacy (*uns*) with him, you become totally oblivious of your external circumstances. This mental attitude to the world is akin to, but not necessarily identical with, *satori* or *kenshō* in Zen Buddhism; *nirvana* in Buddhism; or *apatheia* in Greek Stoicism; and in Gnostic Christianity that was defined by Clement of Alexandria (d. ca. 215 CE) as either "passionlessness" or "a state of serenity of purpose."[16] Arguably, all these psychological states look similar, as they have to do with the lack of suffering, desire, or self-consciousness. Within an Islamic context, this idea is thrown into sharp relief by the early Persian Sufi Abu Yazid al-Bistami (d. 848 or 875).[17] When asked by someone as to what he desires, he responded "I desire not to desire." This statement may appear quite Buddhist at first sight, unless we read how it was interpreted by the thirteenth-century Sufi from al-Andalus (Islamic Spain) Ibn al-'Arabi (d. 1240). In his view, Abu Yazid's response means the following: "Make me desire everything that Thou [God] desirest," so that there may be nothing but what God desires. God "desires" for His servants only "ease, and He desires not hardship" (Qur'an 2:185) for them. He desires good for them, and evil does not return to him, just as has been mentioned in the sound *hadith*[18]: "The good, all of it, is in Thy [God's] hands, and evil does not go back to Thee," even though everything comes from God in respect to the root.[19]

Ibn al-'Arabi's interpretation of the lack of desire declared by an early Muslim mystic is sufficient to make us wary of treating apparent interreligious parallels as an unequivocal evidence of "cultural transfers" into Islam of certain preexisting foreign ideas.[20] As we have just seen, the Sufi concepts that we are dealing with here are undeniably and recognizably Islamic, expressed as they are in the idiom of the Qur'an and prophetic narratives (*hadith*). Whether they can be neatly denuded of their Islamic scriptural vestments and reduced to a trans-religious and trans-historical common denominator is a question that is too complex to detain us here.[21] There is, on the other hand, no denying that Sufi adages such as the one quoted above fit seamlessly not just into the Sufi worldview, but also into Islamic theodicy as a whole.[22] Here are a few more examples of how the concepts that interest us here were extracted from the Qur'an and the prophetic tradition (*sunna*; *hadith*), or, as some might argue, how they were dressed up in an Islamic scriptural garb.

As with other Sufi teachers of the age (the tenth and eleventh centuries CE),[23] in his "Book of the Essentials of Sufism"[24] al-Sarraj begins his definition of the Sufi state of tranquility (*itmi'nan*) by quoting the Qur'an: *"Or soul that has achieved tranquility, return to your Lord, well pleased, well-pleasing! Enter thou among my servants! Enter My Paradise!"* (89:27) and *"Those who believe, their hearts are at rest (or tranquil) in God's remembrance—in God's remembrance are at rest (or tranquil) the hearts of those who believe and do righteous deeds"* (13:28). After providing this necessary scriptural foundation for his discussion of tranquility, al-Sarraj proceeds to quote some pronouncements on the subject of earlier Sufi authorities (*masha'ikh*). One of them, al-Damaghani, explains the Qur'anic verse quoted above as follows:

> Hearts rejoiced by realizing the greatness and majesty of God Most High, are cheered by realizing God's mercy and favor [toward them], then calmed by realizing His sufficiency for them and the truthfulness of His promise [of Paradise], and felt intimacy [with God] in realizing His goodness and tenderness [toward them].

Not entirely satisfied with al-Damaghani's rather straightforward explanation, al-Sarraj puts on his "Sufi hat" and furnishes a rather complex tripartite definition of tranquility that is unapologetically Sufi and elitist in its nature: (1) *The first* type of tranquility belongs to ordinary believers (*al-'amma*), who find peace and tranquility in remembering the mundane bounties that God bestows upon them daily, while at the same time warding off woes and afflictions that are about to befall them. (2) *The second* type is characteristic of the elect (*al-khusus*) believers, who apply themselves strenuously in fulfilling divine commands and are patient in tribulation, while being aware of their acts of piety and obedience toward God and taking pride in their worshipful accomplishments. (3) The third type belongs exclusively to the elect of the elect (*khusus al-khusus*), who acknowledge that their hearts cannot remain tranquil in the face of God's unfathomable, awe-inspiring majesty, incomparability, and uniqueness and, as a consequence, will never find rest nor satisfy their thirst for intimacy with God. Therefore, the Sufi possessors of such restless hearts keep plunging ever deeper into the infinite and bottomless sea of divine knowledge. Unlike the second group, they are no longer aware of themselves or their acts, being totally absorbed in the worship and contemplation of God.[25]

To sum up al-Sarraj's discussion of the spiritual state of tranquility:

1. In principle, any believer is capable of experiencing it; however, the tranquility of the Sufis is way above the ken of the ordinary believers.

2. This conclusion, in its turn, implies that the Sufis, or, rather, their cream of the cream as defined by al-Sarraj, are in possession of a special, privileged knowledge (*ma'rifa*) and character traits that are unattainable for the generality of the faithful. Elsewhere, al-Sarraj implies that among those who are unable to acquire this privileged knowledge and these superior character traits are not just common believers, but also exoteric scholars of Islam, namely, *ashab al-hadith* and *fuqaha'*.[26]

3. Finally, within the Sufi community (*al-qawm*; *ashab hadhihi 'l-ta'ifa*) itself there is a hierarchy of perfection with some individuals surpassing others in their dedication to serving God, knowing him and doing his will. God apportions his revealed, inspired knowledge to his saintly friends (*awliya'*) according to their level of spiritual and moral purity and intensity of dedication.[27]

In the later Sufi tradition, we witness a subtle but significant re-focusing of Sufi attention from psychological states to modes of mystical cognition. This tendency comes to the fore in the influential works of the aforementioned Andalusian mystic Ibn al-'Arabi who recasts Sufi psychology into a full-fledged mystical gnoseology. In discussing the station of satisfaction (*rida*) with the divine predestination, Ibn al-'Arabi indicates that, contrary to what the earlier Sufi tradition says, satisfaction and quietude are not always desirable, especially when it comes to knowing God. In his words,

> God is much vaster than that a person should be satisfied with a little of what comes from Him. Rather, one should be satisfied with Him, not what comes from Him, since satisfaction with what comes from Him cuts off mystics from their aspirations (*himma*).[28]

Because God constantly manifests himself in the "infinity of the possible things" and because there can be no repetition in divine self-disclosures (God being above a mere mechanical repetition), the mystic must follow them constantly instead of being satisfied with one or the other aspect of divine self-disclosure. Seen from this ontological and gnoseological vantage point, satisfaction amounts to complacency insofar as it prevents the gnostic (*'arif*) from recognizing and appreciating God in all of his infinite hypostases. In the words of Ibn al-'Arabi,

> Some people do not know that at every instant God has a self-disclosure which does not take the form of the previous self-disclosure. When such a person lacks this perception, he may become the unceasing companion of a single self-disclosure ... They imagine that the situation is not changing, and so a curtain is let down over them because of the boredom which leads to irreverence, after God has deprived them of knowledge of themselves and him.[29]

Re-exteriorizing Sufi Internality

Bearing in mind the close attention that Sufi masters like al-Sarraj, al-Ghazali, and Ibn al-'Arabi pay to the psychological and cognitive states experienced by Sufi seekers of God, it may appear that the material world in which they lived in the past and continue to live today was and is of little, if any, value in their eyes. Indeed, one may assume that the Sufis have been indeed preoccupied primarily, if not exclusively, with exploring either their own spiritual states or the invisible realm of 'true realities' (*haqa'iq*) of which this world is but a pale, imperfect reflection unworthy of the attention of the truly devout and single-minded ascetic-mystic. This old Platonic idea, as well as the idea of the human soul as the epitome of the Universe, has shaped decisively and profoundly the thought and behavior of countless ascetically-mystically inclined Muslims in the Mediterranean basin and beyond until today. In principle, this impression is accurate. However, the Sufis' preoccupation with the parallel world of true realities and disembodied prototypes of empirical existence,[30] as well as psychological and gnoseological ways of accessing it, was (and still is) neither monomaniac nor exclusive. Acutely aware of their mundane surroundings, Sufi theorists were eager to explore the challenges of living in the imperfect, unjust, and potentially seductive and corruptive world of ours. In particular, they tried to understand how one can maintain serenity and purity of dedication to God amidst the hustle and bustle of mundane activities.[31] After all, the earthly life is given to us so that we could prepare ourselves for the eternal and blissful life to come. In the words of the Sufi poet and writer Farid al-Din 'Attar (d. 1221), "this world is a sowing field for the other world. Therefore, sow this seed, for now it is the time to sow!"[32]

In his "Revivification Religious Disciplines," which we quoted earlier on in this chapter, al-Ghazali (d. 1111) offers ways of harmonizing one's life in this imperfect world with one's aspiration for the perfect life in the hereafter. This monumental theological and legal summa is often described as an attempt to reconcile the principles of moderate Sufism with the values and practices of mainstream Sunni Islam. To some extent, this description is accurate, albeit simplified. al-Ghazali's intellectual legacy being vast and variegated, I will focus here only on those aspects that are pertinent to our discussion of the Sufis' quest for internal tranquility and quietude, on the one hand, and their inevitable engagement with the material world in which they lived. On the other, one thing that al-Ghazali's "Revivification" demonstrates clearly is the problematic nature of the Western conceptual dichotomies pertaining to various types of asceticism-mysticism and their relationship with society. They can be traced to the seminal works of the German sociologist Max Weber (1864–1920) whose *Sociology of Religion*[33] introduces what has become the paradigmatic dichotomy of *world-rejecting mysticism* versus *inner-worldly asceticism*. Based on his conceptualization of Calvinism as a typical *inner-worldly asceticism*, Weber uses it as his benchmark to present Sufism as a curious combination of "contemplative and mystical" elements with "inner-worldly activism" and even militancy in the name of religion. In the final analysis, however, Weber's lack of familiarity with Sufism's original texts and overall negative view of Islam[34] leads him to relegate Sufism to the status of "orgiastic, spiritualistic, contemplative" (i.e., *world-renouncing*) religious and intellectual attitude, rather than a form of *inner-worldly* asceticism-mysticism whose adherents are actively involved in reforming the world and, for Weber, are exemplified by the Calvinists with their "Protestant ethic." Helpful as this dichotomy may be pedagogically and heuristically, it is, like Weber's other "ideal types," not without serious flaws.[35]

My study of Sufism's history has convinced me that the predicament of being in the world while also striving to transcend it by focusing mentally on God was intimately familiar to pre-modern Sufis and their modern-day successors. They realized that one could not and perhaps also should not remain permanently immersed in contemplating God and his mysteries, conversing with him in one's "heart of hearts" (*sirr al-sirr*) or following his ever-changing manifestations in the things and phenomena of material existence. To secure the leisure to engage in such otherworldly meditations, the seeker of God had to leave his spiritual retreat (*khalwa*) if only to earn his livelihood.[36] It was the extent and consequences of this engagement with society that preoccupied many Sufi teachers, causing them to spill much ink to formulate a viable compromise between being in this world and avoiding its treacherous entanglements and enticements.

Let us return to al-Ghazali and his "Revivification of Religious Disciplines." Challenging the rigid Weberian dichotomy just described, the medieval thinker argues that abandoning this world is, in fact, much easier for the Sufi than engaging with it, and thus less meritorious, in the eyes of God. The goal of "breaking the soul and overcoming its drives," according to al-Ghazali, is best achieved through living amidst ordinary folk and being subject to their abuse, ridicule, and moral faults. Life in the crowd, insists al-Ghazali, is more conducive to taming one's animal soul (*nafs*), which constitutes the ultimate goal of every devout ascetic-mystic and the surest way to salvation in the hereafter. That is why, concludes al-Ghazali, Sufi teachers instruct their followers, the inhabitants of Sufi lodges (*ribatat*), to engage with the world outside their protective walls. This move allows the ascetic-mystics to serve the people of the marketplace by praying for them and dispensing divine blessing (*baraka*) to them.[37] In so doing, the precious experience and knowledge of God possessed by the community's spiritual elite are dispersed graciously and unselfishly across the masses of ordinary believers.[38]

About three centuries later, the great North African historian and theologian Ibn Khaldun (1332–1406) brings home the same message, quoting a famous saying of the Prophet that encourages his followers to strike a delicate balance between serving God and heeding the demands of the human nature and society's needs. Like al-Ghazali before him, Ibn Khaldun advises aspiring Sufis not to seclude themselves (*'uzla*) selfishly from the company of ordinary believers, but to rub shoulders (*mukhalata*) with them in the streets and marketplaces of towns and villages.[39] The persistence of this line of Sufi thinking is further attested by the fact that 400 years later the same idea is reiterated by the prominent Maghrebi Sufi of the Shadhiliyya-Darqawiyya order Ibn 'Ajiba (1746–1809). Commenting on Q25:20 that describes the Biblical and Qur'anic prophets as "eating food and walking through the markets," he argues that this description is fully applicable to the Sufi "friends of God" (*awliya'*), or "saints." They, too, says Ibn 'Ajiba, should walk through the markets, mix and eat with the people of the bazaar if only for the sake of [self-]reflection and edification. It is only among the teeming crowds (*ziham*) of the marketplace that they can catch the fleeting glimpses of God's presence, thereby drawing closer to him in their daily lives. In 'Ajiba's own words:

> Isolation is necessary at the beginning, before [the Sufi] enters the realm of true realities of existence. Once he has entered this realm, he should choose the crowd over isolation, so that his heart could achieve equanimity in both crowd and solitude. Isolation from people is the isolation of the weak, whereas isolation in the midst of people is the isolation of the strong.[40]

In sum, internal peace and tranquility are achievable and even desirable without a total seclusion or withdrawal from the world.

Moving closer to al-Ghazali's birthplace in the Muslim East, well before it was formulated by Ibn 'Ajiba, the same principle had been adopted by the Naqshbandiyya Sufi order that originated in Central Asia and bears the name of its founder Baha' al-Din Naqshband (1318–89) of Bukhara. Articulated in Persian as *khalva dar anjuman* ("solitude in society/crowd"), it has been the guiding principle of its followers in the same way as Ibn 'Ajiba's advice motivated the members of his Shadhiliyya-Darqawiyya order in the Maghreb and Egypt.[41] In more recent times, it has found another, recognizably modern, expression in the teaching of the controversial Turkish religious thinker Fethullah Gülen (b. 1941), who insists that his followers should not only live among the masses of believers, but also provide public services to them, especially education. This principle (*hizmet*; meaning "service" in Turkish)[42] has given the name to Gülen's entire movement.[43] The underlying goals of the *hizmet* movement may be disputed, especially in the aftermath of the attempted coup d'état in Turkey in July 2016, but its debt to the pre-modern Sufi tradition, including al-Ghazali, is undeniable.[44] The principle of being and acting in the world, while conversing with God in the secret recesses of one's heart, remains unchanged with Gülen and his "neo-Sufi" followers, his putative political ambitions and aspirations notwithstanding.

As I have demonstrated elsewhere, the social and political implications of introvert–extravert relations with the world under the aegis of Sufism, given Sufi psychological and gnoseological states related to internal peace and tranquility, confirm Marshall Hodgson's conclusion that in Sufism a tradition of intensive interiorization re-exteriorized its results and was finally able to provide an important basis for social order. Perhaps more than their peers in any other major cultural environment, the Sufis succeed in combining a spiritual elitism with a social populism.[45]

All I can add is that, for the majority of Sufis, the sense of responsibility for the spiritual and moral wellbeing of their fellow-believers has eventually triumphed over the ascetic-mystic's egotistic quest for personal tranquility, serenity, and, in the final account, salvation. Peace has to be found and cultivated not within the ocean of one's inevitably selfish soul but in society with all its inevitable disturbances and imperfections. How this quest for harmony with social realities and moral-ethical uprightness might have affected the Sufis' psychological peace and serenity is the subject of another study.

Notes

1   Helmut Ritter, *The Ocean of the Soul: Men, the World and God in the Stories of Farid al-Din 'Attar.*, trans. by John O'Kane and Bernd Radtke (Leiden and Boston: E.J. Brill, 2003), 34–5.
2   For numerous examples of this world-rejecting and devaluating attitude among Sufis, see ibid., 55–76; cf. Alexander Knysh, *Islamic Mysticism: A Short History*, 2nd edn. (Leiden and Boston: E.J. Brill, 2010), 5–10.
3   See, e.g., chapter 1 in Annemarie Schimmel's *Mystical Dimensions of Islam* (Chapel Hill: University of North Carolina Press, 1975); cf. Mark Sedgwick, *Western Sufism* (Oxford: Oxford University Press, 2017), 1–12.
4   For two typical examples, see Abu Nasr 'Abdallah b. 'Ali al-Sarraj al-Tusi, *Kitab al-luma' fi 'l-tasawwuf.*, ed. R.A. Nicholson (Leiden and London: E.J. Brill and Luzac, 1914), 41–2; al-Harith b. Asad al-Muhasibi, *al-Tawahhum. Rihlat al-insan ila 'alam al-akhira.*, ed. Muhammad 'Uthman al-Khusht (Cairo: Maktab al-Qu'an), 1984), 31–2.

5   On him see Knysh, *Islamic Mysticism*, 43–8.

6   al-Muhasibi, *al-Tawahhum*, 89–91.

7   *The Book of Wisdom by Ibn 'Ata' Illah. Intimate Conversations by Khwaja 'Abdullah Ansari*. Introduction, translation, and notes of *The Book of Wisdom* by Victor Danner and of *Intimate Conversations* by Wheeler M. Thackston (New York: Paulist Press, 1978).

8   See, e.g., al-Sarraj, *Kitab al-luma'*, 41–72; Arthur Arberry (trans.), *The Doctrine of the Sufis* (Cambridge: Cambridge University Press, reprint, 1991), 80–134; Alexander Knysh (trans.), *Al-Qushayri's Epistle on Sufism* (Reading: Garnet, 2007), 75–111; Reynold Nicholson (trans.), *The Kashf al-mahjub. The Oldest Persian Treatise on Sufism* (Leiden: E.J. Brill and London: Luzac, 1911), 367–92; Shihab al-Din 'Umar b. Muhammad al-Suhrawardi, *'Awarif al-ma'arif.*, ed. Abu Sahl Sayyam (Cairo: al-Muqattam, 2009), 456–513.

9   See the chapter on early Sufi literature in Knysh, *Islamic Mysticism*, 303–11.

10   For the lack of a clear boundary between Sufi states and stations, see Knysh, *Islamic Mysticism*, 305 and William Chittick, *The Sufi Path of Knowledge: Ibn al-'Arabi's Metaphysics of Imagination* (Albany: State University of New York Press, 1989), 280.

11   Knysh, *Islamic Mysticism*, 118–20.

12   Al-Ghazali, *Ihya' 'ulum al-din* (Cairo: al-Maktaba al-tijariyya al-kubra, 1962), vol. 4, 243–355.

13   For a discussion of an intimate link between trust in God and certitude, see ibid., 260: "Trust in God is only perfected by the strength of one's heart and certitude." These two spiritual states are, in turn, closely linked to tranquility; ibid.

14   Ibid.

15   Ibid., 354–5.

16   Bernard McGinn, *The Foundations of Mysticism.* vol. 1. *The Presence of God: A History of Western Christian Mysticism* (New York: Crossroad, 1991), 105.

17   On him see Knysh, *Islamic Mysticism*, 69–71.

18   A saying of the Prophet Muhammad.

19   Chittick, *The Sufi Path*, 307.

20   For a detailed, and overall convincing, articulation of the theory of cultural transfer within the context of Sufism and Islam generally, see Sedgwick, *Western Sufism*, Part 1.

21   For a detailed discussion of the issue, see Steven Katz (ed.), *Mysticism and Language* (Oxford: Oxford University Press, 1992).

22   As discussed, for example, in Ritter's *Ocean of the Soul*, 34–45, 91–106, 188–97.

23   See Knysh, *Islamic Mysticism*, 116–18.

24   Usually translated into English as "Book of Flashes"; see, e.g., John Renard (ed.), *Knowledge of God in Classical Sufism: Foundations of Islamic Mystical Theology* (New York: Paulist Press, 2004), 65.

25   Al-Sarraj, *Kitab al-luma'*, 67–8.

26   Ibid., 67; see also ibid., 1–20.

27   Cf. al-Ghazali, *Ihya'*, vol. 4, 358–9 and Alexander Knysh, *Sufism: A New History of Islamic Mysticism* (Princeton and Oxford: Princeton University Press, 2017), 70–81.

28   Chittick, *The Sufi Path*, 104. I have slightly modified Chittick's translation of this passage from Ibn al-'Arabi's "Meccan Openings (Revelations)."

29   Ibid., 105–6.

30   See Knysh, *Sufism*, 82, 99–100, 105, 107.

31   See, e.g., Abu Bakr 'Abd al-Hadi (ed.), al-Harith al-Muhasibi, *al-Masa'il fi a'mal al-qulub wa l-jawarih wa 'l-makasib wa 'l-'aql* (Cairo: al-Maktaba al-azhariyya, 1437/2016).

32 Ritter, *Ocean of the Soul*, 190.
33 Max Weber, Sociology of Religion Trans. by Ephraim Fischoff (London: Methuen, 1965).
34 See, e.g., London: Bryan Turner, *Weber and Islam: A Critical Study* (Routledge and Kegan Paul, 1974).
35 As discussed in my *Sufism*, 170–4.
36 Bryan Turner, "Towards an Economic Model of Virtuoso Religion," in *Islamic Dilemmas: Reformers, Nationalists, and Industrialization*. ed. Ernest Gellner (Berlin: Mouton, 1985), 49–72; for a Sufi view, see Abu Bakr 'Abd al-Hadi (ed.), *al-Harith al-Muhasibi*.
37 Knysh, *Sufism*, 171–2.
38 Marshall Hodgson, *The Venture of Islam: Conscience and History in a World Civilization* vol. 2. (Chicago, IL: University of Chicago Press, 1974), 187–90.
39 Knysh, *Sufism*, 172.
40 Ibid.
41 Knysh, *Islamic Mysticism*, 114–17.
42 From the Arabic *khidmat* with the same meaning.
43 For an insider view, see Muhammed Çetin, *The Gülen Movement: Civic Service without Borders* (Izmir: Blue Domem, 2010); for an outsider view, see Joshua Hendrick, *Gülen: The Ambiguous Politics of Market Islam in Turkey and the World* (New York and London: New York University Press, 2013); for a post-coup re-assessment of the movement, see Haqan Yavuz, and Bayram Balcı (eds.), *Turkey's July 15th Coup: What Happened and Why* (Salt Lake City: University of Utah Press, 2018).
44 See, e.g., Jane Schlubach, "Gülen and Ghazzali on Tolerance." November 12, 2005. Online publication: https://fgulen.com/en/gulen-movement/conference-papers/the-fethullah-gulen-movement-i/25513-gulen-and-ghazzali-on-tolerance. Accessed December 1, 2019; *Ghazali on the Principles of Islamic Spirituality: Selections from The Forty Foundations of Religion*. Trans. by Aaron Spevak. Foreword by Fethullah Gülen (Woodstock, VT: Skylight Paths, 2012).
45 Hodgson, *The Venture of Islam*, vol. 2, 218; see my *Sufism*, chapter 6.

5 PRINCIPLED PACIFISM IN ISLAMIC WEST AFRICA

Rudolph Ware

The centerpiece in the story I want to tell here has to do with a vision of Shaykh Ahmadu Bamba Mbacke (1855–1927).[1] He will be our narrator for an important part of this discussion. He authored 200 separate works in the Arabic language, some of them large collections of long poems, some of them with as many as 5,000 lines. He also founded and nurtured a Sufi order, the Muridiyya, that has an absolute and total commitment to nonviolence. Let us look through the window of Shaykh Ahmadu Bamba at this question of peace and principled pacifism in Islam. As I argued in my first book, *The Walking Qur'an*, the goal of traditional Qur'an schooling in West Africa is to inscribe the book of God onto the flesh and blood of human beings so that they become like a Qur'an *walking upon the earth*, in accordance with the saying of the Prophet Muhammad.[2] Their goal is to transmit that achievement from one generation to the next. This theme involves the history of a thousand years of Qur'an schooling, particularly embodiment and the role of embodiment in the transmission of Islamic knowledge in West Africa.

I make an argument in *The Walking Qur'an*, especially in the introduction, about why Islamic studies scholars and African studies scholars ought to be paying more attention to Africa when they study Islam, rather than leaving it out of the story. A sixth of the world's Muslims, more than 320 million persons, live in sub-Saharan Africa. There are more than twice as many Muslims south of the Sahara than there are north of the Sahara, in North Africa. There are more Muslims in Nigeria than there are in Egypt, more Muslims in Ethiopia than there are in Iraq, a higher percentage of Muslims in Senegal than in Syria.[3] Yet, Africa tends to be systematically ignored when we discuss Islam. Especially if we consider peace studies, Africa figures prominently because traditions of tolerance and peaceful interpretations of Islam predominate in sub-Saharan Africa. Moreover, dark-skinned Muslims were exemplars of knowledge and piety in the early days of Islam. The Prophet—peace be upon him—paid attention to them, we ought to as well.

Many of the arguments of my book are informed by the histories and sensibilities of the Muridiyya Sufi order, a Sufi order that claims roughly 5.5 million adherents, most of whom live in Senegal but many of whom are dispersed in diaspora communities throughout the world. The main story, and there will be a few other stories nested within it, is going to be about him and about his approach to peace.

Here, I will discuss briefly four West African scholars. The framework will be provided by Shaykh Ahmadu Bamba Mbacke (1855–1927), scholar and poet, and his approach to peace. The second is Shaykh Musa Kamara (1864–1945) also from Senegal—another scholar who was explicitly pacifist and nonviolent in his literary scholarship.[4] He authored at least forty-seven distinct works, and he was more of a prose writer, whereas Bamba wrote poetry. He was also a historian. Some of Shaykh Musa Kamara's histories are more than 800 manuscript pages in length, and he wrote forty-seven books.

Then there was Shaykh al-Islam Ibrahim Niasse. Both of these two men were from the Tijaniyyah Sufi tradition, but from different branches of it. The community of Shaykh Ibrahim Niasse, the Jama'at al-Faydah (literally "community of the flood"), today claims as many as 75 million disciples worldwide.[5] Most of them are in West Africa, from Senegal to Sudan, but adherents also live in Detroit, Chicago, and South Africa. This community of the flood has poured out all over the world. It may well be the largest single Sufi movement, depending on how a "movement" is defined, in today's world, though it is not as well known as it should be.

Tierno Bokar Salif Tal (1875–1939), who lived in the French Sudan, what is now Mali, will also figure in this talk, but in a less direct way. He was the descendant of the founder of one of the largest so-called Jihad states, in nineteenth-century West Africa. Perhaps in reaction against the carnage of earlier generations, Tierno Bokar Salif Tal articulates quite clearly and forcefully arguments about tolerance and pacifism.[6]

These principles of pacifism or principles of tolerance are all shared by the four scholars just mentioned. Primarily in order to offer readers a mnemonic device, I will point to the way in which each exemplifies a particular value, thus:

1. Human liberty—Shaykh Ahmadu Bamba Mbacke
2. Pacifism—Shaykh Musa Kamara
3. The centrality of love and compassion in the Islamic tradition—Shaykh al-Islam Ibrahim Niasse
4. The universality of truth—Tierno Bokar Salif Tal

With regard to Ahmadu Bamba and the first principle, of human liberty, Muslim scholars trained in the classics of their tradition return again and again to the proposition that humanity's basic condition is freedom, being exempt from slavery.[7] The default for humanity is freedom, and for it to be taken away, a reason must be demonstrated. This conviction led to remarkably forward thinking about the abolition of the slave trade in parts of Islamic West Africa.

Another principle common among these scholars is that the jihad of the soul is above the jihad of the sword. They further hold that truth is universal, and denial of that is prideful. In other words, it is a form of chauvinism on a religious basis, which they view as sinful. It is born of pride. The prophet asserted in an authentic Hadith that it is denying the truth and holding people in contempt. It is denying the creator, who is *al-Haqq* (the Truth) in Islamic tradition, and it involves contempt for the creation. I argue that underlying all these principles is the Islamic vision for the value of a human being. That vision in turn underlies way that you see these principles being played out in West African history.

The fourth central idea here is that love is the reason for the creation. This is in accord with the holy hadith, "I was a hidden treasure and loved to be known. Therefore, I created the creatures, that they might know me."[8] West Africans often observe that if God loves something other than human beings, he certainly has not said so in the scripture. As a result, human beings hold a particularly esteemed position, and honoring them is honoring what God has honored. Love, they hold, is the very reason for the creation of the human being in the first place. They conclude that love should constitute a core value in human beings' relationships with one another.

Yet another principle they share in common is that scholarship spreads Islam better than proselytizing.[9] The term Jakhanke refers to an order of Muslim clerics that began in town of Diakha and spread throughout West Africa.[10] They played a central role early on in promulgating Islam in West Africa, carrying it out without military or political engagement. They systematically abstained from politics and from military activity. They also avoided aggressive proselytizing. The goal was never to proselytize (*da'wa*); the goal was teaching and scholarship in their own communities and providing an example for others to emulate. That model is predominantly responsible for transforming West Africa from a completely non-Muslim society in 900 CE to an overwhelmingly Muslim one today. This transformation was the educational struggle (*jihad*) of the wooden board, the small tablets on which one learns the Qur'an on, rather than the Jihad of the sword.[11]

I want to tell a single story that unites and connects all of these four, and they are all embedded in Ahmadu Bamba's vision of peace. His roughly 200 works make up the largest single entry for anyone in the *Arabic Literature of Africa* series. They probably only represent about a third of his actual scholarly production. Many of his works have not been catalogued. He destroyed others when he wrote new works he felt superseded the previous ones and were superior to them. He was deeply embedded in the Islamic scholarly tradition, trained first and foremost as a legal scholar. He wrote legal opinions about peaceful approaches to dealing with the French occupation, amongst other things (he lived during the colonial period when Senegal was ruled by France).

His life was in a sense composed of text, and in Senegal he is often represented in calligraphic form. Murids, members of the Muridiyya order, say he is the author of "The Seven Tons." In town where he settled, the holy city of Touba, on a typical Friday as many as 80,000 people will come to pray in the mosque. Every year on the 18th of the Muslim month of Safar, about 3.5 million people come to the city of Touba on a pilgrimage that is meant to commemorate an important moment in the life of Ahmadu Bamba. That important moment will frame the rest this discussion.

Let us open with his pacifist principles. In 1895, he made a spiritual retreat at a mosque during the last ten days of Ramadan, in Touba—the town that he established seven years previously, in 1888. Touba at that time did not have a big mosque, just a small wooden building. When Bamba made his spiritual retreat, he had a waking-state vision of the Prophet Muhammad, who came to give him a message.[12] It was not the first time Bamba has seen the Prophet. On authoring one of his first poems praising previous Sufis, he began seeing the Prophet Muhammad— peace be upon him—in dreams and also in waking states. He usually saw him as a being whose limbs appeared to be made of light as they extended from his robes, or he glimpsed a person veiled behind a screen of light, without being able to see him clearly, though the Prophet identified himself. On that day in 1895, sometime in the last ten days of Ramadan, he saw the Prophet Muhammad again, in a waking state rather than in a dream. This time no veil interceded, and his view was unobstructed.

This narration of the vision of the Prophet comes from two of Ahmadu Bamba's sons and one of his earliest disciples. Bamba never wrote openly about it, but he never discouraged others from setting down about what he had told them. He said that the Prophet always spoke first. He said, "Peace be upon you O servant of the messenger." When the Prophet gave him that ontological title in those first visionary experiences, Bamba adopted it. His aspiration was service first and foremost, and he was rewarded with the title "Servant of the Messenger." Bamba responded, "Peace be upon you O' Prophet, and God's blessing and mercy." Then he asked a question, because when the veil of light was removed he noticed something that he had not perceived before. The Prophet was surrounded by throngs of people. Bamba asked him, "Messenger of God, who are these that are with you?" The response was "These are the people of Badr. They never leave my side, not even for a moment." Badr was, according to the tradition biographies of the Prophet, the first major military conflict in the Hijaz. The biographers wrote that 313 champions of the new religion stood against as many as a thousand pagan foes. As the tradition had it, the 313 were poorly armed, with at best six suits of armor and eight horses among them, and they were going up against enemies in full mail, but they routed the more numerous enemies. It is said that the Prophet threw a handful of pebbles in the direction of the enemy camp. This incident is mentioned in the Qur'an, where the voice of God addressed the heroes of the battle of Badr who had bravely cast their spears: "and when you threw, it was not you that threw, but God threw" (*The Spoils* 8:17). This means that God threw the weapons at the enemy and it is further said in the Qur'an that God reinforced the Muslims with a party of angels to bring the victory on that day: "When you were calling upon your Lord for succor, and He answered you, 'I shall reinforce you with a thousand angels riding behind you'" (*The Spoils* 8:9). In the Islamic tradition, Badr is a rhetorically powerful and central moment because without that victory in that place Islam might well not exist. It might have been extinguished in a military defeat at that moment. The people of Badr therefore have an honored station with the Prophet and that is why they are with him at all times.

Let us return to the vision. Bamba said to the Prophet, "I love you. I too want to be someone who is never absent from you. What do I have to do in order to join their company?" The Prophet responded,

> What you ask is going to be difficult. Because the ones that you see with me spilled blood when they didn't want to spill blood. And they had their blood spilled when they didn't want their blood spilled. The time for spilling blood has past. No one can command it any longer. Therefore, you have no sacrifice that you can offer that would make you worthy of their measure.

This exchange is worth pondering.

It is not that Sufism or Muslim mysticism is intrinsically pacifist. Sufis had fought imperial occupation on any number of occasions. Abdul-Qadir al-Jaza'iri led the resistance to the French occupation of Algeria.[13] He was also the greatest living interpreter of the medieval Andalusian mystic Muhyi al-Din Ibn 'Arabi (d. 1240) in his time. And he was somebody who, personally, found fighting odious.

Al-Hajj 'Umar Tal (d. 1864), whom I mentioned previously, also fought the French in the 1850s and 1860s, this time in the Senegal River Valley.[14] Al-Hajj 'Umar Tal's scholarly library was stolen when the French conquered Mali. They moved the whole library, all 4,100 pieces to the French national library, the *Bibliothèque Nationale*, where it still is today. Such scholars led this resistance. Usman Dan Fodio in what is now northern Nigeria fought a war not against foreign occupation but war against slave trading kings, at the end of the eighteenth century and early part of the nineteenth century.[15] These men were all Sufis, one a follower of Ibn al-'Arabi, another a member of the Tijani Sufi order, the third a Qadiri.

There can, then, be no simplistic equation between Sufism and pacifism. Still, there is a close link between Sufism and pacifist discourses in the Islamic tradition. One of the first Sufi sayings that I learnt in Wolof is "The Sufi is the one who, when he finds a fly drinking ink at the tip of the pen, will not write again until the fly has had its fill. How could one who is so gentle with a fly take the life of a human?" Our colleague Cheikh Anta Babou wrote a great study of Shaykh Ahmadu Bamba, "Fighting the Greater Jihad." The title is a reference to the *hadith* or saying of the

Prophet Muhammad, "We return from the lesser jihad to the greater jihad. What is the greater jihad? The jihad against the lower soul of passions."

In *The Walking Qur'an* I talk how it was the Atlantic slave traded that brought scholars, especially those Sufi scholars, to enter into the realm of political activity and military activity. They did so despite their adherence to models like the Jakhanke model, which advocated maintaining pious distance from power and not engaging in military activity. This massive new phenomenon provoked a certain group of Muslim clerics to conclude that there was no nonviolent solution to the problem of Muslims enslaving other Muslims and selling them for bottles of rum.

The scholars took up arms beginning in the seventeenth century and all the way down to the nineteenth century. They developed an indigenous abolitionist tradition, one that was recognized by the founder of the London Society for the Abolition of Slavery, in the very first work that he wrote on the abolition of the slave trade, twenty years before the British abolished the slave trade in 1807. He described Abdul-Qadir Kane, the leader of that first revolutionary movement, as a person who "is certainly more to be respected than any of the sovereigns of Europe, inasmuch as he has made a much nobler sacrifice than they, and has done more for the causes of humanity, justice, liberty, and religion."[16] We have an Anglican priest praising an African Muslim for abolishing slavery in the Senegal River Valley in the 1770s and 1780s.

That same West African emancipatory and abolitionist tradition arrived at these very shores in the bodies of enslaved Africans. A man from Futa Toro in 1806 observed, when he was being sold on the dock of Savannah, that the law of the Muslims does not allow believing persons to own another believing person and their descendants in perpetuity. So, if you Christians are doing that I'm not interested in your religion.

With regard to the first principle, human liberty, let us begin with Ahmadu Bamba before his vision, when he was starting to become a great Shaykh, starting to become someone of note. A disciple came to him and made a gift (*hadiya*) of a slave to him in order to make his ritual submission (*beyah*) to Ahmadu Bamba. And Bamba's response is recorded famously in the oral tradition. He said, "You own him?" The man said, "Yes." Bamba said, "If you own him, then you own me, because he and I have the same master." That is, there is a critique of slavery from within Islam.[17]

The devotion is not only to liberty but also to equality. For instance, there is the tradition of female scholarship on which I focused heavily in *The Walking Qur'an*. Today many Qur'an schools have more girls than boys, nor is that a recent phenomenon. Female scholars play an important role within the Muridiyya and actually within all of the Sufi movements at issue here. All of these West African traditions of tolerance, because of the way that they approach the question of basic human dignity, provide space for women in ritual devotion. For example, amongst the Jakhanke, because men are required by law to lead the prayer, after the prayer women engaged in the ritual supplication (*dua*), often using both the

Arabic language and vernacular languages, so that people can hear the prayer that is offered for the health and protection of the people in their mother tongue, in their African languages. Two of Shaykh Ahmadu Bamba's daughters, Sokhna Muslimatu Mbacke and Mayumuna Kabira Mbacke, wrote extensively in Arabic and, in their case, in the Wolof language using the Arabic script.

Let us return to the day on the 18th of Safar when 3.5 million people come together. What is it that they are celebrating? They're celebrating what happens next in Bamba's vision of the Prophet. Remember, the dialogue has gone as follows:

Bamba: "What do I do to join the company of the people of Badr?"
The Prophet: "What you ask is going to be difficult, because the ones you see with me spilled blood when didn't want to spill blood, they had their blood spilled when they didn't want to have their blood spilled ... The time for spilling blood is over."

The most well-known telling of the story reports the Prophet as having replied, "No one can command it any longer." Another narration has "It ended with them. It ended with the people of Badr. It ended with the generation that fought alongside the Prophet."

This nonviolence in the Muridiyya is not an unthinking commitment to nonviolence that says violence is always bad. It's a commitment to nonviolence that sees the early physical struggles in conflicts in Islam as expiatory, as fulfilling the need for physical conflict for the establishment of Islam, and as therefore having obviated the conditions that would require it for later times.

In the vision, the Prophet says, "The time for spilling blood has ended, there is no sacrifice that you can offer that will make you worthy of their measure." You can imagine that Bamba would be crestfallen by hearing this news. He just said he loves the Prophet and he wants to be with him all the time and now he is told that he cannot come. But the Prophet is always gentle and displays the best of manners. He says, "But I come with good news. In three months you will become the axial saint of your time, the pole of the era." The delay derived from the principle that no one reaches that status before they have reached the age of forty. Why the age of forty? That was the age of the Prophet Muhammad when he first received revelation. It is the age of maturity. Bamba's entire vision reenacts the original inception of the revelation to the Prophet. This foundational vision takes place in exactly the same context, the spiritual retreat (i'tikaf). Why has he engaged in this retreat? What is it for? It is to commemorate the Prophet's retreat at the cave on Mt. Hira in 610 that led to the first revelations. Bamba now has his own Revelation in his own vision. He will be made the axial saint of his time. Because no one can be that until they have had their fortieth birthday. The Prophet then says, however, "But this is only a formality. You will be 40 in three months. If you want I will make you the axial saint beginning today."

This whole dialogue, by the way, took place in Arabic, whereas Bamba narrated it in Wolof, so I will follow the Wolof. He replies, and the way he worded it became famous, "That would be lovely, that would be beautiful, but my ambitions now surpass this. Being the greatest living Sufi of the time is no longer good enough for me. I want to be amongst those who are never absent from you. I love you. And I can't bear the thought of ever parting with you."

Bamba would later write about the great status enjoyed by those people of Badr, the expiatory function that they had served, and why they were so important and so central, why he wanted to join their company. In one of Bamba's poems that I translated, he began by praising the first four Orthodox Caliphs, and then specifically Ali, the fourth:

139. On the Near and Dear, the Lion of War, may He Who Answers grant ascendancy.
140. Upon the Cohort, who answered the call in darkest hours, His honor and clemency.
141. In troubled times, they were victor and vanquished, theirs is dignity, O Such Men!
142. On the day of Humility, the day of Appeals, May He Who Hears, be pleased with them.
143. Founts of good for seekers of gain, sources of pain for seekers of hostility.
144. They rose to the occasion, in confrontation, full of bravery and loyalty.
145. Such gallant knights! Such brave defenders! Slaying antagonists without cowardice.
146. By their grace I've pardoned, without malice, by them I've banished the slanderous.
147. Divert my foes, avert all harm, by the kind listener, who rids of tyranny.
148. I entrust my affairs, to Him my renewer, and those at Badr, with certainty.

The poetry conveys that the sacrifices that were made in that time create this space in which Bamba can articulate his nonviolence. His nonviolence is not a negation of the armed conflict and struggle at the beginning of Islam but rather it is an understanding of the longer-term function it serves in setting him free.

This principle leads to the philosophy of nonviolence in the Muridiyya, and not only in the Muridiyya. A person like Shaykh Musa Kamara also writes specifically about the principles of nonviolence. I mentioned before his forty-seven distinct works. He was not just an archival historian who worked with Arabic documents, but he traveled the countryside in Futa Toro, his place of origin, and interviewed the descendants of clerical families in order to write their history based on oral history as well. He was an extraordinary scholar. He also praised the people of Badr in similar terms, devoting to them a ninety-four-page work, of which twenty pages consist of a devotional poem on how believers can bring blessings upon themselves just by using the names of the individuals at Badr in a formula when sending blessings upon the Prophet. His most important work in this vein, written around 1922, castigates the jihad tradition, arguing that "most Lovers of jihad after the Prophets wanted to make names for themselves and dominion in the land and were not concerned with God's servants who died in jihad."

He argued that jihad caused one to be very delicate and careful with human life. He does not hold that jihad is never warranted under any circumstance. He admits that sometimes self-defense may require it. He maintains, however, that the French occupation was no such circumstance because the Muslims are forbidden from committing suicide. The French were capable of killing so many resisters without suffering casualties themselves that it was unethical to try to resist occupation. That he came to this conclusion is important because he hailed from the same region that gave rise to the most important nineteenth-century Jihadi scholar. The argument was framed by the hadith, "The ink of the scholar is more sacred than the blood of the martyr."[18] That saying may or may not be authentic, but it was nevertheless influential. These are basic principles running throughout West African Islamic thought: that the jihad of the wooden board is a better instrument for spreading Islam than the jihad of the sword, and that the clerics do that work do it through teaching and providing benefit to people.

The Jakhanke specifically articulated this as positive principle, and other well-known teachings that came to be acknowledged throughout Jakhanke communities across space and time.[19] Its basic components were:

1. Unbelief is a result of ignorance (*jahl*) rather than wickedness.
2. It is God's will that some remain in *jahiliyya* longer than others.
3. There is no obligation in religion, and true conversion occurs in God's time.
4. Jihad is not an acceptable means for converting non-Muslims.
5. Jihad is legitimate only in self-defense to protect Muslims' survival.
6. Muslims can and should support non-Muslim rule if Islamic practice is allowed under it.
7. And Muslims must present an example to be emulated so non-Muslims will be attracted to Islam. You don't preach to them.
8. And the way you bring that second to last point to life is by making scholarship the center of life.

The contemporary Sufi scholar Imam Fode Drame, now based in Vancouver, participated willingly with us in campus events because he sees bringing Jakhanke teachings into a classroom environment as a basic extension of the Jakhanke mission in West Africa. In that tradition, they are just trying to teach people about Islam, confident that then they will make up their own minds. That teaching is accomplished through scholarship, not just schooling but scholarly production. All the scholars we have been discussing were extremely productive.

They were, moreover, committed to carrying out these tasks in a way that maintained a pious distance from power, just as the Jakhanke did. I can illustrate this point with a famous anecdote about Ahmadu Bamba. When he was asked to come serve as the chief judge for the most powerful pre-colonial kingdom before the establishment of French colonial rule in Senegal, he politely declined six or seven times. They kept asking him, however, because they sought his prestige at the court. Finally, he sent a letter to the king. The king's scribe prepared to read the letter to him. The scribe opened the letter and read it. He remarked that it began with blessings and invocations. And then the scribe becomes visibly angry. The king asks him, "What does the letter say?" He replied, "No I'm not going to read it, this is very offensive to me, I'm not going to say it out loud."

The king insisted, "What does it say?"
The scribe says, "No, this harms me personally, I am not going to read it."
I'm your king, I command you—what does it say?!

In the letter, Bamba had quoted an aphorism of Ibn Maslama, one of the early Muslims, that compares the scholar who curries favor at the court of a sultan to a fly feeding on a pile of feces. So, the king says, "I don't know what you're so upset about. He's comparing you to a fly. He's calling me a pile of shit."[20]

This anecdote expressed Bamba's stance of maintaining pious distance from power. If you could sum it up in a single phrase, it was a sort of separation of church and state, not to protect the state from the church but to protect the church from the state. After all, whenever religious authority becomes too closely tethered to political authority, there are grave moral and ethical risks. If scholars are responsible for providing an autonomous ethical critique of rulers, Bamba held, who will be left to carry out this task if the scholars have become the rulers? He held that one then ends up with bad religion and bad politics.

Let us return to the vision, which I will paraphrase. Bamba says, "That would be lovely, that would be beautiful. But my ambitions now surpass this. Now that I know that there are people who never leave your side even for a moment, my heart cannot rest with less than this."

The Prophet says to him: "Do you think you're the only one who ever loved me? All of the saints in my religion love me the way that you love me. And I appear to them the way that I am appearing to you. But this thing that you have asked has neither been asked nor has been given to any that came before you."

Bamba responds: "Listen, I don't know what you want from me. I've told you how much I love you. I've told you that my heart can't settle on less than you. And I'm willing to pay any sacrifice that would be required in order to join the company of the people of Badr."

The Prophet says to him, "Are you sure?"
He said, "Oh, I'm sure."

The Prophet then said, according to narrations of the vision,

Then you must go out and face your enemies in your time, the way that they faced their enemies in their time. You are, however, forbidden from spilling so much as a single drop of blood. If you shed blood, your compact with me is broken. I am not of you and you are not of me. If you are going to do that, you must leave this city of Touba that you love, because when you came here you prayed to the Almighty in my name that he protect this place until the Day of Judgment and that prayer has already been answered. So, you will leave this city that you love and face your enemies in your time.

Bamba finished his fast, he celebrated the Eid, and he packed his bags. What he did not know was that African chiefs, jealous of his growing authority, had been conspiring with the colonial regime all this time. He was abruptly arrested on trumped-up charges and was sent away into exile for seven years and nine months. Colonial regimes, often infused with an ideology of white supremacy, often carelessly committed great injustices against the colonized, and a sentence such as was pronounced on Ahmadu Bamba could easily have turned into life imprisonment or death. He, however, came back. The annual celebration during which 3.5 million people come to Touba does not commemorate the day that Bamba returned from exile. It takes place on the anniversary of the day that Bamba was banished, since at that time he began to pay the required price that would allow him to achieve the lofty station of those believers who made sacrifices in the early days of Islam. It is how he was able to draw near to the Prophet through love.

That theme of love is highlighted in another Sufi movement, the Fayda Tijaniyya, though there is only space here to make a few remarks about it that cannot do it justice.[21] Ahmad al-Tijani (1735–1815), the founder of the Tijaniyya order, in speaking of God's love, said, "All of the worlds are included in this love, even the disbelievers (kuffar)."[22] The bumper sticker that you will see among Tijanis in Chicago is "Love is God's Signature on Creation." And the basic reason for this is that the only times the phrase "God loves" appears in the Qur'an, the object of the verb is human beings. The Sufis held that the reason for which God would create human beings who are then capable of turning their backs on him is that it is beneath God's dignity to love a thing that is forced to obey. In order for God to have something in Creation that is worthy of His love, that thing has to be able to choose freely. This principle is the root of Islamic humanism in West Africa, grounded in understanding the investment that God has in every single human being. They hold that love for humanity is cultivated through cultivating love for the Prophet, as the best of creation. And by loving him through poems that praise him and his companions, through sending blessings upon the Prophet, the believers draw near him and their hearts become more expansive and capable of love. But in order to realize that, they must follow the Prophet's command. An authentic hadith says, "You will not enter the garden until you have believed, and you will not have believed until you have loved one another."[23]

Shaykh Ibrahim Niasse expanded on this saying: "You will never have faith until you love each other. Shall I tell you what will make you love each other? Spread peace between yourselves. By the One in whose hand is my soul, you will not enter Paradise until you are merciful." They said, "we are merciful." He said, "It's not mercy between yourselves, it's mercy in general, it's mercy in general." In his Qur'an commentary, Shaykh Ibrahim speaks of the universality of the prophetic message and says that all of the faiths have brought the same message.

Tierno Bokar Salif Tal also expands on that idea in one of his works, not just the universality of the prophetic message that is renewed for all of Humanity, but the universality of truth. He describes three categories of faith.[24] Solid faith (*sulb*) is the first degree.

> It is suitable for the masses, and teachers who are attached to the letter. [It is] channeled by prescriptions imposed by a law drawn from revealed texts, be they Jewish, Christian, or Islamic. It has a precise form and is subject to rigorous determination which admits no foreign element. This degree of *sulb* is heavy and immobile like a mountain. At time it prescribes armed warfare if this is necessary to gain respect and to assure its position.

But this is the outer layer, the layer that corresponds to Islam and the hadith of Gabriel. The layer that corresponds to faith (*iman*) in the hadith of Gabriel is liquid (*sa'il*) faith. It is the faith of those who have faced up to the trials of the law.

> They have triumphed over their faults and now they value Truths from wherever they come, considering neither their origin nor the date of existence. It gathers them and assembles them in order to make from them a body in perpetual movement, not arranged in one particular form. Rather they effect a flow which is constantly forward, like the flow of molecules of water which emerge from the mountain hollows and trickle across varied terrains, flowing together and increasing in size, becoming streams which finally, now as rivers, are thrown into the ocean of the truth (*al-Haqq*). This faith, due to its subtle, liquid nature, is strong, eroding the rocks of intolerance, pouring faith and taking a shape that is not fixed—as is the case with solid faith, but borrowing the form of its receptacle. It neither changes its essence nor retreats. Liquid faith manifests itself as gigantic mystical waterfalls, falling from the mountain into the ravine of active life. It contracts into a sinuous thread to traverse the steep pass. It expands into a great flood plying across a country. This faith is vivifying.

"The final form which corresponds to altruism (*ihsan*), which is the Sufi way, is decidedly more subtle, it's an affair of the elite, ethereal faith-and-charity. The faith of the sphere of truth emerges entirely from this last form. Those who reach it adore God in truth in a colorless light. On this sublime plane, solid faith (emerging from revelation) and liquid faith (emerging from this uncompromising path) both vanish to make way for one sole thing, the truth (*al-Haqq*), which flourishes in the fields of Love and Truth."

And anything other than the pursuit of love and truth, for Tierno Bokar Salif Tal, does not fulfill the conditions of Islam or charity (*ihsan*).

We'll give Tierno Bokar Salif Tal the last word. In his discussion of the jihad of the soul, he said: "We know only the jihad of the soul; as for the other jihad 'it is the mutual killing to which the children of Adam submit one another in the name of God whom they pretend to love very much, but whom they worship poorly by destroying part of his work.'"[25] To this we can only add that this human being is not only part of his handiwork from the standpoint of the Qur'an, but the most favored element in all creation. All the traditions of tolerance and the principles of pacifism in Islamic West Africa are rooted in that same basic humanistic understanding of what a human being is.

Notes

1   Cheikh Anta Babou, *Fighting the Greater Jihad: Amadu Bamba and the founding of the Muridiyya of Senegal, 1853–1913* (Athens: Ohio University Press, 2007).
2   Rudolph T. Ware III, *The Walking Qur'an: Islamic Education, Embodied Knowledge, and History in West Africa* (Chapel Hill: The University of North Carolina Press, 2014).
3   Ware, *The Walking Qur'an*, 17–19.
4   See, e.g., Wendell Marsh, "Reading with the Colonial in the Life of Shaykh Musa Kamara, a Muslim Scholar-saint," *Africa: The Journal of the International African Institute* 90, no. 3 (May 2020): 604–24.
5   Rüdiger Seesemann, *The divine Flood: Ibrahim Niasse and the Roots of a Twentieth-century Sufi Revival* (Oxford: Oxford University Press, 2011); A. Brigaglia, "The Fayda Tijaniyya of Ibrahim Nyass: Genesis and Implications of a Sufi Doctrine," *Islam et sociétés au sud du Sahara*, nos. 14–15 (2000): 41–56.
6   Louis Brenner, *West African Sufi: The Religious Heritage and Spiritual Quest of Cerno Bokar Saalig Taal* (Berkeley: University of California Press, 1984).
7   See, e.g., Rudolph T. Ware, "Slavery and Abolition in Islamic Africa, 1776–1905," in *The Cambridge World History of Slavery*, vol. 4, ed. David Eltis et al. (Cambridge: Cambridge University Press, 2017), 344–72.
8   William A. Graham, *Divine Word and Prophetic Word in Early Islam* (The Hague: Mouton, 1977), 71–2.
9   Lamin Sanneh, *Beyond Jihad: The Pacifist Tradition in West African Islam* (Oxford: Oxford University Press, 2016).

10 Ivor Wilks, "The Transmission of Islamic Learning in the Western Sudan," in *Literacy in Traditional Societies*, ed. Jack Goody (Cambridge: Cambridge University Press, 1968); Lamin Sanneh, *The Jakhanke: The History of an Islamic Clerical People of the Senegambia* (London: Routledge, 2020 [1975]).

11 Ware, *The Walking Qur'an*, chapter 2.

12 Fallou Ngom, *Muslims beyond the Arab World: The Odyssey of `Ajami and the Muridiyya* (Oxford: Oxford University Press, 2016), 125–34 and sources cited.

13 The bibliography is large, but see, e.g., Tom Woerner-Powell, *Another Road to Damascus: An Integrative Approach to 'Abd al-Qadir al-Jaza'iri (1808–1883)* (Berlin: Walter de Gruyter GmbH, 2017) and `Abd al-Qadir al-Jaza'iri, *The Spiritual Writings of Amir `Abd al-Kadir*, trans. Michel Chodkiewizc (Albany: State University of New York, 1995).

14 Amir Syed, "Islamic Authority in 19th Century West Africa" (PhD Diss., University of Michigan, 2017); David Robinson, *The Holy War of Umar Tal: The Western Sudan in the Mid-nineteenth Century* (Oxford: The Clarendon Press, 1985).

15 Ibraheem Sulaiman, *The African Caliphate: The Life, Works & Teaching of Shaykh Usman dan Fodio (1754–1817)* (London: Diwan, 2009).

16 Thomas Clarkson, *Letters on the Slave Trade* (London: Phillips, 1791), 80; see also Thomas Clarkson, "Lettres nouvelles sur le commerce de la Côte de Guinée, 1789–1790," William L. Clements Library, Ann Arbor: University of Michigan.

17 I make this point in Ware, "Slavery and Abolition in Islamic Africa, 1776–1905."

18 Ware, *Walking Qur'an*.

19 Wilks, "The Transmission of Islamic Learning in the Western Sudan;" Sanneh, *The Jakhanke*.

20 Babou, *Fighting the Greater Jihad*, 59.

21 Seesemann, *The divine Flood*; A. Brigaglia, "The Fayda Tijaniyya."

22 Zachary Valentine Wright, *Realizing Islam: The Tijaniyya in North Africa and the Eighteenth-century Muslim World* (Chapel Hill: University of North Carolina Press, 2020), 107.

23 Sahih Muslim, 54.

24 Cf Amadou Ba, *A Spirit of Tolerance: The Inspiring Life of Tierno Bokar*, trans. Fatima Casewit (Bloomington, IN: World Wisdom, 2007), 147–48.

25 Cf Ba, *A Spirit of Tolerance*, 148.

6 RASHID RIDA AND THE 1919 PARIS PEACE CONFERENCE

Elizabeth F. Thompson

In December 1918, the famous Islamic reformer Rashid Rida sat in his home office in Cairo, preparing a new issue of his magazine, *al-Manar*. He had "blogged" the war since 1914, translating documents and summarizing battles for his readers. Now, a month since the November 11 armistice, he looked forward to the opening of the Paris Peace Conference.

To mark the start of new era, Rida decided to write a special introduction to a new volume of *al-Manar*, volume 21. Like many intellectuals from the Arab provinces of the Ottoman Empire, he hoped that the Allied victory would bring hope for an end to wartime tyranny. Arab troops had shared in the conquest of Damascus on October 1, and Prince Faisal had declared an autonomous Syrian-Arab regime.

"Praise to the Almighty, the All-powerful One who created the universe with perfection," Rida wrote, invoking a Qur'anic verse about the Day of Resurrection. God's justice has prevailed, he continued. The Almighty has punished states that oppressed weaker nations: first, Russia withdrew, then Austria and Bulgaria surrendered. "Then the shadow of the Turks receded from Arab, Armenian and Kurdish lands, where the tyrannical Unionists spilled blood. Their corruption surpassed all limits."

God had saved Europe from the German threat by using

the hand of the great nation least prepared for war and battle, the power farthest from seeking sovereignty over other nations and from ambitions over other countries. That nation is the United States of America. It tipped power in favor of the Allies with moral strength more than with troops and materiel. Indeed, its president (Dr. Wilson) called for building peace on the basis of his proposed principles of truth and universal justice.[1]

That Rida discerned the hand of divine justice in the Turks' defeat and in the Americans' victory might surprise those who regard him solely as the student of Jamal al-Din al-Afghani and the grandfather of the Muslim Brotherhood. For scholars familiar with Rida's career as a journalist and political activist, however, his attitude is more comprehensible. Rida was a pragmatist, open to pursuing any available means toward his goal. His goal was sovereignty. Rida found hope for peace and justice in Wilson's opposition to European colonial expansion after the war. National self-determination would permit peoples to forge the terms of their own governments, unhindered by foreign intervention.

Rida regarded Wilson's principles as universal because he was a liberal of the nineteenth-century kind. He shared a belief with his mentors that Islam shared in universal civilization. For him, there was no cultural conflict between Wilson's vision of a liberal world order and Islamic principles of justice and peace. He therefore unreservedly embraced Wilson's project at Paris.

In 1919, Rida would travel to Damascus to participate in the General Syrian Congress, which declared independence and drew up a constitution for the Syrian Arab Kingdom. However, by then Wilson had fallen ill and the American Congress had voted against participation in the League of Nations. Left to themselves, Britain and France proceeded to occupy the Arab portions of the defeated Ottoman Empire. In July 1920, French troops invaded Syria and dismantled the Syrian-Arab state. Rida struggled for two more years to save Syrian sovereignty and its constitution. Only when the League of Nations rejected his appeal to ratify the French mandate did Rida lose faith in the Paris peace process and the liberal world order it established.

This chapter brings a historical perspective to the study of Islamic peace. It argues that we cannot understand Rida's views on Islamic peace solely by reference to his scriptural expertise. We must understand the context within which the December 1918 issue of al-Manar was published. In other words, the study of Islamic concepts of peace must be understood in the historical context within which they were formulated, and with reference to the practice of peacemaking by Muslims. This chapter is part of a broader effort to bring the historical study of social movements into dialogue with the intellectual approaches to Islamic peace.[2]

Such an approach throws new light not only on the nature of Islamic peace, but also on reasons why concepts of peace—and Islam—change. The story of Rida's engagement with the Paris Peace Conference highlights a critical moment of such transformation in the Arab-Islamic world. While historians have spilled much ink on the diplomatic story of what David Fromkin called "The Peace to End All Peace," they have made little or no reference to the views of Middle Eastern political actors. His view of peacemaking is restricted to the negotiating table, where Arabs and Muslims were not permitted. For Fromkin, Paris did not establish peace in the Middle East because of Britain's "lack of conviction," not because of anything local people did or believed.[3]

Erez Manela granted greater historical agency to Arabs and Muslims in The Wilsonian Moment. Nationalists in Egypt, India, China, and Korea were "savvy political actors who ... sought to harness Wilson's power and rhetoric to the struggle to achieve international recognition and equality for their nations." However, Manela suggests that these anti-colonial activists were responsible for the outbreak of post-war violence. In Manela's view, Wilson had never intended to apply self-determination beyond Europe. Nationalists stirred independence revolts to no avail. They had misunderstood Wilson and they were too weak to resist the superior agency of the imperial powers at Paris.[4] There is no place in Manela's framework to account for Rida's vision of universal peace and justice.

For international historians like Fromkin and Manela, political violence in the 1920s Middle East stemmed from the tragic miscalculations of a few leaders. These historians have ignored the growth of mass politics in the region, before and after the war. And they have neglected the engagement of the active middle class with the peace process. Middle Eastern peoples did not simply react to the Great Powers, or blindly adopt Wilson's Fourteen Points. They brought to the era of the Paris peace conference their own political strategies and ideals.

Rida's views on the peace process—expressed in a magazine read widely by the educated middle class across the region—may be read as a barometer of popular response to the decisions taken at Paris. They were subtler and more profound than simple frustration at the failure to obtain independence. The treaties issued from Paris wrought a profound change in popular conceptions of civilizational values that Muslims shared with European Christians.

This chapter suggests that Rida's embrace of Wilsonism was a last stand for the high tradition of liberal Islam that had inspired constitutional movements in Egypt in 1881 and the Ottoman Empire in 1908. Re-reading *al-Manar* in the context of Rida's political activism suggests that the denial of sovereignty at Paris sparked the rise of Islamic movements that rejected liberalism and international law as unjust. Just as punitive peace treaties fueled violent anti-liberal movements in the vanquished countries of Central and Eastern Europe, so too might we understand the rise of violent Islamic movements as a response to specific circumstances, not the expression of a theological essence.[5]

The chapter begins by sketching the historical *context* for the texts in *al-Manar*, with a brief summary of war events and Rida's responses to them. Next, the chapter addresses the *text* of the December issue of *al-Manar* as a product of Rida's war experience. It argues that the texts were strategic political gestures that nonetheless reflected Rida's liberal convictions. Finally, the chapter examines how Rida's views changed after the Great Powers at Paris authorized France to destroy the constitutional monarchy he had helped to found in Syria. It was the appropriation of Wilson's League of Nations (founded to guarantee national rights and international law) for the purposes of colonization that broke Rida's faith in universal, liberal peace. Out of this moment grew the roots of a new vision of Islamic peace based on opposition to European liberalism.

The War Years

Historians have recently argued that the First World War destroyed cross-sectarian coexistence in the Arab provinces of Syria—especially in its southern district of Palestine. Michelle Campos' book *Ottoman Brothers*, for example, is an elegy to the brief promise of Ottomanism that flowered before the war. Likewise, Abigail Jacobson has argued that wartime foreign philanthropy undermined neighborliness among Jews, Christians, and Muslims in Jerusalem, and that the British occupation of 1917 finally polarized Jewish and other groups.[6]

In *Year of the Locust*, Salim Tamari argues that Ottomanism in Palestine was "erased" during the war. He paints a devastating picture of how the young soldier, Private Ihsan Turjman, loathed Cemal Pasha and the Turkish elite. In his diary, Turjman condemned the abuse of Christians and Jews assigned to garbage battalions and welcomed news of Sharif Hussein's revolt. The war, Tamari argued, "decisively undermined progress toward a multinational, multiethnic state and gave rise to narrow and exclusivist nationalist ideologies."[7]

For these and other historians, the First Word War forged an intolerant Muslim society that broke with the pluralistic traditions of the Ottoman Empire. Muslim Syrians joined Turks in mobilizing for total war based on Muslim solidarity, even as Christians in Mount Lebanon were persecuted as potential traitors.[8] While pre-war reforms had required non-Muslims to serve in the Ottoman military, they were now disarmed and relegated to labor brigades.

The Ottoman Empire formally declared holy war on November 14, 1914, in front of the mosque of Mehmed the Conqueror in Constantinople. The declaration rested on five fatwas approved by twenty-nine ulama and Sultan Mehmed V. It was read out in Istanbul by the custodian of the fatwas, Ali Haydar Efendi.

Mustafa Aksakal argues that it was issued to rally ordinary Muslims to the war, but also to express anger and revenge for the Ottoman defeat in the Balkan wars of 1912–13. Greece, Serbia, and Bulgaria, Christian nations once ruled by the Ottomans, expelled thousands of Muslims, who arrived in the Ottoman capital as refugees. The Young Turk regime saw the outbreak of war in 1914 as an opportunity to "end Christian rule over Muslim peoples." In September 1914, it cancelled treaties that had granted privileges to European states of the Entente and their clients within the empire. With the declaration of jihad, they ended Ottoman pretensions to belong to the European state system.[9]

This set the stage for the 1915 decision to expunge the existence of Armenian Christians from Anatolia. In April of that year, Young Turk leaders ordered their mass deportation and murder. While most historians of the wartime Ottoman Empire agree that about 1 million Armenians died, a minority disputes that the intent was genocidal.

There is reason to doubt, however, that the majority of Muslims in the mixed societies of the provinces of Greater Syria and Iraq supported the Young Turks' turn to homogeneity and intolerance. Historians of the Great War in Europe understand that intolerant nationalism did not cause the war; rather, it was the product of it. This also appears to be the case in Syria.

Ihsan Turjman, the Muslim Arab private in Jerusalem, sympathized with non-Muslims forced into menial labor like cleaning streets. That was a primary reason he turned against the Ottomans. The memoir of the governor of Mount Lebanon also suggests that Syrian Arabs held fast to pre-war ideals of Ottoman brotherhood. An Armenian Catholic, Ohannès Pasha Kuyumcuyan's mother came from a Catholic family of Aleppo. He was appointed governor of Mount Lebanon shortly before the Young Turks' coup in 1913. A highly respected, long-serving Ottoman bureaucrat, he was dismissed for non-cooperation by the Young Turks in 1915, just as the first waves of deported Armenians arrived in Greater Syria. Ohannès Pasha's 1921 memoir describes how he returned to Istanbul that summer, in hope of finding friends, the "good old Turks" who had supported the 1908 constitutional revolution against the "bad Turks" of the Young Turk regime.[10]

Ohannès Pasha expressed a lingering liberalism that had survived the inhumanity of war—not just the annihilation of Armenians but also the famine that killed a half-million Syrians and Lebanese. He was not alone. We have reports of Ottoman governors and generals who resisted genocidal orders and worked to rescue non-Muslims from their plight.

Rashid Rida considered himself a Syrian, despite his long residence in Egypt. He was born in 1865 in Qalamun, just south of Tripoli, in the Ottoman state of Syria. He moved to Egypt in 1897 to study with the great Islamic reformer and mufti, Muhammad Abduh, and to escape Ottoman censorship. The next year Rida founded al-Manar, which printed stories concerning the political affairs of Muslims alongside fatwa collections and religious essays. Rida, unlike Abduh, was a committed public intellectual and journalist who sought to spread principles of modern Islamic reform to ordinary believers.[11]

In November 1914, Rida published an open letter to Syrian Muslims in al-Manar, titled "The Abolition of Foreign Privileges and Threat of Civil Strife." He praised their loyalty to the Ottoman state, but warned that their obedience should not extend beyond the letter of its law. Contrary to rumor, their non-Muslim neighbors are not disloyal simply because they have sympathies for foreign powers. A higher law forbids them from resorting to vigilante justice: "The Islamic Sharia does not impose punishment on inclinations, love, or hate or matters of the heart. Moreover, it is the authorities who impose punishment, not individuals."

Rida urged Syrian Muslims to shun the "Devil's whispers" that might push them toward fitna or public disorder. The Arab future must rest on "agreement with your race and with those not of your religion, who the sharia grants equality to you in public rights." Rida supported the Ottoman state's entry into the war to defend its sovereignty. But defense must not cause alarm to Syrian Christians. And Syrians must not capitulate to the Young Turks' Muslim nationalism.[12]

A February 1915 article addressed Christian panic about the declaration of jihad. Rida argued that jihad must not be understood as a war on non-Muslims. Contrary to assertions made in newspapers (he was reading Syrian-American papers) jihad was not an authorization to kill Ottoman Christians. The war, he insisted, has instead brought Muslims and Christians together in solidarity. Attacks on Armenians (he had heard about early instances) were made on political, not religious grounds. Rida apparently believed propaganda that Armenians cooperated with the Ottomans' enemy, Russia. Armenians were attacked, he argued, not because they were Christian, but because they were traitors.

Rida contrasted the limited nature of these early attacks on Armenians to the massive brutality of war in Europe, where the Germans had killed thousands of civilians in Belgium and where soldiers were slaughtered in trenches by machine gunfire and chemical weapons. Rida assured his readers that Islamic laws of war were more just and merciful than European law. Jihad is permitted only in self-defense, he wrote. And Islam does not permit the killing of non-combatants.[13]

While Rida blamed the outbreak of war on modern European materialism, he did not sustain a polarized religious discourse. The war violated the principles of all religions. "For those who understand it, Christianity is a religion of peace and humility," he wrote. "The more people in a nation [who believe this], the more chance there is for peace." Rida was pleased to hear that the war had revived religious feeling in Europe. He even approved of conscientious objectors in England. "Had Christianity been in the hearts of [all] the people, they wouldn't have allowed this war to happen."[14]

Rida's opposition to the war grew. In November 1917, as the Ottomans entered their fourth year of war, he published a two-part article entitled "War and Peace." He condemned European leaders' rejection of peace initiatives proposed by President Woodrow Wilson and Pope Benedict XV. Rida's loyalties had by then shifted. In the preceding two years, famine and Armenian refugees had deluged Syria with disease and death. The Ottomans executed dozens of leading Arab intellectuals as traitors. Rida turned against the Ottomans and their allies. The German government, Rida wrote, was a "war-mongering" state with "evil intentions."

Rida now looked to the Allies to bring a fair a lasting peace. According to the Qur'an, he wrote, high morale, patience, and strategy would prove more decisive than materiel in winning the war. He credited England for its skill building a strong alliance and in luring the United States into the war. "The British proved their superiority in these areas, which will lead to their victory over the Germans," he wrote.

While Rida turned against the Ottomans, he still defended Muslim sovereignty. "We ask Allah to grant victory to truth and justice and to grant freedom to the oppressed nations!"[15] He counted the Arabs among those oppressed nations. He had by then thrown his support to the Arab Revolt launched by Sharif Hussein of Mecca in 1916. In October of that year, Rida was caught in Mecca distributing inflammatory pamphlets warning Muslims that the French planned to destroy the Kaaba and carry the black stone to the Louvre.[16] He tried to unite the Arab sheikhs of the Gulf into an association to resist British imperialism. But Sharif Hussein balked. He disdained cooperation with his rival Ibn Saud, and went so far as to ban *al-Manar* in the Hijaz region of Arabia.

The British warned Rida to stay out of politics. Mark Sykes, the British agent who only months earlier had negotiated the Sykes–Picot agreement to divide post-war rule of the Ottoman Arab provinces with France, interviewed Rida. "He is a hard uncompromising fanatical Moslem, the mainspring of whose ideas is the desire to eliminate Christian influence and to make Islam a political power in as wide a field as possible," Sykes reported to his superiors. "He said that the fall of Constantinople would mean the end of Turkish military power, and therefore it was necessary to set up another Mohammedan state to maintain Mohammedan prestige." Men like Rida were not open to negotiation, Sykes advised: "Force is the only argument that they can understand."[17]

Rida pushed back against British attempts to equate Muslim rule with the massacre of Christians. He published multiple articles praising the Arab revolt and condemning the Turks' crimes against all Syrians, Muslim and non-Muslim. He also condemned Europeans' oppression of Muslims. In May 1918, Rida wrote in apocalyptic terms of the millions dead, and the fact that "hundreds of thousands of men and women who were once engaged in production are now engaged in destruction." Civilian suffering only deepened, especially in Egypt, as inflation and shortages caused mass misery.[18]

Rida warned the British that annexation of Arabia, Iraq, or Syria would provoke revolt. In his view, only Arab sovereignty would bring peace. In that belief, he joined the many activists in the Arab World, Egypt, India, and other colonies who called for independence not just as a reward for war service, but as the basis for post-war peace.

The Text: *al-Manar,* December 1918

This is the context in which Rida composed the December 1918 issue of *al-Manar.* The Ottomans had signed an armistice at the end of October. Prince Faisal, Sharif Hussein's son, had claimed rule of Syria, under the aegis of British occupying forces. In late November, Faisal departed for the Paris Peace Conference to seek formal recognition of an independent, Syrian-Arab state.

Rida barely mentioned Faisal in the issue. The north star of Arab hope was to be the American President, Woodrow Wilson, who received a rapturous popular welcome upon his arrival in Paris in mid-December. In his preface, Rida praised Wilson for proposing an "impartial peace" and a "revolution" in international affairs. Rida then devoted half of the issue to translations of four speeches Wilson gave in 1918 and to a review of British and French promises to guide Arabs to independence. Given Rida's experience with the British during the war, we might reasonably suppose that he viewed Wilson as the sole force in Paris that might block British and French colonial designs on Ottoman Arab lands.

Wilson called not just for peace among nations, Rida remarked, but also for the independence of their peoples and equality between the strong and the weak. The American president challenged the old hierarchies of power, Rida wrote, to demand the "victory of moral power over military and financial power, which was prepared to battle all mankind." Rida urged world leaders to seize this auspicious moment, to open their hearts to God's grace, and to revolutionize relations among nations. He worried that people would soon forget the calamity of war and revert to the same lies and injustices that had caused it.

"After seeing the terrible consequences of war, the only peace in the world exists in equality and justice, leaving behind the politics of conspiracy and hypocrisy, of secret treaties," Rida wrote. This requires "the independence of peoples under the command of their chosen governments; the constitution of a league of experts from [great nations] to judge disputes; and the abolition of most secret agreements …. This is what Pres. Wilson called on all warring factions to do."

Rida warned the Great Powers at Paris that Wilson's plan was a moral duty. "If you don't do it, you will cause a *fitna* (turmoil) on Earth and massive corruption, revolutions, and widespread evil, or the return to war."[19]

To make his point clear—that peace required a revolution in the world system—Rida published Wilson's speeches under the heading "Principles of the Great Social Revolution and Freedom of Nations."[20] He also republished the Fourteen Points which called for an "impartial adjustment of colonial claims" based on consent of the people and "absolutely unmolested opportunity for autonomous development" to peoples of the Ottoman Empire.

Rida presented evidence that Wilson intended self-determination for non-Europeans—contrary to Erez Manela's claim. In his Mount Vernon speech of July 4, printed in *al-Manar*, Wilson assured Americans that the peace would bring freedom and rule of law to all peoples. "Not only the peoples actually engaged (in the war) but many others who suffer under mastery but cannot act; peoples of many races and in every part of the world." In his September 27 speech in New York, also quoted, Wilson again affirmed "that the interest of the weakest is as sacred as the interest of the strongest." The League of Nations would ensure it.

Rida provided extensive comment on this relatively unknown speech. The Cairo-based *al-Muqattam* newspaper promised that the League of Nations would "prevent the outbreak of another great war to afflict humanity." The paper also contrasted Wilson's brand of "socialism" to the Social Darwinism that prevailed in Europe. Wilson gave voice to the universal wisdom of all peoples and creeds.

"So the small nations in all regions of the world raise their hands praying to God to prolong Wilson's life and to grant him the strength needed to realize his dreams," *al-Muqattam* opined. "Indeed, the voice rising from America these days is a prophecy striking the ears of the world with truth and guiding the nations of the world on the path of goodness and survival."

Rida went farther in his praise, calling Wilson Allah's spokesman: "President Wilson is the one who proposed these principles of truth and justice. But he is not the first to call for them. For Allah has done so."[21]

Quoting the Qur'an on impartial justice, Rida applauded Wilson's demand that the peace conference treat all countries by the same standards. Just as Germany must return Alsace to France, so European occupiers must return Arab lands to Arabs. Non-Muslim countries must not be favored over Muslim ones. Rida quoted Wilson's speech to Congress on December 2, 1918, which promised that the "international peace" would apply not only to Europe, but also to Asia and the near and far East.

The December 1918 issue of *al-Manar* suggests that, despite the war, Rida had not lost his faith in liberal, universal ideals of peace and justice. He did not hold an ideal of Islamic peace separate from Christian peace. The war was caused by Europeans' modern materialism, not by deviance from Islam. It is difficult to imagine, today, that a leading Muslim scholar might praise an American president for expressing Qur'anic principles of justice.

Rida portrayed British and French diplomats as the true deviants from universal principles. In the next section of the December issue, titled "The Future of Syria and Other Arab Countries," he urged Arabs to seize independence and to resist promises made by France and Britain. Rida recounted, with contempt, the meeting of French and British officials with Syrians in Paris, where the Europeans cloaked their colonial intentions with promises to "guide" Arabs toward political maturity. "[Arabs] see themselves only as fit for complete independence. They don't ask for a guardian to prepare them for it, because they believe themselves to be adults, not fools or idiots."

"It is up to them [Arabs] to demand what they want," Rida warned. "If they miss this chance and choose slavery over freedom and independence due to the deceptions of colonial advocates, they commit self-destruction and more than that, they kill their entire nation. They will be cursed in history and the history of all nations."[22]

Political Action: The Syrian Congress and Constitution

Rida backed his words with action. In September 1919, he journeyed from Cairo to Damascus, he said, expressly to help found a Syrian state where Muslims and Christians would be equal citizens. Against the Ottomans' crimes, the Arabs would demonstrate the tolerance of true Islam. Rida spent nearly a year in Syria as a deputy in the Syrian Arab Congress. Upon his arrival, Rida joined the Syrian Arab Congress as a delegate from Tripoli. He would defend the sovereignty of the people, against European designs and against Prince Faisal's claims to royal authority.[23]

In essence, the Syrian Arab Congress reached back to the pre-war constitutional revolution of 1908, which had once promised inclusive equality to all Ottoman citizens. On March 8, 1920, Rida joined the Congress in declaring Syria's independence and in crowning Faisal king. In May, Rida was elected president of the Congress. He played a leading role in ratifying a constitution that established a "civilian parliamentary monarchy," limiting the king's power through the legislature and by distributing power to local provinces. The constitution also guaranteed equal rights of all citizens regardless of religion. It guaranteed legislative seats to non-Muslim minorities. No mention of Islamic sharia was made. Indeed, the only way in which the constitution institutionalized Islam was to require that the king be Muslim.[24]

As an Islamic liberal and reformer, Rida could consider the constitution of the Syrian Arab Kingdom as an expression of Islamic principles. He had long promoted the concept of the public interest (*al-maslaha al-`amma*), as an arena beyond the jurisdiction of Islamic law. That arena, which lay outside of direct concern to religion, lay within human jurisdiction. Legislators of each age had to debate and decide upon laws to suit the public interest.[25]

However, the British and French refused to recognize Syrian independence. In the April 1920 issue of *al-Manar*, Rida urged the British to uphold their sacred duty against French claims, now that Wilson's "speeches had floated into the air." The president had fallen ill and the American Congress had voted against joining the League of Nations. "We still have hope that they [the British] will recognize the new social revolution caused by this war ... and overcome their imperial ambitions," Rida wrote. If the British support the interest of Egypt, India, the Arabs, and Persia, these nations will gratefully ally with them and they will establish world peace and Britain's "everlasting greater glory."[26]

His words fell on deaf ears. At the end of April, the British and French signed the San Remo accord, which formally assigned France to rule Syria as a mandate. From that moment, General Henri Gouraud, France's high commissioner, began assembling forces to invade. On July 24, 1920, two weeks after the Congress ratified the constitution, French tanks rolled into Syria.

Faisal fled, and so too did Rida. Left in the dust of history was the Syrian-Arab state and its constitution, perhaps the most democratic constitution ever adopted in the Arab world. The product of weeks of debate, it represented a unique compromise between Muslim conservatives and young nationalist liberals.

Rida struggled for two years to save Syria and its constitution. He traveled to Geneva with the Syro-Palestinian committee (headed by a Lebanese Christian prince) to petition the new League of Nations. The committee argued that Article 22 of the League covenant itself had designated Syria as an "A" mandate, which granted independence on the condition that Syrians accept foreign advisors. Faisal had fulfilled that condition, and Syrians had proved their capacity for self-rule.

In April 1922, Rida stated Syria's case in *al-Manar*. In the Syrian Arab Kingdom, he wrote, "Freedom in all its aspects ruled—including freedom of association, speech, and publishing." Democratic equality had overruled social hierarchy: "The exaggerated salutations and aggrandizement of officials and notables (that Damascus was famous for) disappeared. People sensed their own honor and dignity." Non-Muslims were equal to Muslims in every way, he argued. By contrast, under the European mandates, inequality reigned. Muslims were poorly treated.[27]

The League paid no heed. In July 1922, it upheld the French mandate, depriving Syria and Muslims of the sovereignty that Rida considered the cornerstone of peace. July 1922 was an even more bitter blow to Rida than the invasion of July 1920. The very instrument promoted by Wilson to guarantee "impartial justice" and the rule of international law had been hijacked by imperial powers. Placing Syria under French mandate effectively cast it out of the family of nations. It denied them full humanity, and deprived them of universal rights.

The League's lesson to Arabs was that force, not law, must govern nations. Within three years, Syria broke out in armed revolt. The League had betrayed Muslim and Arab liberals like Rida, who had counseled Syrians to embrace the liberal promise of Paris.

Conclusion: From Universal to Islamic Peace

Rida's actions through 1922 reflect his background and his innate pragmatism in matters of religion. He came of age in an era when it was possible to imagine oneself as both Muslim and liberal. Liberal Islam had weathered the atrocities of war. But post-war politics drove a wedge between liberalism and Islam. At the signing of the Versailles treaty in 1919, Rida had warned that if Europeans colonized and divided Arab lands, then they would make clear that liberal international law and justice are intended for Christians only.[28] Colonization came to pass, and the universal ideal of peace and justice died with it.

It was the particular circumstances of this historical moment that caused the cleavage between liberalism and Islam. The First World War and the Paris peace conference, in my view, were as consequential for the next century of Arab politics as the American Civil War has been in defining the debates in our own politics since 1865.

Rida's constitutionalism was, in retrospect, a last flowering of Islamic liberalism. His views on the terms of peace and justice changed after the League's denial in 1922.

Ahmad Dallal has shown how Rida's conservative turn in the 1920s was rooted in earlier ideas that competed with his liberalism. While he recognized a legal sphere of "*maslaha amma*," he also promoted the expansion of Islamic law into cover all areas of life. This would secure Muslim sovereignty the practices of daily life against the encroachments of European culture.[29]

These competing political motives coexisted in Rida's repertoire as a political activist. This was what made the post-war moment so pivotal. European aggression tilted Rida's intellectual preferences away from liberal constitutionalism toward *salafism* and the vision of a modern, theocratic Islamic state.

In response to the French invasion, Rida wrote in *al-Manar*, "Nobody, anymore, believes the word of the Europeans, nor does anybody trust them, or even perceive them to be qualified to exercise justice and virtue."[30] In the wake of the denial of universal justice at Geneva in 1922, Rida would forge ties with the sole remaining sovereign Arab state, that of the emergent Saudis in Arabia.

After 1922, Rida fought against liberals in Egypt and became a top advocate for an Arab caliphate—the very Islamic government he had rejected in 1920. There is a thread of continuity within this change: Wahhabism supported Rida's own belief in popular sovereignty as a check on the authority of the ruler. Despite its conservative ethos, it offered a more democratic model of religious authority.

By the early 1930s, Rida's rhetoric had utterly transformed. No longer did he regard Christian and Muslim ideals of peace as similar. No longer would he write that an American president gave voice to Qur'anic principles. Rather, in works like *al-Wahy al-Muhammadi* (The Revelation of Muhammad), he would write that the world's salvation lies solely in the message of Islam.[31]

After Rida's death in 1935, populist Islamists whom he inspired, like Hasan al-Banna, turned against liberal pluralism to wage violent campaigns against Egyptian Jews and eventually Christians. Banna built an activist community devoted to reviving a distinctive Muslim habitus defined in opposition to Western liberalism. His famous 1936 letter to King Farouk, "Toward the Light," echoed Rida's view that justice could no longer be found in the West. "Humanity is in dire need of the purifying waters of True Islam."[32]

The Brotherhood's influence in both Egypt and Syria would inspire post-colonial constitutions after the Second World War that established Islamic law as the source of legislation—anathema to the 1920 Congress. Arab nationalists in both countries reacted forcefully against their Islamic rivals. The cleavage between secular/religious, liberal/Islamic became institutionalized in the rival ideologies of regime and opposition. This polarization fueled violence on both sides. The cleavage also split opposition parties, weakening the 2011 uprisings against dictatorship.

The effect of the Paris peace process of 1919 on the Middle East might therefore be profitably compared to that of the Treaty of Versailles in Germany. In 1919 in both realms, an uncertain liberalism bloomed from the battlefields of total war. In both, the people regarded the peace treaties as severe and unjust. In Berlin, Germans condemned leaders of the Weimar Republic for signing the treaty. As a consequence, the republic remained vulnerable to violent, right-wing dissidents.

In Cairo, the Wafd party tried to unite Muslims and Christians, urban middle classes and countryside. But the British weakened the Wafd by imposing a constitution that granted preponderant power to themselves and to the King. The Wafd party foundered its leader, Saad Zaghlul, died in 1927. The following year, Hasan al-Banna saw a political opening for his Islamic movement, which would vie with secular liberals and the Wafd in the 1940s. In Damascus, nationalists broke with Islamic populists to draft a republican constitution in 1928. They remained an elite party, weakened by their association with the French. The secular-religious cleavage persisted after France's evacuation in 1946, and through the post-independence military coups, fueling political violence. This same cleavage weakened the 2011 revolt against the Asad dictatorship, leading to the utter collapse of Syria in the teens of the twenty-first century.

Notes

1   Muhammad Rashid Rida, "Introduction to Volume 21," *al-Manar* 21 (December 1918): 5–6, quoting *The Holy Qur'an*, chapter 74, Surah al-Mudaththir, verses 33–7.
2   This chapter is drawn from a larger book project, Elizabeth F. Thompson, *How the West Stole Democracy from the Arabs: The Syrian Congress of 1920 and the Destruction of Its Liberal-Islamic Alliance* (New York: Atlantic Monthly Press, 2020). I thank the Carnegie Corporation of New York and the Woodrow Wilson International Center for Scholars for supporting the research and writing of the book.
3   David Fromkin, *A Peace to End All Peace* (New York: Owl Books/Henry Holt, 1989), 19.
4   Erez Manela, *The Wilsonian Moment: Self-Determination and the International Origins of Anticolonial Nationalism* (New York: Oxford University Press, 2007), 13.
5   Robert Gerwarth, *The Vanquished: Why the First World War Failed to End* (New York: Farrar, Straus, Giroux, 2016).
6   Michelle Campos, *Ottoman Brothers: Muslims, Christians and Jews in Early Twentieth-century Palestine* (Stanford, CA: Stanford University Press, 2010) and Abigail Jacobson, *From Empire to Empire: Jerusalem between Ottoman and British Rule* (Syracuse, NY: Syracuse University Press, 2011).
7   Salim Tamari, *Year of the Locust: A Soldier's Diary and Erasure of Palestine's Ottoman Past* (Berkeley: University of California Press, 2011), 8.
8   Talha Çiçek, "Visions of Islamic Unity: A Comparison of Djemal Pasha's *al-Sharq* and Sharif Husayn's *al-Qibla* Periodicals," *Die Welt des Islams* 54 (2014): 460–82. Hasan Kayalı, *Arabs and Young Turks: Ottomanism, Arabism and Islamism in the Ottoman Empire, 1908–1918* (Berkeley: University of California Press, 1997).
9   Mustafa Aksakal, "Holy War Made in Germany? Ottoman Origins of the 1914 Jihad," *War in History* 18, no. 2 (2011): 1–16. Quote from p. 13.
10   Ohannès Pacha Kouyoumdjian, *Le Liban à la veille et au début de la guerre*. Revue d'histoire arménienne contemporaine, tome V (Paris: Centre d'histoire arménienne contemporaine, 2003), 177, 184.
11   Dyala Hamzah, "From *'Ilm* to *Sahafa* or Politics of Public Interest (*maslaha*): Muhammad Rashid Rida and his Journal *al-Manar* (1898–1935)," in *The Making of the Arab Intellectual*, ed. Dyala Hamzah (New York: Routledge, 2013), 90–127.

12   Muhammad Rashid Rida, "The Abolition of Foreign Privileges and Threat of Civil Strife," and "How did the Ottoman State enter the War?" *al-manar* 17 (November 1914): 955, 958–60.

13   Muhammad Rashid Rida, "Religious Jihad in Islam," *al-Manar* 18 (Feb 1915): 30.

14   Muhammad Rashid Rida, "A War among Civilized Nations, Not among Religions," *al-Manar* 18 (Nov. 1916): 746–52.

15   "War and Peace," parts 1 and 2, *al-Manar* 20 (November 1917): 199–202 and 20 (January 1918): 246–48.

16   Eliezer Tauber, "Rashid Rida's Political Attitudes During WWI," *The Muslim World* 85, 1–2 (January–April 1995): 114.

17   Mahmoud Haddad, "Arab Religious Nationalism in the Colonial Era: Re-reading Rashid Rida's Ideas on the Caliphate," *Journal of the American Oriental Society* 117, no. 2 (April–June 1997): 268.

18   Muhammad Rashid Rida, "The Disasters of War," *al-Manar* 20 (May 1918): 264–5.

19   Rashid Rida, "Introduction to Volume 21," 8.

20   Rashid Rida, "Principles of the Great Social Revolution and Freedom of Nations," *al-Manar* (December 1918): 17–33. All quotes of Wilson's speeches are from these pages.

21   Rashid Rida, "Comment of *al-Muqattam* and *al-Muqtataf* on this Speech," *Al-Manar* 21 (December 1918): 28–30.

22   Rashid Rida, "The Future of Syria and Other Arab Countries," *al-Manar* 21 (December 1918): 33–6.

23   Mari Almaz Shahrastan, *al-Mu'tamar al-Suri al-`Amm 1919–1920* (Beirut: Dar al-Amraj, 2000), 33–41; George Antonius, *The Arab Awakening* (London: Hamilton, 1938), 292. See also Khayriyya Qasimiyya, *al-Hukuma al-`Arabiyya fi Dimashq, 1918–1920* (Cairo: al-Ma`arif, 1971).

24   The constitution is reprinted in Hasan Al-hakim, *al-Watha'iq al-tarikhiyah al-muta`alliqa bi al-qadiyah al-suriya* (Beirut: Dar Sadr, 1974), 194–213.

25   Dyala Hamzah, " From `Ilm to *Sahafa* or Politics of Public Interest (*maslaha*): Muhammad Rashid Rida and his Journal *al-Manar* (1898–1935)," in *The Making of the Arab Intellectual*, ed. Hamzah (New York: Routledge, 2013), 100.

26   Muhammad Rashid Rida, "The Aftermath of the European Civil War," *al-Manar* 21 (April 1920): 337–44.

27   Muhammad Rashid Rida, "The Second Syrian Trip (10): The Arab Government of Damascus," *al-Manar* 23 (April 1922): 313–14.

28   Memo on Syrian-Arab Demands to British Prime Minister Lloyd George, dated June 25, 1919, quoted from British foreign office archives (FO 371/4232) by Tauber, "Rashid Rida's Political Attitudes," 118–19.

29   Ahmad Dallal, "Appropriating the Past: Twentieth-century Reconstruction of Pre-modern Islamic Thought," *Islamic Law and Society* 7, no. 1 (2000): 342.

30   Emad Eldin Shahin, "Muhammad Rashid Rida's Perspectives on the West as Reflected in *al-Manar*," *The Muslim World* 79, no. 2 (1989): 129.

31   Translated as *The Muhammadan Revelation*, trans. Yusuf Talal DeLorenzo (Alexandria, VA: Al-Saadawi, 1996).

32   Hasan al-Banna, "Nahwa al-Nur," in *Majmu`at Risa'il al-Imam al-Shadi Hasan al-Banna* (Beirut: Dar al-Andalus, 1965), 168. For translation, see "Toward the Light," in *Five Tracts of Hasan Al-Banna (1906–1949)*, trans. Charles Wendell (Berkeley: University of California Press, 1978), 106–7.

7 PARADISE BOUND: RIGHTEOUS OTHERS IN THE WRITINGS OF RASHID RIDA

Mohammad Hassan Khalil

How will God judge non-Muslims in the life to come? This has long been a contentious question in Islamic thought, one with profound implications. Consider, for instance, the case of a believer who holds that all or most non-Muslims will be damned. Such a believer might go to great lengths to convince Others of the truth of Islam, thereby attempting to "save" them; alternatively, the believer might choose to look down upon and be hostile toward God's "enemies." In the present chapter, I shall examine a response to the question at hand offered by the influential modern Muslim scholar Muhammad Rashid Rida—a fascinating inclusivist response that attempts to balance the logic of Islamic tradition and modern realities.

The prevailing doctrine in Islamic thought is that God may excuse—at the very least—those non-Muslims who never encountered Muhammad's message.[1] This is predicated, at least in part, on the Qur'anic principle that God does not punish anyone until He has "sent a messenger" (17:15).[2] Perhaps the most well-known criterion for non-Muslim salvation was developed by the twelfth-century Ash'arite Abu Hamid al-Ghazali (d. 1111) in his famous treatise *Faysal al-tafriqa*. Here we find al-Ghazali asserting, in passing, that God's mercy is so overwhelming that it will encompass many non-Muslims "whose lands lie far beyond the lands of Islam" and whose rejection of the Prophet was hardly informed. Al-Ghazali offers Turks and Byzantine Christians as examples.

In outlining the criterion for non-Muslim salvation, al-Ghazali delineates three categories of non-Muslims: the first are those who never heard of Muhammad; the second are those heard of the Prophet, his message, and his miracles and then chose to ignore or reject Islam; the third are those who heard only negative and false things about Muhammad. According to al-Ghazali, only those who encountered the truth of Islam and then rejected or ignored it (the second category) would be culpable before God. The other two categories of non-Muslims would receive God's mercy. Al-Ghazali goes on to describe what I call his "fourth category" of non-Muslims: these are individuals who encountered the truth of Islam and then actively investigated it before passing away—"sincere" truth-seekers. Although such non-Muslims never converted to Islam, al-Ghazali asserts that they too would be saved on account of their sincerity and, more importantly, God's mercy.

But what about those non-Muslims who encountered the truth of Islam but simply did not find it convincing or compelling enough to investigate? Might divine mercy extend to such non-Muslims, especially if their rejection of Islam was seemingly not due to arrogance or laziness? According to the popular ninth-century Mu'tazilite al-Jahiz (d. 869), God would not damn such individuals on account of their having not accepted Muhammad's message, for, as the Qur'an states, "God does not burden any being with more than it can bear" (2:286).

According to al-Ghazali, al-Jahiz's position is not unreasonable, but it is not supported by revelation. In his book on legal theory, *al-Mustasfa*, al-Ghazali argues that the inability to recognize the truth of Islam reflects a disease of the heart. After all, the Qur'an often rebukes the wicked for their faulty beliefs and suppositions, as when it states, "they think they have something to stand on" (58:18); "it was the thoughts you entertained about your Lord that led to your ruin" (41:23); "that may be what the unbelievers assume—how they will suffer from the Fire!" (38:27); and "they rely on guesswork" (2:78). As such, for al-Ghazali, a righteous non-Muslim would naturally feel compelled to investigate Islam after having encountered it.

Notwithstanding this "restriction," al-Ghazali was ultimately a soteriological optimist: he believed that most of humanity would eventually be admitted into Paradise. Al-Ghazali justifies this optimism by invoking the notion of divine mercy and Qur'an 31:28, which reads, "Both the creation and the resurrection of all of you are as that of a single being." As Ghazali explains,

> Just as most people in the world enjoy health and material well-being or live in enviable circumstances, inasmuch as, given the choice, they would choose life over death and annihilation, and just as it is rare for even a tormented person to wish for death, so too will it be rare for one to dwell in the [Fire] forever, compared to (the number of) those who will be saved outright and those who will ultimately be taken out of the [Fire].[3]

Of course, no one writes in a vacuum. One can only wonder whether, if he were alive today, al-Ghazali would have maintained both his optimism and his particular criterion for non-Muslim salvation, without modifying one or the other. After all, al-Ghazali's criterion was derived not just from revelation but also from the world he knew, a world in which Islam represented the dominant culture. With this in mind, we shall now flash forward to the modern era and examine the views of one of the leading Muslim theologians of the twentieth century, Muhammad Rashid Rida (d. 1935). As we shall see, Rida attempted to reconcile al-Ghazali's widely accepted criterion for salvation with his own modern reality—a reality in which numerous well-educated non-Muslims had been exposed to and familiar with the Islamic message yet chose not to investigate it actively, let alone convert. For Rida, it would be unreasonable to assume that a God of mercy and justice would simply damn these multitudes for not believing in or actively studying Islam at a time when the so-called Muslim world was perceived to be stagnant.

Rida and the Religion of God

Born in 1865 near Tripoli (in present-day Lebanon), Rida is known as one of the leading figures of the Modern Salafi movement. After he moved to Cairo in 1897, he became a prized disciple of Muhammad 'Abduh (d. 1905). Together, 'Abduh and Rida produced one of the most influential and widely circulated Islamic periodicals of the twentieth century, *al-Manar* (The Lighthouse). Following 'Abduh's death in 1905, Rida steered the Salafi publication—giving it a more "conservative" hue— until his own demise three decades later.

Most relevant for our purposes is Rida's Qur'anic commentary in *al-Manar*. We begin by examining his discussion of Qur'an 2:62, a verse that reads as follows: "The believers, the Jews, the Christians, and the Sabians—all those who believe in God and the Last Day and do good—will have their rewards with their Lord. No fear for them, nor will they grieve." Rida tell us that, according to 'Abduh, this passage shows that salvation is ultimately predicated on "true faith" (*sidq al-iman*) in and servitude to God—not religious affiliation.[4] Rida uses this opportunity to cite another Qur'anic verse, 4:123, which reads, "It will not be according to your hopes or those of the People of the Book: anyone who does wrong will be requited for it and will find no one to protect or help him [or her] against God." As Rida notes, this passage was reportedly revealed in response to a dispute between some of the companions of the Prophet and certain Medinan Jews over which of the two groups was now favored by God. For Rida, the Qur'anic response to this debate shows that faith and righteousness trump religious identity.[5]

Rida develops this idea further in his commentary on Qur'an 3:19, which reads, "True religion (*al-din*), in God's eyes, is *al-islam*. Those who were given the Book disagreed out of rivalry, only after they had been given knowledge—if anyone denies God's revelations, God is swift to take account." As Rida presents it, "true religion" is *al-islam* or "the submission" to God, and not specifically the religion of Muhammad. This is why the Qur'an (3:67) refers to Abraham, for instance, as a *muslim*, for he was a submitter to God.

This spirit of inclusion also comes out in Rida's commentary on Qur'an 5:48, the second half of which reads,

We have assigned a law (*shir'a*) and a path (*minhaj*) to each of you. If God had so willed, He would have made you one community, but He wanted to test you through that which He has given you, so race to do good: you will all return to God and He will make clear to you the matters about which you differed.

According to Rida, this passage shows that the revealed laws of various religious communities are all part of the same religion (*din*).[6]

To be clear, however, Rida was not a true religious pluralist. In his commentary on this very passage he presents the path of Muhammad as the only path of moderation. In his eyes, Judaism is extreme in its law, and Christianity is fixated on the spiritual realm. And given that the very next Qur'anic verse (5:49)[7] instructs Muhammad to judge the People of the Book according to what *he* received, Rida holds that the pre-Muhammadan laws were distorted and now abrogated and should not be followed when the Prophet's message is readily available.[8] Incidentally, Rida elsewhere presents the Christian doctrine of the trinity as an example of a "deviation." "It is," he writes, "as the commoners say, 'nonsense' (*kalam farigh*)."[9]

Returning to Rida's commentary on Qur'an 3:19, it is true that he argues for a broad understanding of the term *al-islam*. But he also notes that immediately after the declaration "True religion, in God's eyes, is *al-islam*," the same verse rebukes the People of the Book on account of their divisions and deviations. According to Rida, this shows that, by Muhammad's time, their religions had ceased to represent *al-islam*. To illustrate this point, Rida offers the example of the Christian church, making reference to its internal schisms and various councils, including the Council of Nicaea in 325 CE and the consequent excommunication of Arius (d. 336 CE) and the Arians.[10] This means that with the coming of Muhammad, his religion became the primary path of *al-islam*. It is, as Rida asserts elsewhere, "the religion of all peoples."[11] Any Muslim who fails to adhere to it fails to qualify as a *muslim*, here meaning "one who submits to God." Conversely, any non-Muslim who adheres to it qualifies as a *muslim*, even in the absence of any formal affiliation with the religion called Islam. An example of the latter would be the Ethiopian Christian Negus (al-Najashi), who famously permitted some of Muhammad's followers to remain within his kingdom following their persecution in Mecca. According to Muslim accounts, the Negus secretly submitted to Muhammad's teachings, and the Prophet prayed for him upon learning of his death. According to Rida, the Qur'an speaks of the Negus and other People of the Book who accepted Islamic teachings when it states,[12]

> Some of the People of the Book believe in God, in what has been sent down to you and in what was sent down to them, humbling themselves before God; they would never sell God's revelation for a small price. These people will have their rewards with their Lord; God is swift in reckoning.
>
> (Qur'an 3:199)

Such People of the Book are to be contrasted with those who reject Muhammad's teachings, for "there is no difference between disbelieving in all of the messengers and disbelieving in some."[13] Thus, Rida writes,

No one can be credited with belief (*iman*) who knows [the Qur'an] and yet disagrees with it by preferring his own scriptures .... Everyone reached by the call (*da'wa*) of Muhammad and to whom its truth is evident, as it is to [some People of the Book], but who rejects and resists, as they reject and resist, gains no positive credit for his belief in former prophets and their books. His belief in God is not an authentic belief, one linked to fear of God and submission (*khushu'*).[14]

The careful observer will notice that Rida here only condemns those non-Muslims who have encountered "the call of Muhammad *and to whom its truth is evident.*"

An Old/New Criterion

This brings us back full circle to Qur'an 2:62. In his commentary on this verse, Rida approvingly cites al-Ghazali's criterion for non-Muslim salvation. This is how Rida describes al-Ghazali's three categories of non-Muslims: the first are those who never heard of Muhammad (Rida suggests that these include Americans of "of *that* era" [*li-dhalika al-'ahd*], presumably al-Ghazali's era); the second are those heard of the Prophet, his message, and his miracles and then chose to ignore or reject Islam; the third are those who heard only negative and false things about Muhammad or who did not encounter Islam in a manner that would prompt the "sincere" among them to investigate it.[15] Interestingly, Rida's description of this third category is actually somewhat different from al-Ghazali's. I shall return to this point in a moment. Here Rida does not explicitly mention what I call al-Ghazali's "fourth category," that is, the sincere truth-seekers who pass away without ever becoming Muslim; however, as we shall see, he accounts for them in his later writings.

Like al-Ghazali, Rida maintains that the unreached—the first and third categories—will not be held accountable for not converting to Islam. But whereas al-Ghazali never clarified how or whether the unreached would be distinguished from one another on Judgment Day, Rida asserts that the unreached will not have immunity and be granted paradise on account of their ignorance; they will still be judged by God according to what they knew to be true and good.[16] This criterion for the salvation of the unreached may be nebulous, but as Rida elsewhere insists, people generally recognize good and evil, even if they disagree on the potentially consequential details.[17]

Be that as it may, Rida at times opens the door for the possibility of a test for the unreached on Judgment Day. When considering the Prophet's parents, for instance, Rida takes prophetic reports stating that either one or both of them are "in the Fire" as merely indications of their condition at death, as people are only consigned to Heaven or Hell following the Judgment. As such, he writes, there is yet hope for their salvation should they encounter an eschatological messenger described in certain prophetic reports who will test the People of the Gap, those who never encountered any form of divine revelation in this life.[18]

As for unreached Jews and Christians, that is, those who never encountered Muhammad's revelation, Rida (back in his commentary on Qur'an 2:62) maintains that, however compromised their religious teachings may be, there is enough divine truth in their traditions to separate them from the People of the Gap. Jews, for example, "have the Torah with God's judgment" (Qur'an 5:43); Christians have preserved teachings from the Torah and the Gospel of Jesus.[19] As for the Sabians mentioned in Qur'an 2:62 and elsewhere, Rida notes that these were either a group comparable to the pre-Islamic Arab monotheists known as Hanifs or an offshoot of Christianity that worshipped stars. In the case of the former, they may be considered People of the Gap; in the case of the latter, "like the Jews and Christians," they would have been expected to adhere to their respective religious tradition "until another form of guidance" reached them.[20]

Looking beyond his Qur'anic commentary, we find Rida in *al-Manar* accounting for al-Ghazali's "fourth category," the sincere truth-seekers among the reached. In a June 1903 issue, for instance, Rida submits that God excuses both the unreached and the reached who investigate Muhammad's message "with sincerity" but never convert to Islam.[21] Rida reaffirms this doctrine in a June 1904 issue, in a reply to a letter from a certain Muhammad, a prison clerk residing in Sudan, who had inquired about the fate of non-Muslims.[22] Interestingly, Rida here clarifies that to be reached is to encounter Muhammad's message "in a sound way, one that moves [the sincere] to investigate [it]" (*'ala wajhin sahihin yuharriku ila al-nazari*).[23]

As I indicated earlier, when Rida relates al-Ghazali's third category of non-Muslims—those who have been improperly exposed to Islam—he subtly rewords al-Ghazali's description. Whereas al-Ghazali presents such non-Muslims as those who merely did not encounter the Islamic message in its true form, Rida portrays them as those who *either* did not encounter the Islamic message in its true form *or* did not encounter it in a manner that would spur them to investigate it. Rida's wording suggests that mere exposure to Islam may not be a sufficient incentive for at least some sincere non-Muslims.

In a September 1910 issue of *al-Manar*, in response to a query from an anonymous Tunisian scholar as to whether Christians and Jews could be considered true believers, Rida cites al-Ghazali and goes on to state that what prompts investigation of Muhammad's message varies from era to era. What may have motivated a Christian in al-Ghazali's era to study Islam would not necessarily motivate a modern Christian. And in the absence of a bona fide incentive, the "precondition" for being considered reached is not satisfied.[24]

As for what would prompt investigation in the modern era, Rida maintains that this depends on each individual's state of mind and what is evident to him or her. Nevertheless, for Rida, it would be unthinkable that sincere, righteous Jews and Christians would simply reject Islam once its superiority was made clear to them.[25]

As such, the only non-Muslims who may be deemed culpable for not heeding the Islamic message are (1) those who encounter it and are provided with "enough incentive" to investigate it yet fail to do so and (2) those for whom its truth is apparent yet who reject it out of arrogance and stubbornness.[26]

In making the case for his relatively liberal inclusivist criterion for non-Muslim salvation, Rida invokes Qur'an 4:115[27]: "If anyone opposes the Messenger, after guidance has been *made clear* to him [or her], and follows a path other than that of the believers, We shall leave him [or her] on his [or her] chosen path—We shall burn him [or her] in Hell, an evil destination." According to various Muslim exegetes, this passage was revealed in reference to an apostate named Tu'ma ibn Ubayriq. While in Medina, Tu'ma committed theft and then falsely placed the blame on a local Jew. When his lie became apparent, he fled to Mecca, then under pagan authority.[28] In his commentary on Qur'an 4:115, Rida notes that the divine threat of this verse is worded in a general manner.[29] Accordingly, it must be directed not just at Tu'ma but at all individuals who refuse to accept or investigate Muhammad's message "after guidance has been made clear" to them. And the qualification of this verse—"after guidance has been made clear"—can be taken to apply to other Qur'anic threats directed at Others.

Diversity

In his commentary on Qur'an 4:115, Rida further develops his inclusivist doctrine, which, we learn, was previously espoused by 'Abduh.[30] Reflecting on human diversity and the different ways that individuals respond to Islamic revelation, Rida designates ten groups of people. The first two are (1) those who are absolutely certain about the truth of the Islamic message and (2) those who may not have reached absolute certainty but to whom the truth of Islam is "made clear," meaning that they regard it as a source of divine guidance or, at the very least, a better guide than all others. Individuals of either group who choose to "oppose" Muhammad and not become Muslim (or leave Islam) are truly worthy of damnation. These are people who take "desire as a god" and "whom God allows to stray in the face of knowledge" (Qur'an 45:23). But, according to Rida, few people—examples include Tu'ma and some of the Jewish scholars from the Prophet's era—have actually rejected the Islamic message after its truth was made clear to them.[31] This is because most people prefer "guidance over error, truth over falsehood, and good over evil" when these are evident.[32] As for why anyone would oppose Muhammad after recognizing the truth of his message, 'Abduh had provided two possible explanations: (1) stubbornness stemming from tribalism (*'asabiyya*) or (2) the pursuit of desire.[33] Rida provides a similar yet longer list of explanations: "envy, transgression, love of leadership, arrogance, desire that overcomes the intellect, and tribalism."[34]

The next eight groups are as follows: (3) those to whom the truth of Islam has not been made clear, yet who adhere to it through imitation of their parents and leaders; (4) those who adhere to error through imitation and thus turn away from Muhammad's message and avoid investigating it when it is presented to them—these include most of the People of the Book and Zoroastrians living during the Prophet's era; (5) those who adhere to error through imitation but whose inclination to imitate is not as strong as that of the previous group, and so they are more likely to investigate Muhammad's message—these include many Arab pagans living during the Prophet's era; (6) the argumentative scholars of world religions who, deluded by their incomplete knowledge, "shun" Islam because they follow their masters and fail to investigate it with sincerity; (7) those who were exposed to Muhammad's message but not properly, meaning, they did not encounter the version of the message that is true and that prompts investigation—these include most of the non-Muslims of Rida's era ("this era")[35]; (8) those who, after having been exposed to Muhammad's message (either properly or improperly), investigate it with sincerity yet cease investigating when the truth is not made clear to them; (9) the sincere truth-seekers who actively investigate Islam and, even when they fail to recognize its complete truth, carry on investigating—al-Ghazali's fourth category of non-Muslims; and (10) those who never encountered any divine message—these include the People of the Gap.[36]

According to Rida, Qur'an 4:115 does not condemn individuals from the last eight groups, even though not all are monotheistic.[37] Now if the truth were ever made evident to them and they were then to defy it, they would then be among the first two groups and would thus be condemned. This, however, is not to suggest that individuals from the last eight groups would not be condemned at all. As we saw earlier, Rida asserts that those who may be excused for not heeding the final message will still be judged by what they could discern to be true and good. Thus, Rida is careful to clarify that "opposing" the Prophet and not becoming Muslim constitute just one form of unbelief and error.[38] So rather than guess the respective fates of the individuals of the last eight groups, Rida submits that the most fitting statement concerning them appears in Qur'an 4:115 itself: "We shall leave him [or her] on his [or her] chosen path."[39]

It is worth reiterating that, according to Rida, most of the non-Muslims of his era would be considered unreached, for most belong to his seventh group, those who were *im*properly exposed to the final message. Notice that Rida makes this assessment in an age of widespread literacy and increased contact between different nations. Returning to his September 1910 fatwa, Rida bemoans the fact that Muslims have generally failed to comprehend their own religion and, consequently, to present it properly to non-Muslims.[40] In an April 1933 issue of *al-Manar*, Rida goes so far as to aver that even the intellects of Europe were never exposed to Islam in a manner that would spur them to contemplate its divine origins.[41]

Back in his commentary on Qur'an 4:115, Rida asserts that most modern non-Muslims have heard nothing about Islam "except that it is a religion among the many human-invented religions" and that both it and its adherents propagate "falsehoods."[42] This distorted image of the religion, Rida adds, is comparable to that created by Christian leaders and others just before the Crusades. Thus, most modern non-Muslims think of Islam as being "obviously false"; they do not bother to investigate it "just as Muslims [generally] do not investigate, for example, Mormonism."[43]

The obvious implication of all this is that God will excuse the majority of early twentieth-century non-Muslims. God will even excuse most non-Muslims of Muhammad's era, as Rida presents the majority of such non-Muslims as examples of his fourth group, the blind imitators of error. They had no incentive to investigate Muhammad's message and were oblivious to its truth because they were generally conditioned not to consider the truth claims of any tradition outside of their own. Of course, once any one of these non-Muslims becomes genuinely motivated to contemplate Islam, he or she would no longer belong to Rida's fourth group; failure to investigate the Islamic message at that point would be a cause for damnation.[44]

Closing Thoughts: Rida v. al-Ghazali

All indications suggest that Rida, like al-Ghazali, imagined that most of humanity would one day dwell in Paradise.[45] This is notwithstanding Rida's belief that God will still judge the unreached. As we have seen, Rida holds that most people prefer guidance, truth, and goodness over their opposites. Accordingly, those who reject Islam after its truth becomes evident to them are small in number. Thus, for Rida, the Qur'anic declaration that "most people do not have faith" (11:17) pertains only to "complete faith" (al-iman al-kamil), and the "people" here may simply refer to the people residing in Mecca when this (Meccan) passage was revealed.[46]

I should note that Rida's optimism concerning the afterlife is not always readily apparent. For instance, in his commentary on the Qur'anic pronouncement that "most" of the People of the Book "are wrongdoers" (fasiqun [3:110]), Rida takes this statement to be applicable to contemporary People of the Book, not just those of the past. (As one might expect, Rida rejects the notion that all Jews and Christians are "wrongdoers.") He also maintains that "corruption" (fisq) tends to become more prevalent over time within all religions.[47] "Sinfulness," however, does not necessarily warrant damnation "for ages" (Qur'an 78:23). In other words, one can be "corrupt" or a "wrongdoer" without being a damned unbeliever. Here it is instructive to consider the case of al-Ghazali: although he believed that most of humanity would be saved, he did not think that the majority of these people would attain immediate salvation. As he saw it, throughout the long duration of Judgment Day, many sinners may be briefly chastised "for a second or an hour or some period of time, by virtue of which they earn the title, 'party of the [Fire].'"[48] Many other individuals will simply be taken to account or saved from punishment through intercession. Only those who are truly wicked—a group that represents a small proportion of the "party of the Fire"—will remain in Hell beyond Judgment Day.[49]

But while Rida invokes and borrows much from al-Ghazali, it is their divergence that stands out. Although he cites and endorses al-Ghazali's criterion for non-Muslim salvation, Rida's own criterion is evidently more lenient. It even overlaps with the doctrine ascribed to al-Jahiz, namely that God will excuse non-Muslims who fail to recognize the authenticity of the Islamic message—a doctrine that al-Ghazali explicitly refuted (though one would not sense this relying solely on Rida's writings). As indicated earlier, al-Ghazali held that blind imitators are culpable if they encounter an accurate representation of Muhammad's message and then fail to accept or investigate it, regardless of whether its truth was ever made clear to them. For al-Ghazali, failure to recognize the Prophet's proofs reveals a "disease in their hearts" (Qur'an 2:10).

From Rida's standpoint, however, many individuals' inability to appreciate prophetic proofs may have nothing to do with the heart and everything to do with the intellect. Indeed, if one considers Rida's ten groups, one notices that these represent varying levels of intellectual development. The blind imitators (such as Rida's fourth group), for instance, are inferior to the truth-seekers (the eighth and ninth groups). The truth-seekers who cease investigating the Islamic message after failing to discern its truth (the eighth group) are not as far along as those truth-seekers who find good reason to continue their investigation (the ninth group). And the latter, Rida indicates in a 1905 piece, lag behind those who are able to recognize the truth of the message (as would be the case for individuals of Rida's first two groups).[50] As such, those with a "disease in their hearts" are those who reject the final message after seeing the truth, and not necessarily those whose "mental vision" is impaired in the first place.

From Rida's standpoint, in order to account for the realities of modernity, one must either modify al-Ghazali's inclusivist criterion or abandon the latter's optimism concerning humanity's fate. Al-Ghazali had assumed that to be considered reached, one simply had to come learn about Muhammad, his character, and his miracles. Because so many non-Muslims of al-Ghazali's era were not aware of these things, it was relatively easy for al-Ghazali to justify his claim that the overwhelming majority of people will be saved without violating or modifying his own criterion. But early-twentieth-century non-Muslims, especially the many scholars among them, would have been much more likely to hear of the Prophet and the noble qualities and miracles ascribed to him. Even if most modern non-Muslims had heard mostly negative things about Islam, there were yet many others whose understanding of Islam was generally accurate. If these countless non-Muslims had generally not "seen the light," and if this were likely to be true of many future non-Muslims in an age of technological advancement, damning all these people would surely undermine al-Ghazali's optimism.

Rida appreciated the strong role that social, cultural, and political paradigms and forces play in shaping individuals' and communities' views of the world.[51] And certain paradigms and forces make it unlikely that encountering Islam would induce the kind of response that al-Ghazali took for granted. This is precisely why those things that would prompt the contemplation of Islamic revelation must vary from era to era. In modernity, proper exposure to Islam could not simply entail exposure to the Prophet's attributes and miracles. The dominant paradigms must be offset, but how or at what point this occurs is not entirely clear. What is clear is that Rida regarded his (and 'Abduh's) work as an attempt to rehabilitate Islam's image to provide at least some non-Muslims with "enough incentive" to investigate it.[52] And despite the bleak state of affairs of the early twentieth century, Rida imagined that human civilization would evolve to the point where it would be more likely for people—including Europeans—to investigate and ultimately accept the Muhammad's universal message.[53]

Notes

1   For a more detailed analysis of Muslim scholarly discussions of the fate of non-Muslims in the afterlife, see Mohammad Hassan Khalil, *Islam and the Fate of Others: The Salvation Question* (New York: Oxford University Press, 2012).
2   My translation of the Qur'an, here and elsewhere, loosely follows M.A.S. Abdel Haleem in *The Qur'an: A New Translation* (Oxford: Oxford University Press, 2010).
3   Sherman A. Jackson, *On the Boundaries of Theological Tolerance in Islam: Abu Hamid al-Ghazali's Faysal al-Tafriqa* (Karachi, Pakistan: Oxford University Press, 2002), 129 (translation of al-Ghazali's *Faysal al-tafriqa*).
4   See Rashid Rida, *Tafsir al-Qur'an al-hakim al-shahir bi-tafsir al-Manar*, 12 vols. (Beirut: Dar al-Ma'rifa, 1970), 1:333–336.
5   Rida, *Tafsir*, 1:336–338. See also ibid., 1:428–430, 496; 5:431–434; 6:479.
6   Rida, *Tafsir*, 6:412ff.
7   This verse (5:49) reads as follows: "So [Prophet] judge between them according to what God has sent down. Do not follow their whims, and take good care that they do not tempt you away from any of what God has sent down to you. If they turn away, remember that God intends to punish them for some of the sins they have committed: a great many people are wrongdoers."
8   Rida, *Tafsir*, 6:410–422. Rida develops this point in ibid., 10:279–411.
9   Rida, *Tafsir*, 10:340. See ibid., 6:86–95, 307–310; 10:329–340.
10 Ibid., 3:258–259. The Arians reportedly maintained that Jesus was the *created* Son of God; the Church held that he was "begotten, not made," and coeternal with God the Father. On Rida's polemics on Christianity, see Umar Ryad, *Islamic Reformism and Christianity: A Critical Reading of the Works of Muhammad Rashid Rida and His Associates (1898–1935)* (Leiden: Brill, 2009). Also see Rida, *Tafsir*, 1:338, where Rida presents Christians as "the most insolent community in the world."

11 Rashid Rida, *al-Wahy al-muhammadi* (Cairo: al-Majlis al-A'la li-l-Shu'un al-Islamiyya, 2000), 26. Also see Rida, *Tafsir*, 10:361–362 and Rashid Rida (ed.), *al-Manar* (Cairo: Idarat Majallat al-Manar, 1898–1935) vol. 33, no. 2 (April 1933): 104–5.

12 Rida, *Tafsir*, 4:315–318.

13 Ibid., 6:276. Also see ibid., 6:7–10.

14 Jane McAuliffe, *Qur'anic Christians: An Analysis of Classical and Modern Exegesis* (Cambridge: Cambridge University Press, 1991), 173, 176 (translation of select passages from Rida's *Tafsir*).

15 Rida, *Tafsir*, 1:338–339 (emphasis added).

16 Rida, *Tafsir*, 1:339. See Rida's related remarks in ibid., 6:72–75.

17 Rida (ed.), *al-Manar* 7, no. 13 (September 1904): 496.

18 Rida (ed.), *al-Manar* 20, no. 10 (October 1918): 448; *al-Manar* 33, no. 9 (February 1933): 674–5.

19 Ibid., 1:337. Cf. Rida's (ed.) discussion of pagan elements in the Bible in *al-Manar* 4, no. 12 (August 1901): 448–51.

20 Rida, *Tafsir*, 1:337–338. See Rida (ed.), *al-Manar* 25, no. 3 (March 1924): 227, where Rida proffers that although Buddhism and Zoroastrianism were divinely inspired, they have evolved and been altered to the extent that their divine truths are now concealed.

21 Rida (ed.), *al-Manar* 6, no. 7 (June 1903): 267–8.

22 Rida (ed.), *al-Manar* 7, no. 7 (June 1904): 258–9.

23 Ibid. This particular quote also appears in Rida (ed.), *al-Manar* 4, no. 13 (September 1901): 497; and *al-Manar* 7, no. 13 (September 1904): 496.

24 See Rida (ed.), *al-Manar* 13, no. 8 (September 1910): 572–6. In *al-Manar* 4, no. 13 (September 1901): 497, Rida indicates that, in the modern era, the proper method of calling people to Islam (*da'wa*) differs from that of the Prophet's era. Furthermore, in *al-Manar* 3, no. 21 (September 1900): 481–90 (especially 485), Rida advises fellow Muslims to call people to Islam in a manner that encourages investigation.

25 Rida (ed.), *al-Manar* 13, no. 8 (September 1910): 574–5.

26 See ibid., 572–6.

27 See Rida (ed.), *al-Manar* 13, no. 8 (September 1910): 574–5.

28 See, for instance, al-Tabari, *Jami' al-bayan 'an ta'wil ay al-Qur'an*, ed. A. al-Bakri et al., 10 vols. (Cairo: Dar al-Salam, 2007), 4: 2540; al-Zamakhshari, *al-Kashshaf 'an haqa'iq al-tanzil wa-'uyun al-aqawil fi wujuh al-ta'wil*, ed. "A. al-Mahdi, 4 vols. (Beirut: Dar Ihya" al-Turath al-'Arabi, 2001), 1: 599; and al-Qurtubi, *al-Jami' li-ahkam al-Qur'an*, ed. 'A. al-Turki, 24 vols. (Beirut: Mu'assasat al-Risala, 2006), 7: 130–131.

29 Rida, *Tafsir*, 5:410.

30 Ibid.

31 See ibid., 5:410–412.

32 Ibid., 5:410.

33 Ibid.

34 Ibid., 5:416.

35 Here, when referring to non-Muslims, Rida uses the term *kuffar* (sing. *kafir*). Although this term is used in the Qur'an to designate the unbelievers bound for Hell, Muslim scholars often use it as a technical term to denote anyone who is not legally a Muslim. Rida must have the latter meaning in mind, as he is referring to the unreached.

36 Rida, *Tafsir*, 5:412–413.

37 Ibid., 5:414.
38 Ibid., 5:418. This statement appears at the beginning of Rida's commentary on the next verse, Qur'an 4:116.
39 Rida, *Tafsir*, 5:414–415.
40 Rida (ed.), *al-Manar* 13, no. 8 (September 1910): 575–6.
41 Rida (ed.), *al-Manar* 33, no. 2 (April 1933): 106.
42 Rida, *Tafsir*, 5:413.
43 Ibid. See Rida's related remarks in ibid., 10:345–363.
44 See Rida's related remarks in ibid., 12:220–222, 246; and Rida (ed.), *al-Manar* 13, no. 11 (December 1910): 868–70.
45 Although Rida's thought evolved over the years, and although his polemics intensified in response to Christian missionary activity (see Ryad, *Islamic Reformism and Christianity*), we have no good reason to think that he ever abandoned his liberal, al-Ghazali-inspired form of inclusivism. Rida first compiled and published his Qur'anic commentary from *al-Manar* as *Tafsir al-Manar* in 1927, long after they first appeared in the periodical. Although he occasionally provides corrigenda and addenda in the *Tafsir* (see, for example, Rida, *Tafsir*, 1:492–496), none have any bearing on his discussions of the fate of non-Muslims. Furthermore, none of his other later writings offer an alternative vision.
46 Rida, *Tafsir*, 12:52–53.
47 Ibid., 4:65–66.
48 Jackson, *On the Boundaries of Theological Tolerance in Islam*, 126 (translation of al-Ghazali's *Faysal al-tafriqa*).
49 For Rida, the kinds of evildoers who would only continue to sin if granted everlasting life in this world are a "minority" of the people consigned to Hell (Rida, *Tafsir*, 12:162).
50 Rida (ed.), *al-Manar* 8, no. 4 (April 1905): 154–5. Here Rida indicates that those who are most advanced intellectually and spiritually are "the perfect believers" (*al-mu'minun al-kamilun*) and that they are "small" in number. Between them and the worst of humanity, the rejecters of revelation, are various classes of people, including the truly unreached and those who accept the Islamic message but fail to "uphold its rights."
51 See, for instance, Rida, *Tafsir*, 10:346, 354–355.
52 See Rida (ed.), *al-Manar* 11, no. 8 (September 1908): 615, where Rida asserts that the Muslim scholars of his age had failed to present Islam in a manner that would prompt investigation, that is, until 'Abduh produced his modernist treatise *Risalat al-tawhid* (*The Theology of Unity*). See *al-Manar* 33, no. 2 (April 1933): 106, where Rida expresses his hope that his own work would similarly lead sincere non-Muslims, including European scholars, to contemplate Islam.
53 See Rida, *Tafsir*, 10:355, 362, 384–392.

8 ABDUL GHAFFAR KHAN: AN ISLAMIC GANDHI

James L. Rowell

Who was Abdul Ghaffar Khan, and what did he accomplish? Born in 1890 in the city of Utmanzai (what is today a small town north of Peshawar, Pakistan). "Badshah" Khan, as he came to be affectionately known, lived until the ripe age of ninety-eight and passed away in 1988. Of that long life he spent some thirty years in prison protesting the injustice of the governments of British India, and Islamic Pakistan. Inspired by two figures—Gandhi and the Prophet Muhammad—he devoted his life to the cause of nonviolent civil disobedience. Ghaffar Khan could be called learned in terms of the Qur'an, and Islamic history, but his view of Islam was simple and uncomplicated. He preferred the nonviolent interpretation of his tradition and seemed to filter all violent aspects out.

Abdul Ghaffar Khan grew up in an Islamic context, accepting the Qur'an and the traditions of the Prophet Muhammad.[1] He was taught to memorize the Qur'an by a local mullah, apparently well known for his cruelty and beating of students, Khan included.[2] The Islamic mullahs of his immediate area did not seem to have any positive impact in teaching him a nonviolent Islam. There mullahs seem to have been more intolerant and exclusive in their outlook, refusing even Christians as legitimate dhimmi or "people of the book." One mullah reluctantly let local Pathans read textbooks in English, but rejected the Christian Bible: "Let the boys read English, so long as they do not read the Christian scriptures; for the Christians have tampered with these books and it is no longer lawful for Muslims to read them."[3] The more tolerant, benevolent outlook seems to have been either a natural endowment to Ghaffar Khan, or to have been acquired from his parents. Either way, he would challenge and reject the intolerant view of some of the local mullahs.

Abdul Ghaffar Khan did not set out to be part of the nonviolent movement. He was a six-foot-three-inch Pathan, prime material for a rugged soldier. In fact, he left his high school final examinations in order that he might join "The Guides," a

This chapter first appeared in a slightly different form as James Rowell (2009) "Abdul Ghaffar Khan: An Islamic Gandhi," *Political Theology*, 10:4, 591–606, DOI: 10.1558/poth.v10i4.591. Our thanks to Professor Rowell and to Taylor and Francis for their kind permission to use it here.

corps composed of Sikhs and Pathans that he expected would give him privileged access to a career as a British Officer. It turned out, however, after witnessing an incident of British racism against a fellow Pathan in that same corps, he realized nothing was further from the truth. He resigned from the Guides, and refused to accept a commission, much to the displeasure of his father.[4]

In the next few years he gravitated toward the social education of his fellow Pathans. Inspired by his former high school teacher, Reverend Wigram, he realized he felt the impulse of a social reformer, proceeded to open schools, and to challenge Pathan custom and tradition. Abdul Ghaffar Khan believed that his fellow Pathans were kept ignorant, and badly needed education and enlightenment. Illiteracy rates in the region were reported to be as high as 98 percent, and reportedly even A.G. Khan's own parents could not read or write. Despite the opposition of both the British and the local mullahs (who perhaps feared losing a source of their own Islamic donations), he began to establish schools for Pathan boys and girls.[5]

Khan was married twice, but lost his first wife during an epidemic of influenza, and lost his second wife while traveling in Jerusalem. He had been on the hajj, the religious pilgrimage to Mecca, when in Jerusalem his second wife fell from a staircase and was killed. At least two sons came from these marriages, but after the tragic death of his second wife he determined not to remarry and to dedicate the rest of his life to public service. Abdul Ghaffar Khan viewed Islam in terms of selfless love and service: "It is my inmost conviction that Islam is *amal, yakeen, muhabat*—selfless service, faith, and love."[6] In his own eyes and interpretation, the Prophet Muhammad taught peace.

"Badshah" Khan, as Abdul Ghaffar Khan came to be known, did not immediately come to prominence in the Indian movement for independence. As early as 1920, however, he was attending conferences and becoming politically aware, but it was not until several years later that he would first meet Nehru and Gandhi, and increasingly was pulled into the orbit of the latter. Khan for a number of years was essentially a social reformer, taking pride in his own Pathan heritage, but also realizing it was badly in need of reform.

One of most important aspects of Pathan culture that Abdul Ghaffar Khan wanted to change was that of the *badal* or the blood-feud honor code. If one person had been killed, it was laid upon the honor of his relatives to avenge that killing to maintain one's pride and tribal self-esteem. It was a brutal code of justice and one that invited constant retribution. Eknath Easwaran commented that code of *badal* blood-vengeance was so strong that it largely defined Pathan manhood: "two supreme arts of the Pathan life: how to kill and how to die. Through these he becomes most fully a Pathan."[7] Gandhi himself commented that Hindu boys and girls often grew up in fear of the Pathans as a people with a reputation for violence.[8]

Abdul Ghaffar Khan was much influenced here by his father, who also disliked the *badal* blood-feud code, who kept no enemies, and yet stood out as one highly esteemed amongst the Pathans. Abdul Ghaffar Khan had also thought the tradition was very dysfunctional, and when he heard of Gandhi's message of nonviolent resistance he increasingly gravitated toward it. In his own words:

> As a young boy, I had violent tendencies; the hot blood of the Pathans was in my veins. But in jail I had nothing to do except read the Koran. I read about the Prophet Muhammad in Mecca, about his patience, his suffering, his dedication. I had read it all before, as a child, but now I read it in the light of what I was hearing all around me about Gandhiji's struggle against the British Raj … When I finally met Gandhiji, I learned all about his ideas of nonviolence and his Constructive Program. They changed my life forever.[9]

To further illustrate the context of the culture, we must remember that the Pathan (also variously written or spelled Pakhtun, or Pashtun) culture is the same one that contributed large numbers of talibs or Islamic students to the Taliban movement. The Pathan culture strides the boundary of the Durand line, which was established by Sir Mortimer Durand as far back as 1893 to demarcate the boundaries of Afghanistan and Pakistan.[10] The Taliban of course advocated everything that Abdul Ghaffar Khan spurned. The Taliban approved of purdah, or the seclusion of women, and prevented their education. Badshah Khan opposed purdah and fought for women's equality, and opened schools for girls.[11] The Taliban banned music, except for male voices singing in praise of the Taliban, while Badshah Khan celebrated the use of drums and bagpipes when he started his nonviolent army, the Khudai Khidmatgars or "Servants of God." If the Taliban took Islam in the direction of exclusivity and repression, Badshah Khan took the religion in the direction of openness and equality.

The very existence of Abdul Ghaffar Khan and his movement suggests that a more careful and nuanced understanding of Pathan culture must emerge. Khan's Islamic values would reject and repudiate those of the latter Taliban. Men such as Abdul Ghaffar Khan, from the same region as the Taliban, and existing within the span of a few decades of each other, necessitate more scholarly attention be given to the possible flexibility of Islamic political theology, at least pertaining to this region. Clearly the understanding of Islam in the area has not been entirely belligerent or uniform.

Parallels of the "Two Gandhis"

Abdul Ghaffar Khan and Mohandas Gandhi were kindred religious spirits in many respects, though one was raised a Muslim and the other a Hindu. Khan would apply the concept of dhimmi or favored "people of the book" in the Qur'an not only to Jews and Christians, but also to all believers. Khan also asserted that nonviolence was the essential heart of Islam. Nonviolence was not a mere strategy to him or to Gandhi, it was an essential principle of life. Nonviolence, or ahimsa, was elevated to the level of God and Truth in Gandhi's view: "My uniform experience has convinced me that there is no other God than Truth. And if every page of these chapters does not proclaim to the reader that the only means for the realization of Truth is Ahimsa (non-violence), I shall deem all my labor in writing these pages to have been in vain."[12] Elsewhere Gandhi reiterated this formula: "Truth is God, gives me the greatest satisfaction. And when you want to find Truth as God the only inevitable means is Love, i.e., non-violence."[13] From an Islamic perspective, Khan would come to affirm much the same beliefs, seeing both himself and Gandhi as equals and humble servants of God.

Both Khan and Gandhi remained emphatic in their devotion to nonviolence. While Gandhi himself once affirmed: "I do believe that where there is only a choice between cowardice and violence, I would advise violence;"[14] it must be pointed out here that Gandhi was talking theoretically. Nonviolence was not a method for cowards. Indeed those who lacked the stomach or capacity for it might resort to violence, which Gandhi abhorred. Gandhi at no time in his career embraced or accepted a violent response, and we find that Abdul Ghaffar Khan, who became one of his closest friends and allies, also maintained that consistent pledge. When the Indian National Congress took a more limited, and policy-oriented, approach toward nonviolence under the threat of Japanese aggression in 1939, Gandhi rejected the advice and Abdul Ghaffar Khan resigned from the council that had considered the issue. Khan and Gandhi believed in nonviolence as an unwavering principle, and not a mere policy or stratagem.[15]

Khan affirmed, as did Gandhi, a more universal and inclusive understanding of religion. No person was regarded to be unholy or an "infidel," simply because of the label of their religion. Gandhi refused to accept that any one religious tradition had a monopoly on truth and insisted: "Do people become enemies because they change their religion? Is the God of the Mohammedan different from the God of the Hindu? Religions are different roads converging to the same point. What does it matter that we take different roads so long as we reach the same goal? Wherein is the cause for quarreling?"[16] Further he said: "For me all the principal religions are equal in the sense that they are true. They are supplying a felt want in the spiritual progress of humanity."[17] Gandhi hoped and affirmed that the days of religious intolerance were over: "The time has now passed when the followers of one religion can stand and say, ours is the only true religion and all others are false. The growing spirit of toleration towards all religions is a happy augury of the future."[18]

Biographers of Abdullah Ghaffar Khan indicate an identical inclusive spirit. Gandhi himself noted that A.G. Khan had this open-minded and inclusive religious character: "I was struck by their transparent sincerity, frankness, and utmost simplicity. He was consumed by a deep religious fervor. I found him to be universalist."[19] Author and biographer Attar Chand also described A.G. Khan: "He was a devout Muslim but had genuine love for all religions, and he firmly believed in the brotherhood of man."[20]

Abdul Ghaffar Khan established a nonviolent army of Pathans committed to the Gandhian technique of nonviolence. This very remarkable fact is one too often neglected in popular media, which is essentially concerned with the violent character of Islam. Although media do often exonerate the tradition of Islam from accusations of violence, the importance of men such as A.G. Khan is now overlooked.[21] Khan himself affirmed that universal outlook toward humanity in creating this band of nonviolent Islamic warriors:

> The Prophet has said that the most pious and God-fearing youth is he who brings comfort to the creatures of God. The mission of the Khudai Khidmatgars is to give comfort to all creatures of God. Remember this also that the Muslims alone are not the creatures of God. The Hindus, Sikhs, Muslims, Jews, Christians, and the Parsis, in short, all the creatures that live in this world are the creatures of God. The mission of the Khudai Khidmatgars is to give comfort to all creatures of God.[22]

Abdul Ghaffar Khan affirmed a universal regard for all religions as an essential duty; hence, his concept of dhimmi, or "people of the book," would have invariably been extended to Hindus as well as to Jews and Christians. A.G. Khan (reporting from prison) admired Hindus and Sikhs for their religious spirit and dedication to God.[23] The view of the essential equality of human beings and our religions was a basic tenet of this faith.

Martin Luther King, Jr. once commented about Gandhi: "Nonviolent resistance had emerged as the technique of the movement, while love stood as the regulating ideal. In other words, Christ furnished the spirit and motivation, while Gandhi furnished the method."[24] Khan actually understood Gandhi's contribution in a similar regard. For Khan, however, it was the Prophet Muhammad who had originally been nonviolent, and it was Gandhi who had revived this spirit of nonviolence. In Khan's interpretation, Gandhi was speaking no less of the core values of Islam.

Scholars of Khan's life also generally affirm that Khan could not separate religion and politics. Here we see the obvious connections with Gandhi, who also affirmed very similar ideas about religion and politics.

> For me there is no politics without religion—not the religion of the superstitious or the blind, religion that hates and fights, but the universal Religion of Toleration. Politics without morality is a thing to be avoided.
>
> Politics bereft of religion are absolute dirt, ever to be shunned. Politics concerns nations and that which concerns the welfare of nations must be one of

the concerns of a man who is religiously inclined, in other words, a seeker after God and Truth … Therefore in politics also we have to establish the Kingdom of Heaven.[25]

Abdul Ghaffar Khan would echo much the same sentiment: "It is my inmost conviction that Islam is *amal, yakeen, muhabat* [work, faith, and love] and without these the name Muslim is sounding brass and tinkling cymbal. The Qur'an makes it absolutely clear that faith in One God without a second, and good works, are enough to secure a man his salvation."[26] This quote reflects possibly the Christian influence in his life, as Khan received education from a Reverend Wigram, who perhaps encouraged and fostered his outlook as a social reformer.[27]

In review, an "Islamic Gandhi" is one who is nonviolent, universal in outlook, religiously and politically engaged, and finally of course rooted in the belief of Islam. Many sources of course confirm Khan's piety and dedication to the Muslim way of life, not the least of whom was Gandhi who never saw Khan miss a prayer, except when illness prevented it.[28] One of the most remarkable achievements of Khan's religious devotion culminated in his political efforts to establish nonviolence as the proper Islamic response to oppressive rule. This would of course lead to the creation of the Khudai Khidmatgars.

The Khudai Khidmatgars

The most remarkable of Khan's achievements was the conversion of his own Frontier Afghans—the Pathans or Pashtuns, to the service of nonviolence. The Pashtuns had an historic reputation as warriors. The tribal code of *badal* or blood vengeance prepared them to strike back not only within their own society, but against foreign aggressors. Based upon Abdul Ghaffar Khan's own testimony, many Pathans were born, bred, and raised with a fighting spirit dedicated to maintaining pride and honor. Badshah Khan decided, however, that violence was not really the solution; it was just part of the problem. The very belligerence that was part of the Pathan culture made it all the more remarkable that Abdul Ghaffar Khan was able to teach them nonviolence. Jawaharlal Nehru observed:

There is nothing so surprising about our Frontier Province as the conversion of a war-like people to the doctrine of non-violence. That conversion is, of course, far from complete and the Pathan does not worry himself about philosophical or metaphysical speculations. But it is patent that in action he has been remarkably non-violent. The man who loved his gun better than his child or brother, who valued life cheaply and cared naught for death, who avenged the slightest insult with the thrust of a dagger, has suddenly become the bravest and most enduring of India's non-violent soldiers. That was due undoubtedly to the influence of one man—Abdul Ghaffar Khan—whose word was almost law to his people, for they love him and trusted him.[29]

Nehru made more favorable comments about Khan in his own Autobiography,[30] and Nehru was not alone in his observations. Joan Bondurant once wrote that a people with no prior exposure to ahimsa, to nonviolence, showed a remarkable capacity to adopt and practice it.[31] The miracle of the conversion of the Pathans to nonviolence would seem almost surreal to Mohandas Gandhi: "That such men who would have killed a human being with no more thought than they would kill a sheep or a hen should at the bidding of one man have laid down their arms and accepted nonviolence as the superior weapon sounds almost like a fairy tale."[32]

Yet it was not a fairy tale, it was historical reality. Khan was able to convert some 80,000–100,000 of his own Pashtun people to the belief in nonviolence. This, as evidenced by the Pathan cultural appetite for battle and badal, was certainly no easy task. Yet in 1929 he was able to first form the nonviolent brigade of Pathans, the Khudai Khidmatgar, also known as the "Red Shirts" (for the particular dye they used on their garments) or the "Servants of God." Appealing to the Pathans on the grounds of practicality, and of Islam, Abdul Ghaffar Khan became known as the "Badshah" Khan, the "King" of Khans, and as great a leader to his Pathans as Gandhi had been to much of the rest of India. The solemnly sworn oath is a serious thing in Pathan culture, and so it was that the Pathan "Red Shirts" or "Servants of God" were convinced by the force of Khan's personality, perseverance, and argument to take the following vow:

I am a Khudai Khidmatgar; and as God needs no service, but serving his creation is serving him, I promise to serve humanity in the name of God.

I promise to refrain from violence and from taking revenge. I promise to forgive those who oppress me or treat me with cruelty.

I promise to refrain from taking part in feuds or quarrels and from creating enmity.[33]

But how was this accomplished? What arguments could Khan appeal to? Gandhi had observed that the dream of a nonviolent Pathan was something more like a fantasy, but Khan had made it a reality. It was not, as Gandhi suggested, something out of fairy tale. This was a hundred thousand Pathan Muslims—a very significant portion of the total population of the Frontier region at the time. Badshah Khan persuaded them to pledge their lives to nonviolence, traveling some twenty-five miles per day on foot, going from village to village to promote nonviolence, education, and social uplift.[34] As Martin Luther King Jr. suggested that nonviolence was the only practical solution for American blacks, Badshah Khan evaluated his own historical reality and suggested that nonviolence was the better strategy to be pursued by Pathans:

> Two types of movements were launched in our province ... The violent movement [the uprisings before 1919] created hatred in the hearts of the people against violence. But the nonviolent movement won love, affection and sympathy of the people ... If a Britisher was killed [during the violent uprisings] not only the culprit was punished, but the whole village and entire region suffered for it. The people held the violence and its doer responsible for repression. In the nonviolent movement we courted self-suffering ... Thus, it won love and sympathy of the people.[35]

Based upon his experience, and his religious convictions, Khan told the Pathans that nonviolence was their best hope. It was not only their best hope, it was also their greatest weapon: "I am going to give you such a weapon that the police and the army will not be able to stand against it. It is the weapon of the Prophet, but you are not aware of it. That weapon is patience and righteousness. No power on earth can stand against it."[36] Badshah Khan's faith and confidence in nonviolence were based upon a personal creed and sincere devotion, but extended to an analysis that it was also the superior tactic.

The Khudai Khidmatgars helped to keep the Frontier Province out of violent conflict when elsewhere in India violence had erupted. Their service and the memory of Abdul Ghaffar Khan continue to be held high today in India, but it is a tragic fact of history that the movement was systematically pulled apart after the Independence and partition of India and Pakistan. Upon Badshah Khan's death in 1988, some authors point out that India may have mourned his loss more than Pakistan. A sad, but realistic fact about nonviolence is that it does not always or inevitably prevail. Indeed, after partition Badshah Khan felt as if he and his Khudai Khidmatgars were "thrown to the wolves" in Pakistan, that he was alone, in an unsympathetic political climate (he had opposed partition and later Muhammad Ali Jinnah in pursuing Pathan freedom).[37]

Gandhi had once promised that he would never abandon Badshah Khan and that he would always be there to struggle nonviolently beside him. Gandhi once said, "We will fight Pakistan if they maltreated you. It is true that I believe in nonviolence, but it will be for the Government of India to help the Pathans to keep their honor and the right of self-determination."[38] Sadly, however, the Mahatma was not able to keep that promise because a militant Hindu assassinated him on January 30, 1948. Instead of "two Gandhis," one in India and the other on the Frontier (now Pakistan), there was only one. Badshah Khan now wrestled with the unresponsive government of Pakistan, while sympathetic Indians such as Jawaharlal Nehru looked on, without intervening in the internal affairs of Pakistan. Perhaps because of his extensive time in jail in Pakistan, and the failure to keep his mission alive there, we know less of the Islamic Frontier Gandhi than we know of the Mahatma.

Badshah Khan and Gandhi

We typically understand jihad as violent struggle, as advocated by Osama bin Laden, and practiced by Muhammad Atta, amongst others. Such men, however, would be in Badshah Khan's eyes apostates who had actually abandoned the true spirit of Islam. Badshah Khan saw in Gandhi and in the Prophet Muhammad his role models for nonviolence. Operating in complete opposition to the concept of radically violent jihad which we know today, he elucidated his own concept of jihad:

> This is our jihad, our crusade. Before we can fight the British, we must first end the violence and murder in our own hearts. Remember that overcoming our personal weakness is the greater jihad, the greater crusade. It is what God wants of us.[39]

Substitute satyagraha for jihad in the above context, and these words might easily have been spoken by Gandhi. Replace jihad with nonviolence, and the British with "American racism," and the quote might be put in Martin Luther King Jr.'s mouth. Yet it is odd that in cataloguing the heroic efforts of nonviolence, the name of Badshah Khan so rarely comes up. Too much time and effort are put into showing the dysfunctional side of Islam. And while one cannot deny it is there (that would be to pretend that Bin Laden did not exist, or 9/11 never happened), one must appreciate that Islam is not alone in having a historical legacy of bloody conflict—Christianity has had its share, without argument. Hopefully men like King, Gandhi, and Badshah Khan can point to the more redeeming and positive aspects of political theology in the future.

Badshah Khan became a staunch proponent of nonviolence and an equally staunch supporter of Gandhi. It is important, however, to reiterate that he saw this as a Muslim duty. That the ideas of nonviolence and Islam are essentially compatible is something that may seem jarring for many people today, but for Badshah Khan and his converts to nonviolence it became the truth of their life, and the truth of their religion.

Was Ghaffar Khan's interpretation of Islam genuinely based in Islam? Or did Ghaffar Khan just affirm everything the Mahatma said? Badshah once did say that he placed a great deal of trust in Gandhi's decisions, even going so far as to see them inspired by one who had devoted himself to God:

> Whenever a question of great pith and moment arises in Gandhi's life and Gandhi takes an important decision, I instinctively say to myself, this is the

decision of one who has surrendered himself to God, and God never guides ill. I have never found it easy to question his decision for he refers all his problems to God and always listens to His Commands. After all I have but one measure, and that is the measure of one's surrender to God.[40]

Even in this statement we see a Muslim interpretation of Gandhi as one who has submitted to God. It shows also how Badshah Khan equated the God of Islam with that of Hindus, a remarkable extension of the notion of dhimmi. Badshah Khan did think in terms of Islam, but he did not think narrowly in terms of Islam. His Islam was a universal calling to faith, devotion, and nonviolence. If one lived up to those callings, one could infer that Badshah Khan would have thought Allah was well pleased.

But serious attention must be given to the critics who have pointed to the violence that they see in the Qur'an, and in the tradition of Islam. How do we reconcile these, and how did Badshah Khan also reconcile them?

The Qur'an and Jihad in Islam

Abdul Ghaffar Khan knew the Qur'an, as he had been required to memorize it by his mullah. Do we find nonviolent messages in the heart of Islam, in the Qur'an itself? The Qur'an does distinguish right and wrong, and accordingly rewards or punishes: "What! Do those who seek after evil ways think We shall hold them equal with those who believe and do righteous deeds—that equal will be their life and their death?" (Qur'an 45:21).[41] Further the Qur'an speaks of love and doing good deeds: "Allah gives glad tidings to his servants who believe and do righteous deed. Say 'No reward do I ask of you for this except the love of those near kin'" (Qur'an 42:23). Good deeds are superior to evil deeds: "Nor can goodness and evil be equal. Repel (evil) with the better, then will he between whom thee was hatred become as it were thy friend and intimate"[42] (Qur'an 41:34).

The patient enduring nonviolence of Mohandas K. Gandhi is one that Badshah Khan saw as essentially inspired by the Divine God. To Badshah Khan, Gandhi was no less a holy person than any given Muslim, and indeed it was Gandhi's nonviolence which he took to heart and interpreted at the essence of his own Islam. Believing this, Badshah Khan himself became known as the "Frontier Gandhi."

There are, of course, troubling verses in the Qur'an that run against this grain: for example, the verses which plea for making war against the unbelievers when the holy months have passed (Qur'an 9:5), or to lop off the heads of the unbelievers on the battlefield (Qur'an 47:4). The Qur'an has comments which speak critically of Jews and Christians, but also seem to uphold them as dhimmi, "people of the book," who have received a genuine revelation and whose Prophets are acknowledged. In my own assessment, the Qur'an does not have an unambiguous interpretation. While it speaks in terms of stern judgment, and awaiting hellfire for the unbelievers and those who doubt, it also speaks consistently of God as merciful and kind, and essentially smiling upon persons who "do good works, and have faith."

But can we look to the Prophet Muhammad as a role model for nonviolence? How could one reach this conclusion, given the fact that we know the Prophet Muhammad also fought in combat? The Qur'an states the need to "lop of the head of the unbeliever" (in Muhammad's case, the opposing Meccans) in combat, when peace has failed. The Prophet Muhammad was indeed no Gandhian, he physically did take up a sword, he did not just speculate as Gandhi did that violence was preferable to cowardice. The Prophet was a warrior, and as even Gandhi once complained, "The sword is too much in evidence among the Muslims. It must be sheathed if Islam is to be what it means—peace."[43] Ghaffar Khan certainly agreed with the Mahatma that Islam meant peace, and did his best to live out that example. If the Prophet Muhammad had to defend the Muslim faith, Ghaffar Khan must have thought it had been an unpleasant or necessary duty, and not the pinnacle or intent of Islam.[44] Ghaffar Khan was not a systematic theologian any more than Gandhi was. Both were campaigners, and pragmatists, who desired to see their faith put into positive action.

Badshah Khan might have simply not accepted that the Qur'an was an infallible document, as Gandhi assumed his own Hindu tradition was not without flaws. No definitive statement, writing or reflection, however, has so far come to this writer's attention to suggest how Ghaffar Khan read the Qur'an—literally, or liberally. If the Qur'an is thought to be fallible, objectionable parts of it might be dismissed just as objectionable parts might be dismissed in the Judeo-Christian tradition. If Abdul Ghaffar Khan did object to parts of the Qur'an or of his Muslim tradition, it certainly seems that it was his prerogative to do so.

How Abdul Ghaffar Khan reconciled the textual ambiguity of these verses and traditions in Islam is not fully known by this writer, but what is clear is that he decisively concluded that the proper interpretation of Islam, in his own eyes, was thoroughly nonviolent. As previously noted, Badshah Khan said:

It is my inmost conviction that Islam is *amal, yakeen, muhabat* [work, faith, and love] and without these the name Muslim is sounding brass and tinkling cymbal. The Qur'an makes it absolutely clear that faith in One God without a second, and good works, are enough to secure a man his salvation.[45]

Badshah Khan took a simple, peaceful, and very universal understanding of his religion. It seems possible to extend the idea that any man, of any religion—Christian, Muslim, Jew, Sikh, or Hindu—who had good faith, and did good works, would be accepted by the overarching mercy and forgiveness of Allah, who was God of all. Whatever our petty differences amounted to upon this Earth, it was keeping the good faith, and doing good works in the spirit of peace, and nonviolence, which would essentially count toward our salvation here and in the hereafter. This was his simple view of Islam.

Conclusion: The Legacy of Badshah Khan

The great tragedy of Khan's life is that with the partition of India and of Pakistan, new forces and new voices came to power that were very much opposed to Abdul Ghaffar Khan. His greatest potential friend and ally, Mohandas Gandhi, was assassinated shortly after independence, and Khan's own Khudai Khidmatgars were systematically repressed and taken apart by the new Pakistani government. Scholarship has also suggested that Khan's nonviolent appeal to Islam and ahimsa was not one he could make his own Pathan people accept for very long. In short, the conversion of Pathans to nonviolence was not permanent in some reports.[46] Thus Khan's legacy, while very relevant ideologically and theologically, is sadly now in neglect.

Opposing his new government, Khan would spend another fifteen years in prison for his political agitation, earning him truly the title of "Badshah Khan"— King of Khans, whether he accepted it or not. In fact, if one adds the total time Badshah Khan spent in prison fighting for freedom for the Pathans, it adds up to some thirty years (accounts do vary of exactly how much time he spent in prison, but thirty seems a supportable figure); this is more than Martin Luther King Jr., Jawaharlal Nehru, and Mohandas Gandhi combined. Certainly that should qualify A.G. Khan as one of the great, Islamic nonviolent resistors in our time.

A tragic fact is that since the terrorist attacks of 9/11, the call to violent jihad has imbued Islam with a new and bloody spirit that really betrays the more peaceful nature that it has been proven to sustain. The violence of terrorist jihad is a bloodstain that will not easily wash clean. Sullied by the reputation of those who have perverted its spirit, what is most urgently needed now is a second Islamic Gandhi, of equal or greater renown to Abdul Ghaffar Khan. In particular, if such an Islamic Gandhi were to arise in Palestine, and be able to reconcile peace between Israeli and Palestinian, this would go a long way to restoring the reputation of Islam, and reclaiming it from the terrorists who have done it a great disservice. This may seem far-fetched, this may seem idealistic, but recall the words of Eknath Easwaran: "If Badshah Khan could raise a nonviolent army out of a people so steeped in violence as the Pathans, there is no country on earth where it cannot be done."[47]

This is perhaps too optimistic. Favorable political and cultural factors are essential for the realization of nonviolence. In terms of political factors, we have to have a government or a nation with some residual level of moral conscience that can be appealed to.[48] A totalitarian government—such as existed in Nazi

Germany—would make nonviolent satyagraha—be it Muslim, Christian, or Hindu—very difficult. Similarly in terms of culture, the people have to be ready for or persuaded to nonviolence, and willing to pay the very high price that might be paid to follow it patiently, enduring with great risk and an even greater heart.

Some seeds of nonviolent resistance are already present in Israel-Palestine. Rachel Corrie, an American citizen, was killed by an Israeli bulldozer in a nonviolent protest of the demolition of Palestinian homes. Mubarak Awad, a Palestinian Christian, was called briefly by the press a "Palestinian Gandhi" for his efforts to support nonviolent civil disobedience amongst the Palestinians. The title, however, is one he has been too humble to claim. Mr. Awad has made some remarkable accomplishments, but it is difficult to say with conviction whether he has or will equal the impact of Gandhi, King, or Badshah Khan.

Magnetism and charisma are undoubtedly qualities not to be underestimated, and are especially valuable to give direction, hope, and popular energy to nonviolent religious movements. Such charisma is not something Khan or Gandhi would have voluntarily owned up to (both were somewhat embarrassed by their titles of "Badshah Khan—King of Khans" and "Mahatma or Great Soul"), but it is arguably indispensable for giving the necessary motivation and inspirational leadership that nonviolence requires. Such leaders are always imaginative, optimistic, universalistic in their thinking, and unfortunately in many regards far too rare, and far too unique. It is, however, a long century, and with patience we wait. Perhaps only a Muslim Gandhi, able to convict the conscience of Muslims, and non-Muslims alike, will have the patience and fortitude to wash the bloodstains out of Muslim politics, and restore it to a path hopefully in accord with its own Prophet. Abdul Ghaffar Khan would have wanted no less.

Notes

1   Attar Chand, *India, Pakistan and Afghanistan: A Study of Freedom, Struggle and Abdul Ghaffar Khan* (New Delhi, India: Commonwealth Publishers, 1989), 8.
2   Jean Akhtar Cerrina, *Islam's Peaceful Warrior: Abdul Ghaffar Khan* (Bloomington, IN: Xlibris Corporation, 2003), 32–4.
3   Eknath Easwaran, *A Man to Match His Mountains: Badshah Khan, Non-Violent Soldier of Islam* (Berkeley, CA: Nilgiri Press, 1984), 56.
4   Ibid., 55–9.
5   Chand, *India, Pakistan and Afghanistan*, xliii, 27, 37.
6   Easwaran, *A Man to Match His Mountains*, 12.
7   Ibid., 99.
8   Chand, *India, Pakistan and Afghanistan*, 55.
9   Easwaran, *A Man to Match His Mountains*, 141.
10 Stephen Tanner, *Afghanistan: A Military History From Alexander the Great to the Fall of the Taliban* (Cambridge, MA: Da Capo Press, 2002), 218.
11 Easwaran, *A Man to Match His Mountains*, 104.

12   Mohandas K. Gandhi, *Gandhi, An Autobiography: The Story of My Experiments with Truth*, trans. from Gujarati by Mahadev Desai (Boston, MA: Beacon Press, 1993), 503–4.

13   Shriman Narayan, ed., *The Selected Works of Mahatma Gandhi*, vol. 6 (Ahmedabad, India: Navajivan Publishing House, 1968), 100.

14   D. Mackenzie Brown, *The White Umbrella: Indian Political Thought from Manu to Gandhi* (Berkeley and Los Angeles: University of California Press, 1964), 148.

15   Easwaran, *A Man to Match His Mountains*, 167.

16   Narayan, *Selected Works of Mahatma Gandhi*, vol. 4, 137.

17   Ibid., 266.

18   Ibid., vol. 6, 272.

19   Cerrina, *Islam's Peaceful Warrior*, 126.

20   Chand, *India, Pakistan and Afghanistan*, 175.

21   One video biography of A.G. Khan exists, while multiple biographies can be found of Martin Luther King, Mother Teresa, or Mohandas Gandhi. Additionally, books about A.G. Khan's life are becoming older, or more frequently are out of print.

22   Chand, *India, Pakistan and Afghanistan*, 185.

23   Cerrina, *Islam's Peaceful Warrior*, 87–90. See also Chand, *India, Pakistan and Afghanistan*, 36, 178.

24   Martin Luther King Jr., *A Testament of Hope: The Essential Writings and Speeches of Martin Luther King Jr.*, ed. James M. Washington (New York: HarperCollins, 1986), 17.

25   Narayan, *Selected Works of Mahatma Gandhi*, vol. 6, 435.

26   Easwaran, *A Man to Match His Mountains*, 63.

27   Ibid., 63.

28   Chand, *India, Pakistan and Afghanistan*, lvi.

29   Ibid., 107.

30   Jawaharlal Nehru, *An Autobiography, Centenary Edition* (New York: Oxford University Press, 1989), 265, 274, 556.

31   Joan V. Bondurant, *Conquest of Violence: The Gandhian Philosophy of Conflict* (Princeton, NJ: Princeton University Press, 1988), 138–9.

32   Easwaran, *A Man to Match His Mountains*, 20.

33   Cerrina, *Islam's Peaceful Warrior*, 96.

34   Chand, *India, Pakistan and Afghanistan*, 31, 63.

35   Easwaran, *A Man to Match His Mountains*, 138.

36   Ibid., 117.

37   Chand, *India, Pakistan and Afghanistan*, 86, 138.

38   Ibid., 13.

39   Cerrina, *Islam's Peaceful Warrior*, 104.

40   Chand, *India, Pakistan and Afghanistan*, 175.

41   Abdullah Yusuf Ali, translator of *The Holy Qur'an* (Beltsville, MA: Amana Publications, 1989).

42   Other translation by N.J. Dawood reads: "Good deeds and evil deeds are not equal. Requite evil deeds with good, and he who is your enemy will become your dearest friend. But none will attain this attribute save those who patiently endure; none will attain it save those who are truly fortunate."

43   Chand, *India, Pakistan and Afghanistan*, 177.

44   One finds actually a diametrical opposition in thought of Abdul Ghaffar Khan, and Osama bin Laden. The latter once stated that violent jihad was the peak of Islamic

duty; see Bruce Lawrence, ed., *Messages to the World: Statements of Osama bin Laden* (New York: Verso, 2005), 49.

45 Easwaran, *A Man to Match His Mountains*, 63.
46 M.S. Korejo, *The Frontier Gandhi: His Place in History* (New York: Oxford University Press, 1993), 57–9.
47 Easwaran, *A Man to Match His Mountains*, 189.
48 James L. Rowell, "Gandhi and Bin Laden: Polar Extremes," *Journal of Conflict Studies* 26, no. 1 (2006): 35–54.

9 ISLAM AND PEACE: A MUSLIM FUNDAMENTALIST PERSPECTIVE

Sherman A. Jackson

I would like to begin with a cautionary note of sorts. Today, whenever the concept of peace is invoked, it is almost invariably against the perceived threat of physical, martial force. Peace, in other words, is routinely thought of as the simple absence or cessation of violence. This heightened focus on aggressive, physical conflict is especially acute whenever the topic of discussion is religion and all the more so today if the religion in question happens to be Islam. Meanwhile, for those of us who are members of the academy, there is an additional element informing our analytical gaze. Violence is the instrument of coercion par excellence; coercion is the nemesis of philosophical liberalism; and philosophical liberalism permeates the epistemological ether of the contemporary Western academy, as it does the socio-political culture of America at large. Cumulatively, this contributes to an unspoken criterion that holds religion to be acceptable only to the extent that it is domesticated and shorn of all powers of coercion, ensuring its inability to challenge the state or the dominant culture. Those who are contemptuous, suspicious, or dismissive of religion often recline upon this criterion in binding the state with the task of "protecting" society from religion. Meanwhile, those who are supportive of religion are often so eager to avoid any indictment or criticism thereof that they are incapable of critically engaging its liabilities and messiness, including the challenge it can pose to peace.[1] Both groups, however, run the risk of self-deception and seeing their respective commitments and contributions to the cause of peace as being much greater, much purer, and much more innocent than they may actually be.

In his classic essay, *Moral Man and Immoral Society*, the celebrated Christian theologian Reinhold Niebuhr reminds us of just how treacherous would-be commitments to peace can actually be.

> So persistent is the cry of peace among the ruling classes and so strong the seeming abhorrence of every form of violence and anarchy that one might imagine them actuated by the purest pacifist principles, were it not or the fact that they betray no pacifist scruples when they consider international affairs.[2]

Of course, in these our times of Eric Garner, Sandra Bland, Ferguson-Missouri, and the like, we need not restrict our gaze to the international arena. As Niebuhr himself would go on to observe, there is an even more subtle liability lurking beneath the surface of many calls to peace. The tendency to equate peace with the simple absence of violence, he notes, often masks a false consciousness that fails to recognize just how devastating nonviolent injury can be. The nonviolent abuse of economic, political, intellectual, or cultural power, or even the power differential between a parent and a child, can be just as easily and badly exploited as are bombs, bullets, or the authority to police.[3] Indeed, a single-minded commitment to "social justice" can occlude the evils that lurk behind the lack of commitment to "cognitive justice," where cognitive frames, cultural sensibilities, and epistemological presuppositions are manipulated to normalize the misrecognition of legitimate self or communal interests.[4] As the Qur'an notes in this regard, "domination is worse than killing" (*wa al-fitnatu ashaddu min al-qatl*).[5] In such light, to target only those forms of injury toward which the West (or the dominant culture in the West) feels vulnerable, namely destructive physical violence in such forms as terrorism, while ignoring those forms of injury—violent and nonviolent—to which non-Westerners (or minority groups within the West) feel vulnerable can hardly amount to a genuine or meaningful commitment to peace.

None of this is to deny that ideological and practical commitments to wanton violence *are* a major impediment to peace. And given the magnitude and persistence of religiously motivated violence in certain parts of the world, especially the Muslim world, it seems fitting for Western scholars and students of Islam to address violence as a problem. Still, I think we should be careful about surrendering too easily and perhaps too self-righteously to false or self-serving criteria that render us party to an effective conspiracy to promote a kind of peace that serves the interests of some while blithely or callously ignoring the legitimate right of others to a dignified and more holistically peaceful existence.

Peace, Violence, and Fundamentalism

The Muslim fundamentalist perspective on Islam and peace on which I shall focus here is part of a contemporary Islamist group's self-critique of violence as the primary medium of exchange in negotiating political conflict over the public role and status of Islam. This singular focus on violence, however, should not be taken to imply that the group equates peace with the simple absence of physical force, as if to say that once violence ceases to exist everything must be accepted as fine. As we shall see, they are neither pacifists nor dead to the fact that society can be quite unhealthy and oppressive even without violence. For them, the problem goes beyond the simple fact or occurrence of violence to the actual status of violence as an Islamic commitment. Their argument, in other words, is essentially against the tendency of Islamist movements to see violence as a duty that Islam imposes upon Muslims as an absolute, non-negotiable ideal. Obviously, on such an understanding, Islam could hardly be reconciled with the value of peaceful coexistence in a world replete with alternative perspectives on life. But beyond this, the fundamentalist imputation of panacean powers to violence obliterates the recognition of the many other necessary constituents of a meaningful, effective, and dignified existence. This oversight is a major constituent of the fallacy that these Muslim fundamentalist critics want to correct.

Of course, "fundamentalist" is an ambiguous and much abused term. My use of the word has nothing to do with any commitment to a literalist approach to Muslim scripture or the intellectual tradition of Islam.[6] Fundamentalism in a Muslim context refers, rather, to a particular mode of insisting on the public recognition of the authority of Islam—especially *shari'ah* or Islamic law—as *the* organizing principle of Muslim society. While many Muslims who are not fundamentalists also share this commitment, what sets fundamentalists apart is their recognition of violence as the primary if not exclusive medium of exchange between them and those perceived to stand in the way of this goal. According to the group under consideration, this valuation of violence is grounded not so much in any literal reading of Muslim scripture as it is in a very particular reading, valuation, and deployment of Muslim history. As this was a history in which violence was recognized as both a given and an effective geopolitical negotiator, the net result of taking it as the lens through which to read Muslim scripture and tradition (as well as contemporary reality) is to convert violence into a *transcendent* value that appears to draw its legitimacy not from historical experience but from scripture itself. In this capacity, violence becomes *the* Islamic language of socio-political negotiation, scripturally mandated, permanently normative, and universally applicable in all times and places. In this context, the persuasiveness and allure of Muslim fundamentalism reside not so much in any literal authority it accords Muslim scripture but in the uncritically inflated authority it accords a particular reading of the pre-modern Muslim past, a reading that is effectively rendered invisible *as a reading* by the fact that it resonates so powerfully with the modern Muslim predicament, where, like their pre-modern forebears, Muslims see Islam as being under mortal threat. In sum, this reading produces an interpretive prism that is essentially composed of *history idealized, internalized and then essentially forgotten as history*. As peaceful coexistence was often part of the pre-modern Muslim *unimaginable*, this perspective renders peaceful coexistence between Muslims and non-Muslims unimaginable for modern Muslim fundamentalists today.

To be sure, Muslim fundamentalists are not alone in rejecting or doubting the possibilities of peace between Muslims and non-Muslims. The group under review is keenly aware of American imperial designs and attitudes regarding the region, especially following the fall of the Soviet Union but actually since the end of the

Second World War. In addition to the views of the likes of former President Richard Nixon in his book, *Seize the Moment*, and Francis Fukuyama in his book and essay, *The End of History*, they cite Samuel P. Huntington's damning assessment in his book, *The Clash of Civilizations and the Remaking of the World*: "The underlying problem is not Islamic fundamentalism; it is Islam; for Islam has problems with modernity."[7] But even in the face of this, their argument is essentially that violence, especially in the name of religion, cannot be the sole and exclusive response. For, American designs are often not motivated by religion at all,[8] and Muslim weakness is neither overcome nor offset by the kind of wanton violence practiced by Muslim fundamentalists. On the contrary, the surfeited focus on violence actually preempts the development of the kind of power and standing that would actually serve the Muslim *ummah* in this regard.

The Muslim Fundamentalist Critique

On October 6, 1981, the entire world was shocked by the brash spectacle of Egyptian President Anwar al-Sadat's assassination. This was part of a plan to take over the country and establish an Islamic state, the legal, social, economic, and political order of which would be explicitly defined and regulated by *shari'ah*.[9] This attempted "coup" had been orchestrated by an amalgamation of militant Islamist groups brought together the previous year under the banner of "Egyptian Jihad Incorporated" (*Tanzim al-Jihad al-Misri*) or more simply Jihad Inc. (*Tanzim al-Jihad*).[10] Jihad Inc. was headed by Muhammad 'Abd al-Salam Faraj, and it included two other formal groups, one led by Kamal al-Sa'id Habib, the other a contingent largely from Upper Egypt headed by Karam Zuhdi under the name "*al-Gama'ah al-Islamiyah*." It is upon the latter and some of its members that I shall focus for the remainder of this chapter.

Sadat's assassination was paralleled by an attempt by *al-Gama'ah al-Islamiyah* to take over the city of Asyut and from there march on to Cairo. The Cairo-faction of Jihad Inc. succeeded in assassinating Sadat, as a result of which Faraj, Khalid al-Islambuli, and three others were executed. But the *Gama'ah*'s mission in Upper Egypt ended in failure, as a result of which all of its leaders and scores of its members landed in prison. In prison, internal differences led to the dissolution of Jihad Inc., and the *Gama'ah* resumed its status as an autonomous organization. This was also the beginning, however, of a new, more violent relationship with the Egyptian state and society. From the time of Sadat's death through the first half of the 1990s, the number of people killed by the *Gama'ah* was estimated in the thousands, including Egyptian officials, Coptic Christians, Western tourists, secular intellectuals, security forces, and innocent bystanders.[11] This was met, of course, by brutal government retaliations, including summary executions, mass incarceration, and torture. At one point, the number of *incarcerated Gama'ah* members alone was placed between 15,000 and 30,000, making the *Gama'ah* easily the largest radical jihadist movement in Egypt and the Arab world at the time.[12] As both the Egyptian government and the *Gama'ah* saw themselves engaged in an epic battle for their very existence, by the mid-1990s there was no end in sight to the vicious cycles of violence that raged between them.

On July 5, 1997, however, the *Gama'ah* stunned the nation. At his trial in a military court (in which *Gama'ah* members were routinely tried) on charges of trying to blow up a bank, one of its members stood up in open court and read a statement signed by six first-tier *Gama'ah* leaders.

> The Historical Leadership of *al-Gama'ah al-Islamiyah* calls upon their brethren from among the leadership and the rank-and-file to terminate, without stipulation and with no prerequisites, all armed campaigns and communiqués that call for such, both inside and outside of Egypt, in the interest of Islam and the Muslims.[13]

This was the beginning of the *Gama'ah's* so-called "Initiative to Stop the Violence." A few years later, in 2002, they issued four manifestos under the series title, "Correcting Misunderstandings (*Silsilat tashih al-mafahim*)."[14] The explicit aim of these tracts was to repudiate the *Gama'ah's* old commitment to violence as their primary medium of exchange and to set the group upon a new ideological cum-tactical foundation. Importantly, the *Gama'ah* insisted that their new perspective was explicitly grounded in their new understanding of *shari'ah*, which their years of incarceration had allowed them to study and actually learn, as opposed to simply imagining, as they had in the past. According to their own testimony, their study of *shari'ah* brought them to appreciate the importance of properly assessing the situation on the ground as a prerequisite to a proper application of the religious law, what they came to refer to as "*fiqh al-waqi'*" or "jurisprudence of factual reality."[15] On this basis, they insisted that their approach to applying *shari'ah*—including any duty to execute *jihad*—must recline upon two fundamental constituents: (1) a proper assessment of actual reality on the ground, along with its practical implications, and (2) *shari'ah*-proofs from the Qur'an, Sunna, or other recognized sources of the religious law. Only through a proper assessment of reality on the ground, in other words, could they determine whether a particular application of a validly deduced rule would actually serve the underlying goals and objectives (*maslahah*) for which it was legislated. In the past, they admit, they paid no attention to any of this but simply waged *jihad* based on what they took to be the plain dictates of scripture, mediated, of course, through the romanticized prism of Muslim history. Now, by contrast, they understand that a factual assessment of reality might be even more probative than the plain dictates of scripture in determining whether or not a rule should be applied. This new insight was at the heart of the "misunderstanding" that they now wanted to correct:

> The mistake we made in the past was that we used to privilege (individual) texts over the broader aims and objectives of the law, allowing the texts to run rough-shod over these aims and objectives. We used to engage in *jihad* without taking any account of the benefits or harms that would accrue to our action. Now, however, our understanding has changed: it is the broader aims and objectives that determine the application of the text. So, if the text says, e.g., wage *jihad* against the Jews, I must first determine the benefit to derive from this *jihad*, i.e., will my interests be realized by fighting or by not fighting. This is the sound approach (*wa hadha huwa al-sahih*).[16]

What are these "broader aims and objectives" to which the *Gama'ah* repeatedly refers? Chief among them, they insist, is "to guide humanity to God"[17] to "endear the people to their Lord and Creator and direct them to the straight path of God, through the least burdensome means and easiest route."[18] Violence, for its part, *might* be prescribed as a means of serving or protecting this mission, but only if it bears a practical relationship thereto and the resulting benefits are projected to outweigh the harms. And here they seem to recognize that just because a religious injunction was carried out in a particular way in the past, even by the Pious Ancestors or other heroes of the tradition, this does not mean that this rule must be applied in the exact same fashion today, given the known differences between past and present reality. *This*, and not simply its status as a scripturally mandated institution of organized violence, is the litmus test to be applied when contemplating a decision to wage *jihad*. Otherwise, according to the *Gama'ah*, *jihad* today can end up undermining the very aim that it was instituted to serve, again, guiding people to God and endearing them to their Lord and Creator.[19]

Of course, most people today would dismiss any connection between violence and guiding people to God as both ineffectual and beyond the pale, especially given the collective memory of the Western experience with the so-called Wars of Religion. But while the *Gama'ah* is keen on noting the differences between past and the present reality, they are equally alive to their commonalities. Power, they recognize, including the deployment of violence, remains as critical a factor in modern geopolitical relations as it was in the pre-modern past. And especially as a civilization (and not just a religion) Islam will neither be able to sustain its integrity nor promote its message as a prostrate, subjugated client. This goes beyond the purely coercive properties and effects of power. For, power almost always exerts a deep psychological influence on contending groups, especially the overpowered.[20] As the celebrated Ibn Khaldun put the matter, "the vanquished are always enamored of following the ways of the victor."[21]

On this understanding, the relationship between power and the attractiveness of its wielder's message may not be as distant as we may be commonly (and comfortably) used to assuming.

And yet the *Gama'ah* seems to recognize that power is not necessarily the same as violence. Nations such as China or Russia are spared attack, exploitation, and undue influence not because they practice the kind violence deployed by Muslim fundamentalists but because they are powerful. Indeed, the *Gama'ah* observes that the misapplication of violence can actually weaken, rather strengthen, the Muslim community, by rendering it the target of overwhelming military force that it lacks the ability to repel (as when the Americans "retaliated" against Afghanistan after 9/11) or by sapping the internal strength of Muslim nations by forcing them to devote so much of their attention and resources to domestic terrorism. None of this negates the religious duty to stay prepared to wage *jihad*.[22] Indeed, Muslims must be collectively strong in order to deflect the practical and psychological effects of power directed at them by others. Strong, however, is one thing, wantonly violent another.

At the time they inaugurated the Initiative to Stop the Violence, the *Gama'ah's* primary focus was the domestic scene in Egypt. But their recognition of the importance of considering the difference between pre-modern and modern reality and how this informs the use of violence and the effective application of the law would ultimately take their critique beyond Egypt to contemporary jihadism in general and to *al-Qa'idah* in particular. In 2004, its leadership jointly published the previously cited book entitled *Istratijiyah wa Tafj'irat al-Qa'idah: al-Akhta' wa al-Akhtar (Al-Qa'idah's Strategy and Bombings: Mistakes and Dangers)*.[23] While they are careful to insist that they mean no disrespect to "Shaykh" Usamah b. Ladin, nor to impugn *al-Qa'idah's* intentions or downplay America's negative role in the region, they explicitly speak of *al-Qa'idah's* misunderstanding of *shari'ah*, including their failure to effect a proper assessment of reality on the ground. Specifically, according to them, *al-Qa'idah* tends to proceed on a pre-modern division of the world into believers and unbelievers and then allows this to do all of their thinking for them. Whereas such a division *may* have implied lethal hostility between Muslims and non-Muslims in the past, in the modern world, the existence of such a negative relationship must be factually determined and not merely assumed. Whereas *al-Qa'idah* assumes that US and Muslim interests are completely and permanently contradictory, based on the legacy of Muslim–non-Muslim relations in the historical past, the *Gama'ah* holds up concrete contemporary examples that challenge this assumption, such as America's support for the Afghan *mujahidin*.[24] Similarly, while *al-Qa'idah* holds any kind of truce, negotiation, or alliance with America to be tantamount to Islamic treason, the *Gama'ah* points out that such a position contradicts well-known practices of the Prophet Muhammad himself, who made treaties and alliances with the same pagan Arabians who opposed, vilified, and attacked him and his religion.[25]

Again, none of this should be misunderstood. The *Gama'ah* points explicitly to America's abject bias regarding the Arab–Israeli conflict, its hypocritical, self-serving promotion of democracy, human rights and the protection of women and religious minorities, not to mention US economic exploits in the region. All of this the *Gama'ah* roundly condemns, even as they recognize the Muslim *ummah*'s obligation to confront these challenges, even if such should entail a principled resort to *jihad*. The question, however, both from the standpoint of a proper understanding of geopolitical reality *and* from the perspective of *shari'ah*, is whether the kind of wanton violence and bellicosity advocated by *al-Qa'idah* is the most appropriate or effective response. For, if the overall aim of *al-Qa'idah*'s "jihadism"—indeed of *any* jihadism—is, as it must be from the perspective of the religious law, to promote the broader aims and objectives of Islam, such as guiding people to God, not only has this brand of violence not served this interest, it has gone so far as to turn the entire world not only against *al-Qa'idah* but against all Islamic movements if not Islam as a whole.[26] By contrast, again, without blanketly ruling out *jihad*, the *Gama'ah* seems to anticipate a view more recently articulated by the prominent Egyptian cleric (now resident in Qatar) Shaykh Yusuf al-Qaraḍawi, which clearly recognizes forms and deployments of power other than and beyond violence.[27] According to al-Qaraḍawi, especially in the age of Twitter, satellite TV, rapid transit, and the internet, violence, including Western imperial violence, may no longer be the greatest threat to Islam or, to use Peter Berger's famous term, to Islam's "plausibility structure."[28] To the extent that violence is no longer the primary threat, neither is it likely to be an effective response. As such, rather than more violent *jihadis*, what Islam needs today is

> a massive army of preachers, teachers, journalists and those who are competent in training people in how to address today's public in the language of the age and the style of the times, through voice, image, spoken word, physical gesture, books, pamphlets, magazines, newspapers, dialogue, documentaries, drama, and motion pictures.[29]

Again, this is a clear recognition of the distinction between *power* and *violence*. And, while given the geopolitical realities of the day, it may be absolutely necessary to amass and deploy power in the cause of peace; the same does not necessarily hold for violence.

The Critique of ISIS

At the time the *Gama'ah* issued their corrective manifestos, the overwhelming majority of its leadership was still in prison. Between 2003 and 2005, however, most of them had been released. Once out of prison, support for the Initiative to Stop the

Violence continued apace, and certain members continued to churn out tracts that expanded on its basic theme. This was especially the case with Najih Ibrahim, a stalwart leader who went back to the very beginning and whose signature appeared on all of the corrective manifestos. Following his release, Ibrahim began to develop a progressively more independent voice that may have been more representative of his own rather than the *Gama'ah's* view as an organization. Indeed, signs of tension between him and at least a faction within the group appear in 2014, when the *Gama'ah's* official website announced a temporary pause in its operations, directing those who wished to continue following Ibrahim's views to a separate website. Up to that point, not only had Ibrahim administered the *Gama'ah's* website, his views virtually dominated it. Now, however, the cumulative effects of the Arab Spring, the ascension of Mohamed Morsi to the presidency of Egypt, the "coup-volution" and subsequent crackdown by General 'Abd al-Fattah al-Sisi, including the outlawing of the Muslim Brotherhood, along with the ominous rise of ISIS, were all sowing disagreement within the movement. Ibrahim, along with Karam Zuhdi, who had now been replaced as leader of the *Gama'ah* by another stalwart from back in the day, 'Isam Dirbalah (who died in prison under al-Sisi in 2015), was pitted against a more "restless" faction, who, while sticking to the Initiative to Stop the Violence, at least for the moment, felt that the group should be "doing more" to address the political situation in Egypt and to raising Islam to its rightful place as the ultimate socio-political arbiter.

Against this backdrop Ibrahim teamed up in 2014 with a former rank-and-file member of the *Gama'ah*, Hisham al-Najjar, who had resigned in protest over certain differences with the "restless" faction Sikkīn. Together, they wrote a book in critique of ISIS entitled *Da'ish al-Sikkin Allati Tadhbah al-Islam* (*ISIS: The Knife That Slaughters Islam*).[30] While their critique is pointed most directly at ISIS, it clearly signals a parallel criticism of Islamist movements overall. Based on what I detect of Ibrahim's writing style during his tenure as administrator of the *Gama'ah's* website, about two-thirds of the book appear to be written by him, with the last third being the contribution of al-Najjar.

At the most basic level, ISIS's most fatal flaw, according to Ibrahim and al-Najjar, is its inability to distinguish between *its* interests as a movement and the interests of the Muslim *ummah* as a whole. On this confusion, it sees itself as the exclusive representative of Islam, who will bring victory, majesty, and dignity back to the religion and restore Muslims to their proper place in the modern world. Of course, only those who do not welcome such an agenda could see fit to stand in ISIS's way. As such, anyone who opposes or even fails to support their effort is deemed an enemy of Islam![31] In the West (or perhaps I should say among many Muslims in the West) the tendency is to see all of this in terms of what and how it contributes to ISIS's rush to ex-communication, or *takfir*, accompanied by the wanton intolerance and violence that goes along with such a judgment. But for Ibrahim and al-Najjar, the problem is much broader. While ISIS's violence and intolerance are problems to be sure, it is its navel-gazing, short-sighted perspective overall that is the greater concern. For, this condemns the group to a small-mindedness that preempts its ability to understand the true nature of the challenges facing it or the *ummah* and of the necessity of availing themselves of the kinds of resources and opportunities that might actually serve the *ummah*'s primary and long-term interests. In short, according to Ibrahim and al-Najjar, while ISIS may *speak* of an Islamic *state* or an Islamic *caliphate*, it is actually unable to *think*, let alone *act*, like a state *or* a caliphate. Instead, ISIS behaves like a gang, a militia or a fraternity, whose addiction to violence and bellicosity denies it the ability to understand, let alone achieve, what it takes to thrive geopolitically in the modern world.[32]

This is clearly manifested, according to Ibrahim and al-Najjar, in ISIS's contemptuous behavior toward world powers and their leaders. They cite as an example a letter ISIS reportedly sent to Turkey's Erdogan following his ascent to power, in which they state: "O Mr. secularist, we will soon occupy your country and turn you out of it."[33] They make similar threats against Russia's Putin and to then British Prime Minister David Cameron.[34] To this they add such heinous acts as the beheading of American journalists and the execution of diplomats sent from the Syrian Islamist group *Jabhat al-Nusrah*.[35] They go on to ex-communicate Muslim groups as diverse as the *Nahḍah* Party in Tunis alongside a long list of groups in Egypt, including the Freedom and Justice Party (founded by members of the Muslim Brotherhood), The Light Party (*al-Nur* founded by Salafists), and the Building and Development Party (*al-Bina' wa al-Tanmiyah*, founded by members of the *Gama'ah* itself).[36] All Shiites, of course, are infidels on a fortiori grounds.[37] Again, while these actions are all problematic in and of themselves, Ibrahim and al-Najjar suggest that what is most disturbing is the gross immaturity and naïvité they reflect about what it means to operate as a formal polity, especially one purportedly representative of a global community such as the Muslim *ummah*. For no state, not even a super-power—let alone a caliphate!—can exist or function effectively without allies possibility. Yet, ISIS recognizes neither the concept nor the possibility of "friends" or "allies," except with regard to those who unconditionally accept their party line. Indeed, according to Ibrahim and al-Najjar, ISIS effectively raises the enterprise of creating enemies to the level of a science, earning them what they refer to as "a PhD in creating enemies" (*ustadhiyah fi san' al-a'da*").[38] Yet, none of this is able to conceal or offset the deficits that accrue to such hubris and isolation. And this prompts Ibrahim and al-Najjar to ask what kind of reasonable state or even reasonable activist movement would act like this?

> What kind of caliph is this whose state couldn't even fix the tracks on a tank, service the wheels on a fighter-jet or fix a broken radar, yet will make all kinds of threats and promises to the whole world, in language that is nothing but arrogance, bluster, pettiness and vulgarity, such as the letter they address to "Obama, the Dog of Byzantium" (*kalb al-rum*)?[39]

The reference to President Barrack Obama as the "Dog of Byzantium" is a good example of what Ibrahim an al-Najjar identify as ISIS's myopic relationship with Muslim history. The phrase "*kalb al-rum*" comes from a letter reportedly sent by the 'Abbasid Caliph Harun al-Rashid over a thousand years ago to the Byzantine ruler Nicephorus (al-Naqfur), in response to the latter's refusal to pay a tribute that had been agreed upon by his predecessor, the empress Irene. In response, the Caliph invades Byzantium, defeats the Byzantines, and extracts an even higher tribute. Now, Ibrahim and al-Najjar ask, what has Obama and America to do with the Byzantines? The answer, of course, is nothing: Obama is black and the Americans are a mixture of races and religions. But such phrases as "*kalb al-rum*" are a part of an escapist narrative used by preachers and religious teachers to tickle the emotions of the Muslim masses by reminding them of a powerful and glorious past, without mentioning that this power and glory did not come out of nowhere but was the result of assiduous dedication in all aspects of human civilization.[40] In other words, instead of empowering and instructing its people to the end of actually achieving what they aspire to, ISIS effectively anesthetizes them and puts their faculties of critical analysis, imaginative creativity, and genuine human encounter to sleep.

Again, this misguided approach is not unique to ISIS; it is typical of modern Islamist movements as a whole who repeat the same old rhetoric and the same old stories, time and again, despite the radically different [historical] circumstances out of which these stories emerged. Rather than devote themselves, in other words, to forging the kinds of local and international relationships and acquiring and deploying the kinds of skills and resources that could actually enable them to compete on the world stage, these movements jeopardize the lives and interests of their Muslim constituencies by rendering them prisoners and ultimately victims of this misleading narrative.

To be sure, powerful over-simplifications gleaned from romanticized historical narratives almost always play a role in enhancing the morale and resolve of downtrodden groups in the face of overwhelming odds. As such, this in itself is not the cardinal sin of ISIS. But, taken to the extreme, the kinds of interpretive presuppositions generated by such uncritical and overzealously indulged narratives can totally obfuscate if not dislocate both the words and meaning of scripture. This is a serious problem, according to Ibrahim and al-Najjar, as it threatens not only to distort Islam as a blueprint for a healthy collective existence but also to undermine the very authority of scripture itself. As they note,

> Turning certain chapters of Muslim history into proofs that can be invoked in a manner that rivals the authority of religion and the religious law is among *the* major contemporary crises, especially when the protagonists of these stories from the past are kings and rulers ... Trying to follow in the tracks of an ancient history in times and places that bear no relation, resemblance or likeness to

that history will continue to bring disaster upon disaster upon the Islamic movement and all the *Da'ish*es of the world.[41]

Beyond the question of the practical relevance of these narratives, Ibrahim and al-Najjar note that modern Islamist movements routinely engage in highly selective readings of Muslim history, crafted expressly for the purpose of legitimizing a certain approach to socio-political conflict in the name of Islam, while ignoring or downplaying well-known or even more authoritative alternatives to such renderings. For example, in the case of addressing President Obama or other political leaders, they point to the precedent set by the Prophet Muhammad, who in addressing the non-Muslim rulers of Egypt and Byzantium deliberately used the Arabic honorific *'azim*, "the great," which was clearly intended to convey a sentiment of formal respect: "to Heraclius the Great of Byzantium"; "to Muqaqus the Great of Egypt."[42]

Again, such crassly pragmatic invocations of Muslim history contribute much and directly to ISIS's inflated estimation of violence, as they imagine it to have catapulted their Muslim ancestors to global ascendancy in the glorious past. It does not take much, however, to see that this perspective is reinforced if not partly inspired by what is seen to be the obvious role that violence played in the West's colonial and post-colonial "success."[43] In other words, this in many ways is but a reflection of the common tendency of the vanquished to imitate the victor. But this single-minded focus on violence, according to Ibrahim and al-Najjar, comes at the expense of the *civilizational* dimension of Islam. And it is only as a civilization, a *haḍarah islamiyah* whose groundedness in religion gives it the bearing and confidence to contribute to and benefit from cultural, intellectual, technological, and commercial exchange with other cultures and civilizations that Islam can compete on the global stage and provide for its own long-term sustainability. This is the way it actually *was* in the Muslim past, going all the way back to the time of the Prophet himself. But, again, the narrative generated by ISIS does not recognize the value of culture or civilization. And this is why, according to Ibrahim and al-Najjar, the skills and talents displayed by some of its most gifted recruits are almost never deployed beyond the goal of exercising control over the populace or waging war against its adversaries. In this way ISIS shoots both itself and the *ummah* in the foot. For, "even if they are able to seize control over this or that patch of land, nations and civilizations are not just patches of geography or caches of weapons. They are something much broader, more inclusive and deeper. Nations are extensions of culture, civilization, history and inherited values, as well as social and religious intermingling."[44] This combination, according to Ibrahim and al-Najjar, is what enables nations to sustain themselves, influence others, and thrive in the face of the kinds of challenges and opportunities that typically confront them at home and abroad.

More concretely, ISIS's obliviousness to the value of culture and civilization and its assumption that violence can substitute for these impedes its ability to properly conceptualize let alone build what Ibrahim and al-Najjar refer to as a "modern state," i.e., a "*dawlah 'asriyah*,"[45] not to mention a "super-state" in the form of a caliphate. Here the authors' assessment is couched in a rather sanitized depiction of Europe and America, who are imagined to have completely overcome such challenges as dictatorship, injustice, inequality, lack of freedom, and the treatment of minorities. At the same time, it proceeds on the assumption that the solutions arrived at *by the West* are precisely those anticipated by the broader aims and objections of *shari'ah*. Nevertheless, ISIS, for its part, according to Ibrahim and al-Najjar, recognizes none of this, as a result of which it ignores what the authors identify as the structural socio-political imperatives of Islam, such as serving the commonweal, equality before the law, freedom, justice, administrative accountability, and respect for minorities. Instead, ISIS is willing to forfeit all of this in favor of an almost exclusive focus on the so-called prescribed punishments, or *hudud*, as some sort of symbolic representation of a normative Islamic order. According to Ibahim and al-Najjar, this is based on both an abuse and a misunderstanding of political power in Islam. For, political power, or *sultah*, they insist, is not the private property of the Muslim ruler or caliph, to be used solely to solidify and enhance his position; on the contrary, it is a public trust (*amanah*) that is to be used to promote the public interest. But ISIS, according to them, has no time for such structural imperatives or "constitutional values" (*al-qiyam al-dusturiyah*). As a result, their program remains plain and simple: "autocracy in the name of religion" (*al-istibdad b'ism al-din*).[46]

Of course, there is much in pre-modern Muslim history (like the history of the rest of the pre-modern world) that can be called upon to lend support to non-representative government. And this is why the unhealthy relationship that Muslim fundamentalists groups such as ISIS have with their history is so problematic. For, not only does this reading apotheosize this history, thus retarding Muslim efforts to oppose autocracy in the name of Islam, it weakens Muslims' ability to resist the power and confidence wielded by those who actually enjoy the fruits of representative government. In effect, it renders the socio-political grass outside Islam always seductively greener than anything Muslims can boast or reasonably hope for in Muslim-majority lands. Thus, write Ibrahim and al-Najjar,

Right now, Barack Obama, sitting in his office in the White House in Washington, with his long legs stretched out over his desk, wearing his shiny black shoes, will be able to dismantle this so-called 'caliphate' with the greatest of ease, not with scud-missiles and drones but with the power that the high constitutional principles and values of *shari'ah* confer upon *any* people, even if they are not Muslims.[47]

Again, while ISIS is the direct object of this critique, it is aimed at Islamist movements overall. For, almost *all* of them, in the view of Ibrahim and al-Najjar, are blinded by their inflated estimation of violence and coercive power to the necessity of ingratiating their constituencies with the values, virtues, and possibilities of their religion, en route to establishing a mutually supportive relationship between the rulers and the ruled, Muslim and non-Muslim alike. This, they warn, will ultimately result in a population of hypocrites who thrive on dishonesty, duplicity, and facile opportunism as survival mechanisms, whose intentions are never pure but always provisional, and who come to love, hate, fear, envy, resent, and ultimately covet and cower to power and anyone associated with it. Here incidentally, in their own move to draw on the authority of pre-modern Muslim history, Ibrahim and al-Najjar invoke the reputed father of sociology Ibn Khaldun (d. 808/1406):

When political power is used in a manner that is overly domineering, abusive and quick to punish, constantly seeking to expose people's breaches and enumerate their sins, fear and humiliation invariably grip the people, and they in turn seek refuge in lying and deception, and their inner consciences are thoroughly compromised.[48]

In sum, the kind of "religious autocracy" embraced and promulgated by ISIS and other fundamentalist groups will ultimately result not only in dysfunctional states and a stillborn caliphate but also in a society of scarred and broken people. Feeble replicas of Adorno's "authoritarian personality," this will be a mass of bullies who are also easily bullied, men and women who are subservient not only to rightful guides and loyal superiors but to *anyone* who has, appears to have, or can promise more power than they have, and all of this, alas, perpetrated and legitimized in the name of Islam.

There is one final aspect of Ibrahim's and al-Najjar's critique that I would like to mention briefly, as it impinges directly on the matter of peaceful coexistence. As is known, ISIS espoused a certain apocalyptic vision connected with the Syrian town of *Dabiq*, after which it named its magazine. Ibrahim and al-Najjar do not refer to *Dabiq* directly but take up the general issue of apocalyptic statements attributed to the Prophet, as they see these as another way in which ISIS seeks not only to confer religious legitimacy upon the primacy of violence but to imbue ordinary Muslims and potential recruits with a sense of being religiously bound to support such commitments to blood-letting. Ibrahim's and al-Najjar's response is that, leaving aside the question of whether these reports from the Prophet are all reliable, there is a difference between what they refer to as a "*khitab shar'i*," or "divine injunction" and a *khitab qadari*," or a "divine report."[49] While a divine injunction requires Muslims to *act* in a manner that fulfills that injunction, a divine report requires nothing more than that Muslims *believe* in such reports.

Thus, for example, if the Prophet reports that the caliphate will be dismantled into petty kingdoms (*mulk ʿaḍḍ*), this does not require Muslims to contribute to such dismantling; it merely requires them to believe that this will ultimately occur.[50] In terms of their premeditated actions, divine injunctions may actually require Muslims to conduct themselves in a manner that forestalls or reverses such an inevitable occurrence. The same logic applies to end-of-time reports regarding apocalyptic confrontations between Muslims and non-Muslims. They do not dictate that the interim relationship between the two can only be one of violence.

All of this takes us back to a concern expressed by the *Gamaʿah* way back in 2002 in the Initiative to Stop the Violence. There they expressed deep anxieties about how the acceptance of violence as the exclusive Islamically authentic means for negotiating socio-political conflict can become entrenched to the point that it is raised beyond critique. They wrote,

> We fear that if matters persist as they are and the flames of vengeance continue to smolder in people's hearts that the matter will get out of hand, the tear in the fabric will expand beyond any mender's ability, and it will no longer fall within the capacity of anyone to return matters to their proper course. Similarly, we fear that the continuation of these confrontations will generate new misunderstandings that become normalized with the passing of time, to the point that those who hold such understandings, due to their long familiarity with them, come to believe that they are factually consistent with *shariʿah* and that there is nothing wrong with them. In fact, subsequent generations will come to receive these notions as if they were the very core and spirit of religion.[51]

There are other (in my view less salient) features of Ibrahim's and al-Najjar's critique that time will not permit me to cover. For example, more could be said about the role of sectarianism in ISIS's approach and the charge that ISIS is a godsend to Western powers who want to keep the Muslim world weak and divided. This actually goes back to an aspect of the *Gamaʿah's* self-critique in the late 1990s and early 2000s. At that time, they chided themselves over the fact that their fundamentalist activities kept the Egyptian state, the largest Arab Muslim regional power, turned in on its own internal problems, leaving Israel and the United States to romp about as they pleased.[52] Beyond this, there are a number of points on which one might want to challenge Ibrahim and al-Najjar, such as the sense they give that everything that led to the West's ascendancy was already there in Islam centuries earlier just waiting to be activated, or the impression they occasionally give that Muslim scripture totally devalues violence. Then there is the question of how exactly, i.e., on the basis of what restrictive principles, one is to go about the business of calibrating scriptural interpretations to changes in history. How far can such calibration go. In conclusion, however, again, given the limits of time, there are two final observations that I would like to register before I close.

The first is simply a reminder that, for all the pragmatism displayed in the analyses of Ibrahim and al-Najjar—indeed, by the *Gama'ah* as a whole—their critique is *fundamentally* based in a reading of *shari'ah*. In this regard, it does not differ in kind, even if it may in degree and detail, from critiques put forth by members of the official religious establishment. Perhaps the biggest difference is that *Gama'ah* members tend to take a more macro-approach as opposed to the more detail-oriented, casuistic, or micro-approach reflected, for example, in the *fatwa* of Shaykh Muhammad Ya'qubi or the joint letter sent to Abu Bakr al-Baghdadi by a group of Muslim scholars and clerics from around the world. Nevertheless, the *Gama'ah's* critique should give pause to those who tend to look upon *shari'ah*, or what has come to be known in the West as "*shari'ah*-law," as invariably contributing to the mentality of ISIS or other "extremists" and never fundamentally challenging this. Our authors demonstrate, in other words, that not only can principled critiques of the program and activities of the likes of ISIS come from liberals, secularists, or so-called progressives; they can also come from the pens of bearded men with deep fundamentalist commitments and strong attachments to *shari'ah*.

The second observation relates to the *moral* status of violence in the critique of Ibrahim and al-Najjar. While our authors are explicit in condemning violence on practical grounds, there seems to be little in the way of moral condemnation, i.e., violence as a moral evil that stands in the way of peace as a moral good. This is more a matter, however, of my particular presentation of their views. At several points and under several headings, they strongly and explicitly condemn ISIS's violence on moral grounds.[53] In fact, they insist that ISIS's violence not only violates Islam but the very norms of "manhood" (*rujulah*) and a "normative Arab sense of self" (*urubah*).[54] Indeed, they insist, such violence bespeaks, "a great rupture ... in the basic constitution of human mercy that should reside in the heart of *any* human being, let alone any Muslim, Sunni or Shiite."[55] But I have chosen not to place this moral critique front and center in an effort to avoid the risk of distorting the overall thrust of their message by allowing it to be overly informed by our Western obsession—especially post-9/11—with ISIS's viciousness and barbarity. In the West, we tend to focus on little more than ISIS's violence and intolerance. And in the Muslim community, this is often more for the purpose of distancing American Muslims from such behavior than it is out of any recognition of any broader aims and interests of Islam that might be obliterated thereby. From this vantage-point, it becomes easy for us to recognize critiques of ISIS's *violence* but more difficult to see much beyond this. By contrast, Ibrahim and al-Najjar seem to be saying that while violence is a problem, to be sure, there is *much* more to be considered beyond the question of violence. In fact, their message seems to be that, were ISIS to adopt or acquire a more comprehensive understanding of *shari'ah*, according to which ample attention and priority are assigned to such enterprises as culture, civilization, economics, and the development of political thought and institutions, the very *value* of their brand of violence would be drastically reduced even in their *own* eyes, as it would be seen as being far less relevant to Islam's long-term interests and the restoration of its place in the world. It may be, then, that by *our* focusing so supremely and exclusively on ISIS's and other Muslim extremist groups' violence, *we* may be actually closer to them in our thinking than we care to recognize. For, in maintaining such a focus, we may be ultimately saying that we see little wrong with ISIS other than its addiction to wanton physical cruelty. Clearly, however, going back to the cautionary note with which I began this chapter, this can easily set us up to become in our own context purveyors of a kind of peace for others that, while devoid of violence, falls painfully short of anything that we ourselves would recognize or accept as the foundation of a dignified existence.

Notes

1   As we read, e.g., in Matthew 10:34-35, "*Do not think that I have come to bring peace to the earth; I have not come to bring peace, but a sword. For I have come to set a man against his father, and a daughter against her mother, and a daughter-in-law against her mother-in-law; and one's foes will be members of one's own household." The New Oxford Annotated Bible* 3rd edn., ed. M.D. Coogan (New York: Oxford University Press, 2001), 22 New Testament.

2   R. Niebuhr, *Moral Man and Immoral Society* (New York: Charles Scribner's Sons, 1960), 139. The book was originally published in 1932.

3   See, e.g., Niebuhr, *Moral Man*, 172: "Gandhi's boycott of British cotton results in the undernourishment of children in Manchester, and the blockade of the Allies in wartime caused the death of German children."

4   As Edward Bernays, the reputed father of propaganda, observes: "The conscious and intelligent manipulation of the organized habits and opinions of the masses is an important element in democratic society. Those who manipulate this unseen mechanism of society constitute an invisible government which is the true ruling power of our country. We are governed, our minds molded, our tastes formed, our ideas suggested, largely by men we have never heard of." See his *Propaganda* (New York: Ig Publishing, 2005), 37.

5   Qur'an 2:191.

6   Elsewhere I have argued that Islam never produced a literalist canon. My point of departure, however, was the literalism that characterized Christian fundamentalism in the modern West. There, the insistence on a literalist reading of the Bible served as a dike around Christian doctrine to protect it from erosion. In such capacity, nonliteral readings were looked upon with deep suspicion, the "literal" being equated with the "true." My point was that Islam never developed *this* kind of literalist canon. It is true that Muslims recognized a genre of meaning that was independent of both the speaker and the hearer. But the legitimacy of abandoning such meanings was also recognized, assuming that this was grounded in recognized justifications. In sum, the thrust of my claim was aimed at the basic assumption that, when it comes to religion and scriptural interpretation, the literal meaning is always the true meaning and to

abandon it is to compromise or capitulate to non or anti-religious pressures. See, e.g., my "Literalism, Empiricism and Induction: Apprehending and Concretizing Islamic Law's *Maqasid al-Shari'ah* in the Modern World," *Michigan State Law Review*, no. 6 (2006): 1469–86 at 1474–6. See also, however, R. Gleave, *Islam and Literalism: Literal Meaning and Interpretation in Islamic Legal Theory* (Edinburgh: Edinburgh University Press, 2013), where he appears to challenge this view, noting that there were legal theorists who held the literal meaning to be the only meaning.

7   See K.M. Zuhdi et al., *Istratijiyah wa Tafjirat al-Qa'idah: al-Akhta' wa al-Akhtar Istratijiyat* (Al-Qa'idah's Strategy and Bombings: Mistakes and Dangers) (Cairo: Maktabat al-Turath al-Islami, 1424/2004), 36. This book was jointly authored by the formerly imprisoned leadership of Egypt's *al-Gama'ah al-Islamiyah* following its renunciation of political violence in 1997. See below.

8   *Istratijiyah*, 30.

9   This basic vision is clearly laid out in Faraj's manifesto, *al-Faridah al-gha'ibah (The Neglected Duty)*. While this work was of limited distribution, see N. Junaynah, *Tanzim al-jihad: hal huwa al-badilal-islami fi misr?* (Cairo: Dar al-Hurriyah li al-Sihafah q l-Tiba'ah wa al-Nashr, 1409/1988), 223–73 for a reproduction of the entire text in Arabic. For an English translation, see J.J.G. Jansen, *The Neglected Duty: The Creed of Sadat's Assassins and Islamic Resurgence in Egypt* (New York: Macmillan, 1986), 159–234. Jansen notes that several editions of the tract were published, not all of them congruent. His view (p. 3) is that the most reliable was that issued in 1984 by the Egyptian Ministry of Religious Endowments, which is what Junaynah apparently relied upon in her work. For a fuller treatment of Sadat's assassination and its aftermath, including the renunciation of political violence, see my *Initiative to Stop the Violence*; *Mubadarat Waqf al-'Unf: Sadat's Assassins and the Renunciation of Political Violence* (New Haven, CT: Yale University Press, 2015).

10 At one point or another, members of this amalgamation included such stalwarts as Ayman al-Zawahiri, Sayyid Imam (a.k.a. Dr. Fadl), and Muhammad al-Hukaymah, believed to be Abu Bakr Naji, pen-name of the author of the notorious tract, *Idarat al-Tawahhush (The Management of Savagery)* which many believe to be the operating manual of ISIS.

11 According to H. Bakri, between 1991 and 1994 alone, there were 1,119 deaths among innocent civilians, not counting police or *Gama'ah* members. See his *al-'Unf al-siyasi fi misr: asyut bu'rat al-tawattur al-asbab wa al-dawafi'* (Cairo: Markaz li al-Buhuth wa al-Tadrib wa al-Nashr, 1996), 127. The numbers vary from account to account. For more on this issue, see my *Initiative*, 130–1 nt. 34.

12 See my *Initiative*, 124–5, nt. 4

13 See my *Initiative*, 13.

14 These include: (1) *Mubadarat waqf al-"unf: ru'yah waqi'iyah wa nazrah shar'iyah* (Initiative to Stop the Violence: A Reality-Based Assessment and a Shari'ah-Based Approach); (2) *Taslit al-adwâ "alâ mâ waqa'a fi al-jihad min al-akhta"* (Shedding Light on the Mistakes That Have Befallen the Understanding of Jihad); (3) *al-Nush wa al-tabyin fi tashih mafahim al-muhtasibin* (Advice and Clarification to Correct Misunderstandings among Those Who Police Public Morals); (4) *Hurmat al-ghuluw fi al-din wa takfir al-muslimin* (The Impermissibility of Religious Extremism and of Declaring Fellow Muslims to be Infidels). See my *Initiative*, 51–56 for a full English translation of the first of these manifestos, *Mubadarat waqf al-'unf: ru'yah waqi'iyah wa nazrah shar'iyah*.

15 *Initiative*, 27–32.

16 See M.M. Ahmad, *Mu'amarah am muraja'ah: hiwar ma'a qadat al-tatarruf fi sijn al-aqrab* 2nd edn. (Cairo: Dar al-Shuruq, 423/2003), 118.

17 See their *Taslit al-adwa' "ala ma waqa'a fi al-jihad min al-akhta"* (Cairo: Maktabt al-Turath al-Islami, 2002), 3.

18 *Taslit*, 3.

19 Ibid., 3–4.

20 This is especially so with contending *groups* as opposed to quarreling *individuals*. As Niebuhr observed, "It may be possible, though it is never easy to say, to establish just relations between individuals within a group purely by moral and rational suasion and accommodation. In inter-group relations this is practically an impossibility. The relations between groups must therefore always be predominantly political rather than ethical, that is, they will be determined by the proportion of power which each group possesses at least as much by any rational and moral appraisal of the comparative needs and claims of each group." See *Moral Man*, xxii–xxiii.

21 See Ibn Khaldun, *Muqadimmat al-'allamah ibn khaldun*, ed. H. 'Asi (Beirut: Dar wa Maktabat Hilal, 1986), 101.

22 Indeed, they insist, "jihad is a duty that will remain valid until the Day of Judgment; but it is a duty that is governed by rules and parameters (*dawabit*) that must be observed to ensure its proper execution." See *Istratijiyah*, 17.

23 See note 7 above.

24 Ibid., 33, 67.

25 Ibid., 66–7.

26 Ibid., 85.

27 In fact, Tariq al-Zumar, who played a pivotal role in bringing together the coalition *Jihad Inc.* back in the 1980s, formally joined the *Gama'ah* in prison in 1991 and was released from prison in 2011 (long after he had served his formal sentence), would come to recognize nonviolence (*al-'amal al-silmi*) as a form of strategic power and "among the most important means of advancing the Islamic awakening." See his *Muraja'at la taraju'at* (Cairo: Dar Misr al-Mahrusah, 2008), 30.

28 See P.L. Berger, *The Sacred Canopy: Elements of a Sociological Theory of Religion* (New York: Anchor Books, 1967), 110–13. By plausibility structure, Berger is referring inter alia, to early modern Protestantism's significant success in stripping the world of mystical and super-natural elements that undergirded the meaningfulness of Christianity (and religion in general) in the pre-modern world. The degradation of the plausibility structure has in turn sapped religion's ability to sustain its relevance in the modern world, spawning the rise and diffusion of a secular (i.e., non-religious) worldview.

29 Yusuf al-Qaradawi, *Fiqh al-jihad*, 2 vols. (Cairo: Maktabat Wahba, 1430/2009), 1: 402–3.

30 2nd edn. (Cairo: Dar al-Shuruq, 2015).

31 *Da'ish*, 15.

32 Ibid., 19, 58, 111.

33 Ibid., 47.

34 Ibid., 48.

35 Ibid., 47, 61.

36 Ibid., 46.

37 Ibid., 18, 59.

38 Ibid., 47.

39 Ibid., 48.

40   Ibid., 78.
41   Ibid., 79.
42   Ibid.
43   Ibid., 96.
44   Ibid., 98.
45   Ibid., 99.
46   Ibid., 109.
47   Ibid.
48   Ibid., 140–1.
49   Ibid., 91.
50   Ibid., 91–3.
51   See my *Initiative*, 79–80.
52   *Initiative*, 72–4.
53   At one point, for example, they affirm that taking human life, including non-Muslim life, is an evil or harm (*mafsadah*) that can only be tolerated in the face of a higher benefit. See *Taslit*, 18.
54   *Da'ish*, 51.
55   Ibid., 53.

10 WOMEN, RELIGION, AND PEACE LEADERSHIP IN BOSNIA AND HERZEGOVINA

Zilka Spahić Šiljak

Moral leadership has to do with finding a way for oneself,
pointing a way for others. (Robert Coles)

Bosnia and Herzegovina is a post-war, post-socialist, and ethnically divided country.[*] The war (1992–5) long since ended, but ethnically divided citizens still struggle to live peacefully. Negative peace, in terms of the absence of war, is achieved but with unviable state institutions and ethnic divisions imposed by the Constitution, which was drafted in Dayton in 1995. The constitutional framework of Bosnia and Herzegovina imposes and reifies ethnic divisions. Furthermore, the ethno-nationalist political parties have not done much to make the changes necessary to improve the social and economic wellbeing of their impoverished and anguished people.

Positive peace, in terms of restoration of individual relationships, the creation of social systems that serve the needs of the whole population and the constructive resolution of conflict, is incredibly fragile and compartmentalized among the different organizations and groups that have been striving to bring normalcy in daily life. These organizations work to heal the physical and spiritual traumas of war. They attempt to re-knit the fragile web of interethnic and interreligious solidarity in Bosnia and Herzegovina. However, most of them work in virtual isolation from the state. Civil society organizations, which focused on peace and interethnic reconciliation in Bosnia and Herzegovina, have primarily been supported by international donors.[1] The Bosnia and Herzegovina state has shown little interest in supporting these organizations and has occasionally actively blocked their efforts.

Yugoslavia was a multiethnic country that emerged from the old Austro-Hungarian Empire. Initially a constitutional monarchy, it was invaded and ruled by the Axis during the Second World War. In 1946, the Communist Party took power, but it fell in 1989. In 1990–2, the country broke up into smaller nations on an ethnic basis, including Croatia, Bosnia and Herzegovina, and Serbia-Montenegro, though the latter made expansionist claims under nationalist authoritarian Slobodan Milosevic. In 1992–5, a massive civil war broke out in the multiethnic state of Bosnia and Herzegovina, in which the new countries intervened, which largely targeted Muslim Bosniaks, in which a hundred thousand were murdered and some 2 million were displaced from their homes. It was the most sanguinary fighting seen in Europe since the end of the Second World War, with a genocide in Srebrenica in 1995 that left 8,000 Bosniak Muslims dead.

In the midst of this horror and devastation, women from all ethnic groups devoted themselves to peacebuilding and were the first ones to cross the ethnic borders and gender boundaries imposed by the newly ethno-nationalistic regimes in these countries. Women have been and continue to be in the forefront of peacebuilding activities in local communities. They were among the first to establish civil society organizations and to initiate the promotion of women's human rights, minority rights, peacebuilding, and reconciliation during and after the war, from 1992 forward. Some of them started working in the midst of terror and destruction to make life easier for those who were marginalized and oppressed.[2] Peace scholars emphasize that peace starts at the same moment as conflict.[3] Some very courageous women of different ethnic, religious, and nonreligious backgrounds initiated peace activities to protect their friends, neighbors, and fellow citizens during the war. These same women continued this peacebuilding work after the war in more formal ways, often by joining the nongovernmental sector.

In this chapter, I will first contextualize the role of religion in peacebuilding in post-war Bosnia and Herzegovina. Then I will discuss the key religious teachings that motivated some women to become activists and leaders. Finally, the chapter considers how religious women understand peace leadership and how they perceive themselves as leaders. I argue that religion was not a conversation starter in the first civic and peacebuilding initiatives in Bosnia and Herzegovina, and that religious women who ran in nongovernmental organizations, including the three women I interviewed, started to appeal more explicitly to religion in peacebuilding in the last decade. I also argue that only a few women's organizations have a clear faith-based agendas and programs, while all others operate as secular organizations, employing religion as one argument for peacebuilding. For the purposes of this chapter, I conducted semi-structured interviews with three prominent religious women from two civil society organizations in Sarajevo and one in Bosansko Grahovo. After my research on women and peacebuilding in Bosnia and Herzegovina, which clearly shows that religion was not a conversation-starter in the first civic initiatives in peacebuilding and reconciliation,[4] I decided to interview a few religious women who deploy religion as one of their arguments for peacebuilding, or as the central such argument. I then explore more closely the intersection of faith, activism, and leadership. All three organizations run by the women work on peacebuilding, but the profiles of their organizations differ.

Small Steps

Amra Pandžo is a Muslim woman who runs the faith-based peacebuilding organization "Small Steps," in Sarajevo. She is an observant Muslim woman without formal theological education and like the majority of Muslim women in Bosnia and Herzegovina she does not wear hijab nor find it crucial to her faith.[5] Her faith is one of the most important motivating factors in her peace work and she started her organization to use Islam as a tool in peacebuilding.

Sehija Dedović is an observant Muslim woman with formal theological education and she does wear hijab, which she explains as a sign of her personal piety and choice, which is similar to other hijabi women in Bosnia and Herzegovina.[6] She leads the woman's organization "Nahla" (which means "bee" in Arabic), which she did not portray as religious or Islamic, but as a civil society organization inspired by the teachings of Islam. Sehija clarified that although Nahla was inspired by religion, they started using a faith-based notion after 2004, when that concept became more familiar in the Bosnia and Herzegovina context. Nahla is open to all women, but draws mostly Muslim women with and without hijab, which reflects the current population in cities where they work. Sehija underlines the interreligious openness of her organization and the availability of their programs to all women while some specific religious programs are designed primarily for Muslim women.

Danka Zelić, a Catholic woman, is a leader of the woman's association "UG Grahovo." She is a former police officer and agronomist who dedicated her life to the reconciliation of her neighbors. She is an observant believer, but she does not portray her organization as faith-based, rather as a secular organization that sometimes organizes faith-based activities and interreligious encounters. She uses religion as a tool in peacebuilding, not as the key argument.

Religion in Peacebuilding

The ambivalent ability of religion to divide and reconcile, to destroy and heal, to imprison and liberate has produced ambivalent feelings about the role of religion in the public realm both among nonbelievers and believers.[7] Many believers were aware of the politicization of religion during and after the war by ethno-national elites; therefore, most of them have been cautious to use it for peacebuilding initiatives and thus distanced their first civic initiatives from religion.

Religion is an important part of ethnic/national identity in the Balkan region for all three major ethnic groups. Croats tend to be Catholic, Bosnians Muslim, and Serbs Eastern Orthodox Christians. Since religion and other forms of ethnicity overlap, it is sometimes hard to view religious actors as neutral when the ethnic groups come into conflict. Only when they emphasize core common values, such as social justice, compassion, empathy, forgiveness, and reconciliation, are they able to transcend ethno-national divisions.[8]

After religion had been marginalized in public life during socialist Yugoslavia, the religious revivalism of the 1980s brought hope to many that they would in future freely practice religion without being ostracized or marked as backward. However, the coalescence of ethnicity and religion at the beginning of 1990s resulted in the harsh reality of the war in which religion was used as a tool in the empowerment of ethno-national agendas and goals and to increase distance among the three ethnic groups.

Scholarship in the last two decades about the Balkan region shows an enormous politicization of religion,[9] and the nationalization of religion and God that reduced religions to mere nationalized symbols that celebrate a God who loves and prefers one nation over others and who assists in others' defeat.[10] Some religious authorities went so far as to bless warring activities that resulted in persecution and killing and most were silent about crimes committed in the name of their ethnic and religious groups. As Clark found in her research in Bosnia and Herzegovina, denial was present everywhere and the most prevalent was "interpretive denial," which means that people denied the facts, even assigning them different meanings and sometimes replacing facts with myths as counter-memory—for instance, how the ethnic group suffered in the Second World War.[11] Mitja Velikonja has described the role of religious communities as antagonizing and confronting rather than inclined to peace and reconciliation.[12]

The lack of an open and honest approach to suffering and victimhood by the highest religious authorities has distanced many from institutionalized religions, but not necessarily from religions per se, as the spiritual and ethical foundations of their lives. Another reason why religious leaders were not more involved in peacebuilding was a lack of human resources in religious communities to undertake peacebuilding activities and also a lack of understanding of peacebuilding and reconciliation concepts in general. Clark presents an example from her research, when one Orthodox Christian priest in Sarajevo said that there "are no mechanisms that can alter time and make people to forgive and forget. They can only give people faith."[13] But having in mind the authority they enjoy and the relevance of their work, they can do more than giving faith; they can do what Appleby concludes: build coalitions across ethnic and religious and nonreligious lines and invest time to "channel the militancy of religion in the direction of the disciplined pursuit of justice and nonviolent resistance to extremism."[14] For

Appleby, peacebuilding is a comprehensive process, which entails collaboration and the involvement of different actors, both religious and nonreligious; and since religion is often used to justify warfare, it should be used also to build peace and heal wounds.

However, there is a different dynamic between the clergy at the highest level and the clergy in local communities in terms of possibilities for action. John Paul Lederach distinguishes the role of highest religious leadership from local religious leaders, because religious leaders "are generally locked into positions taken with regard to the perspectives and issues in conflict.[15] They are under tremendous pressure to maintain a position of strength vis-à-vis their adversaries and their own constituencies." While local leaders have more freedom for interaction and collaboration, their voices are not heard, nor strong enough to bring about more profound change.[16] Their own communities very often oppress them, as Paul Mojzes found in his research, because they go against the nationalists.[17]

With all the obstacles mentioned above, religion still remains as powerful source for peacebuilding and reconciliation. It gives meaning, identity, and spiritual strength to believers who are thereby more resilient and confident in facing adversaries. Religious institutions for many believers are still trustworthy authorities and the credibility they have can be used to overcome divisions and bring people together around common causes in local communities. However, as the three religious women from Bosnia and Herzegovina show, not everything is up to the religious leadership; believers also can initiate and act as agents, inviting religious communities into partnership. I therefore decided to interview local women leaders who are religious and who use religion as an argument for peacebuilding. However, these women also collaborate with religious leaders and faith communities because they know how much authority these institutions still have for many in Bosnia and Herzegovina.

Religious Women and Peacebuilding

Important things to explore in this research were: the understanding of peacebuilding among religious women, how they reflect on their peace work, and how it is linked with religion. As mentioned earlier, women in Bosnia and Herzegovina have been engaged in peace initiatives mostly within secular, local nongovernmental organizations. At the beginning of their work they were inspired to do something for their neighbors, friends, and those less privileged or excluded from society. One of the peacebuilders in the book *Shining Humanity* described the beginning of her work as merely a desire to bring people back together and to rebuild destroyed houses: "We did not know what projects were ....For us projects were like literally building a house."[18] As such, women tend to use a broad definition of peacebuilding that includes various kinds of activities, such as psycho-social therapy, the protection of wartime rape survivors and survivors of other gender-based violence, conflict resolution and conflict transformation, peace education, humanitarian aid, the empowerment of women in politics, and any action that would bring one human being closer to another human being and reconcile neighbor with neighbor.

For some of the women whom I interviewed, peacebuilding is not work; rather it is a life calling. For example, Amra Pandžo does not divide her life into private and professional spheres; she is not a peace worker in the office and a mother in the home. Amra does not believe that it is possible to divide her life into these two halves because peacebuilding is not merely a profession; it is her identity and her way of being in the world, her "vocation" as she calls it. She emphasized this at the very beginning of our conversation to underline the importance of peacebuilding, which is usually a hard profession to grasp. One of the world's greatest contemporary peacebuilders, Pope John Paul explained the same conundrum: "When I say I work in support of conciliation processes, it is rarely sufficient to give people a sense of what I do."[19] Amra is faced with the same questions and inquiries to clarify what exactly she does professionally.

Sehija, like Amra, does not describe her activism as something separate from her being, her life and her work, because her understanding of Islam requires searching first for an inner peace which should be reflected in her actions, her relationships with people, and convictions. Many Muslims do not separate their lives into religious and secular spheres and living Islam as a path, a way, they tend to be fully involved and present as believers with consciousness of God's presence.[20] When I asked her when she started peacebuilding, Sehija told me that all of her work was peace work, and that peace is an inseparable part of what it means to be a Muslim. However, she said that after 2004, her organization began to formally use the language of faith-based peacebuilding initiatives, although their work from the beginning was inspired by faith.

Danka Zelić does not formally elevate her peace work to a life calling, although everything she has been doing is indispensably related to both her private and professional lives as a human rights activist and conciliator. She also does not perceive her peacebuilding as a career or profession, because she does not separate her life from the destiny of the people with whom she works, which is primarily a returnee population in western Bosnia and Herzegovina. For her, peace is about proper communication and building relationships between people. Peace is repairing broken friendships and mending torn families. Peace is learning how to build trust among neighbors because sustainable relationships require trust. These three women as well as many other activists whom I have interviewed were not aware of the academic theories about peace, feminism, and gender equality when they started their work. They were not concerned with naming and theorizing, because they did what they thought was right to make life easier for people who suffered and to answer their immediate needs. Later, when they started attending various educational seminars and training sessions, they learnt that their work falls under the theoretical category of "peacebuilding" in the broadest sense. However, in the beginning their approaches were genuinely grassroots—do it first, theorize about it later. All of them are women of action.

Sehija, for instance, elaborated that upon her return to Bosnia and Herzegovina after the war, she was searching for something she could do to help women, primarily religious women whose concerns and needs were overlooked by existing secular NGOs as well as different Islamic organizations. She found that Muslim women tended to be marginalized and reduced to some sectors and logistical activities. They were passive members of these organizations, waiting for men to offer them some role within these predominantly male organizations:

> I understood that the empty space was the space for women … I saw that various organizations—humanitarian, educational, and religious—employed similar methods in terms of marginalizing their female members … they decided what they would do with women in their annual plans … I was unhappy being perceived as a marginal part of these organizations … and I thought that many women would also be unhappy, and that we needed to offer a kind of alternative to that.

She did not want to replicate the work of numerous organizations in Bosnia and Herzegovina, but to offer something that was missing in the tapestry of women's organizational work—to provide a kind of sanctuary and safe space for Muslim women, but also for other women to be accepted and recognized with their full religious and nonreligious identities and needs intact.

Amra was engaged in secular organizations right after the war, but she also noticed that something was missing—a faith-based approach to peacebuilding— therefore she decided to start Small Steps, an organization that gathers volunteers and not professional peacebuilders. She wanted to bring up an important argument of religion in peacebuilding but also to deconstruct the media image of Islam, which is of terrorism, oppression, and backwardness.

Danka's work found her when she started her new career as a police officer in Bosansko Grahovo. When she peered into the faces of her returnee Serb neighbors she could no longer follow the dictates of politics and government, but she succumbed to the dictate of her heart—she decided to help returnees and over time she quit her job in the police in order to fully engage with peacebuilding and reconciliation work.

All three peacebuilders recognized the needs of their communities and begin to work what they found themselves relevant and useful. They created small islands of peace everywhere they worked and contributed to building a culture of peace that remains fragile and underdeveloped because different social actors have to fulfill their roles and are being obstacles for peace and reconciliation.

Religious Motivation?

What is the role of religion in the peacebuilding work of these three women? How did religion inspire them and what are the key teachings in their traditions that guide their lives?

Amra, Sehija, and Danka have different experiences and social settings in which they operated, but religions have remained important parts of their identities, worldviews, and work. While Amra approaches peace work exclusively from a religious perspective, Sehija, although primarily inspired by religion, does not portray her organization that way because it offers a variety of programs, faith-based and not. And as previously mentioned, Danka's religiosity is not her main motivation for engaging in peacebuilding. Amra and Danka did not refer to religion at the beginnings of their activism because it was not the right time to raise religious arguments, so they approached it first and foremost as humanists who were willing to help their fellow neighbors and citizens. Both emphasized listening and recognizing every voice.

I have already mentioned some of reasons for this exclusion of religious arguments, such as the politicization and nationalization of religion. However, I would like to discuss more what teachings in their faiths motivated them to become activists and how these teachings shape their worldviews and ethical values.

As an observant Muslim woman who wears hijab, with her faith as an inseparable part of her life and work, Sehija was committed to serve her community and her country with the knowledge and skills she gained in several countries where she studied. She wanted to help women, especially Bosnian Muslim women who have not had space for activism within the regular structures of the Islamic community and Islamic organizations. When she finally founded Nahla, her primary goal was to offer a space for women where they could come, learn, grow, and help each other to be better human beings as well as to provide support and comfort for each other.

Nahla is registered as a secular civil society organization for educating women, inspired by religion. At first it was intriguing why a Muslim woman wearing hijab established an organization that primarily gathers Muslim women but does not call itself a religious organization. The answer lies in Sehija's understanding of her faith and the role of religion in public life. She makes a clear differentiation between religious organizations established under the special Law on Freedom of

Religion and the Legal Position of Churches and Religious Communities (2004) and organizations inspired by faith.

As a believer and observant Muslim woman, she does not find it necessary to emphasize the religious roots of her organization, because everything they do, as she explains it, they do as responsible believers and human beings for the benefit of women, families, and society. Being a responsible believer for Sehija means being first and foremost an accountable human being. The two should go hand in hand, and as a Muslim, she runs her entire life according to her faith and the key principles of Islam; therefore, she does not divide her life and work into religious and nonreligious compartments. Her motto for activism is derived from the Qur'anic teaching: "Act! And God will behold your deeds, and [so will] His Apostle, and the believers" (Qur'an 9:105).

Sehija is particularly inspired in this work by the Islamic principle of *ihsan* (doing good), which means that a Muslim should strive for excellence, kindness, and compassion in all actions and interactions. For Sehija, *ihsan* is the highest state of faith, and she is striving to attain that level. In her explanation of *ihsan*, she notes that honoring contractual obligations is an important part of her faith. According to Sehija, one cannot be a true believer if he or she violates contracts. *Ihsan* means full accountability, both before people and before God, because believers are conscious of God's presence in every moment of their lives (*taqwa*). With this intellectual and spiritual approach to her faith, Sehija did not feel it necessary to distinguish peacebuilding as something separate. She believes that being a righteous, accountable, and compassionate Muslim consequently means being a conciliator—somebody who practically lives peace with every breath and step she takes. This is, however, a very high standard for most believers who usually do not reflect upon their faith in this way, but Sehija does no less than that—to seek to attain a state of tranquility and peace inside her heart, which will be reflected in everything she does.

Amra's entire work is faith-based; religion is the prime motivator of all of her actions. She finds it important and relevant to emphasize the religious roots of her activism because, as she explained,

> the [Bosnian] civil sector was separated from anything that was this ethno-national mainstream. In other words, these were the organizations that mostly inherited some of the socialist and communist and atheist ideas. Everything related to nationalism or, God forbid, religiosity was removed from civil society.[21]

However, by religion she does not mean a rigid scripturalism or an unthinking adherence to ritual, although she observes Islam's main rituals (*fard*). Rather, for Amra, religion means conscious prayers and the ethical principles of honesty, kindness, and justice that help her to reflect God's love and spirit in her peace work. Unlike Sehija, she does not explicitly mention the concept of *ihsan*, but everything she strives toward is to attain that state of being—balance and peace with God and people. Being exposed to the various of teachings of Islam, she has come to understand that the principles of her faith should not be wrapped into strict rules for the sake of rules; for Amra only an open heart can reflect mercy toward people. Dialogue is therefore the best channel to open the heart to others and to act out of love. Love is the greatest gift for Amra, and she thinks that only those who manage to encounter life with recognition for the needs of other human beings will reach fulfillment and happiness:

> The key issue for peace for me is love and … [being] able to love, because the happiness of other human beings is important to you. Love is crucial because today many are restless and the reason for this restlessness is that modern civilization makes us turn the reflector [searchlight] away from ourselves. It encourages us to think only about our own needs and wishes … and we became lost in this self-analysis, and we become unhappy …. Therefore, spiritual hygiene is important … a spiritual life encourages us to look around us, and to value the needs of others as highly as we honor our own needs. Only in this way, with this paradigm, can peace come about.

Amra also mentioned the human heart, which is, according to a famous hadith of the Prophet Muhammad, the most important temple: "It is a lesser sin to break the Ka'ba than it is to break a human heart." Driven by these principles, she is determined to take untold risks and to go into the unknown in order to attain peace. Amra wants all voices to be heard, because every voice is a sign of God's creation; to neglect or exclude the different or the marginalized is to deny a part of God's creation. This approach to religion inclines toward a Sufi understanding of faith that is not restricted to mosques and holy sites. As Amra explained, the holiest site is one's heart, which is the beginning and the end of everything.

Although Danka does not use religion as the key argument in her peace work, a critical foundation of her work is the Bible and its Ten Commandments alongside compatible secular humanist values and norms, because serving her fellow human beings for her means serving God. She specifically mentioned the relevance of the messages of Jesus Christ, who showed the path for all people:

> We should all be equal, we should respect each other regardless … we should not envy, but rather strive to be of help and to appreciate the good qualities that people have … We should live our own lives the way Jesus preached and recommended and not interfere in the lives of others unless we want to help them. If we cannot be of help, we should at least try to not cause pain or distress!

Danka's motivation for peacebuilding comes from the Christian teaching that one must act in the service of others because God is watching. Danka believes that she should give if she wants to receive and in that dialectic of giving and receiving she creates moments of happiness and peace. She does not use religious vocabulary to explain this, but moments of happiness and peace are moments of spiritual experience that are sometimes hard to explain with words.

All three women seek to live what their faiths teach and preach and they are determined to do their work and not so much to explain why they do it, on which premises and with which motivation.

Understanding Leadership

The next issue explored was leadership: how do these women understand leadership, do they consider themselves leaders, and did they become leaders by choice or by accident? In the past couple of decades, many studies were conducted suggesting different models of leadership: "command-control type," "heroic" leadership, and "transformative" or "collaborative" styles. At first, leadership studies emphasized the qualities and traits of the so-called great man, a "born" leader and with an innate capacity and talent for leadership. Over time, organizations have moved from this trait-centered approach to more inclusive and collaborative leadership styles. Assertiveness, authoritativeness, and decisiveness were once characteristics assigned to men, while care, compassion, and collaboration were assigned to women. This binary assignation of traits is rife with errors and unnecessary essentialization and can be as harmful to women as a total denigration of their leadership abilities.

Therefore, in order to avoid the intellectual straitjacket of gender binaries, we need to approach women and their leadership styles with flexible, open, and contextualized lenses. Leadership is always contextualized, and as Jean Lau Chin says, "we need to examine the contexts in which they lead. Behaviour occurs within a context and is influenced by the power relationships among the participants."[22] The context of Bosnia and Herzegovina is very complex, and in the process of transition between two differing social, economic, and political systems in the last two decades, women have experienced a "re-traditionalization" of gender roles. Women were faced with the challenge of positioning themselves between and within the competing discourses of local cultural and religious traditions, Marxist socialist values, and neoliberal capitalist values wrapped up in the democratization process.

Given this complicated context, it should be of little surprise that the three women whom I interviewed had a complex and often ambiguous understanding of their own relationship to leadership. For example, Danka explained to me that she did not plan to become a leader. It happened spontaneously over time. Because she trains other women to use their leadership skills, she considers herself a leader, but she also views this term with doubt and uncertainty. She admitted to me, "Somehow,

I always think that everything has happened spontaneously with me." As she worked with other peacebuilders, over time she appeared to be somebody who was trusted and perceived by her colleagues as leader. She set moral example for her colleagues and friends, and they trust her. As Robert Coles explains: "A leader is someone who knows how to persuade others to keep others company, to stand for what she believes in, the good, the one hundred percent right thing to do."[23]

Sehija also depicted her leadership as something spontaneous. She became a leader over time, with the growth of her organization. However, she has reservations about the use of the term "leader" when describing her work with Nahla.

> As a leader, if I may call myself that ... [is] somebody who leads with something in a certain moment. Actually I work and try to show by my own example how something should be done ... but I also leave enough space for everyone in her/his own domain of responsibility.

Her moral leadership is recognized by women in Nahla and more broadly because she has stood firmly for what she believes and she encouraged others to join her in work for the cause of peace.

Whereas Amra is the leader of Small Steps, her understanding of leadership is more oriented toward facilitation and collaboration. She does not like the word leader, particularly because its translation into Bosnian (*voða*) resonates for her with bolshevist images of a dictator and strong (patriarchal) hierarchy. She would prefer to be a facilitator:

> If a leader is a person that affects somebody's life and is able to lead him/her from one to another moment of life then I am a leader, but this means that every one of us is a leader in certain moments of our lives. When I say leader, somehow I think more in terms of a structural system led by somebody.

Amra believes that women exercise leadership every day, but that they are not aware of this because many associate leadership with (male) authority and power in public life. Similarly as Robert Coles points out: "leadership isn't only something in you, in a person—your personality; leadership depends on where you are as much as who you are, and it depends on the company you're keeping."[24] Therefore, Amra understands her role more as a facilitator of the process and flow of actions and reactions between parties and groups.

Although all three women can be described as prominent leaders of their organizations for at least a decade, all of them claim that they had no ambitions toward leadership as such, and were not formally trained for leadership roles. Their assumption of these roles occurred spontaneously. Regardless, these women had the vision, courage, and faith to act within their communities, which distinguishes them as leaders, notwithstanding how they themselves understand their leadership roles and whether they like the term.

Leadership Styles

Even though all three women spoke about spontaneous leadership and that they have never planned to be leaders nor had formal training for that role, they did elaborate on the leadership traits of women and men and even essentialized female leadership qualities.

The leadership traits that these three peacebuilders exhibit can be explained with the IDEA-based leadership model developed by Mary Lou Decosterd (2013). In this leadership model, the key traits are intuition, orientation, directive force, empowering intent, and assimilative nature and they stem from the traditional socialization of women as the "caring" sex. Intuition is about looking at life with vision and embracing the whole picture instead of just a piece of it; directive force refers to an innovative spirit that can get the task done while focusing on the outcome; empowerment means giving authority to make others more confident; assimilation is about bringing people together in constructive ways as well as transforming situations in the sense of solving conflicts. Both males and females, however, can learn and use these key traits effectively with proper education and socialization.

The peacebuilders interviewed spoke from a background of patriarchal socialization in Bosnia and Herzegovina with certain expectations about both sexes as well as an emphasis on femininity and feminine traits. Regine Birite clarifies that "the feminine presence also stems from women's greatest weakness, their long exile from positions of authority inside mainstream institutions."[25] All of them, however, reject winning and losing paradigms, and they rather refer to collaboration, listening, and understanding—qualities that are taken as weak in traditional, male-dominated leadership. They were not ashamed to show vulnerability. They sometime risk their lives and their security, but not out of fear, but from love, compassion, and care, especially for those who have suffered or need help.

These women's work includes challenging the existing norms, family traditions, and local authorities that discriminate against minorities and oppose reconciliation. Danka, for instance, peacefully challenged the local authorities in Bosansko Grahovo who were against the return of Serb refugees. To overcome fear and stand for the needs and dignity of other human beings one needs courage and vision. Katherine Martin (2010, loc. 200–3) adds that "it takes far more courage to challenge unjust authority without violence than it takes to kill all the monsters in all the stories told to children about the meaning of bravery."

Amra and Danka clearly bring their feminist identities into their peace work, with IDEA leadership traits, because they are determined to empower women and to give them a voice. Sehija does not use feminism as her identity or discourse, but her entire work and activism fall under that category because she is also determined to empower women and to stand for equality, equity, and justice. In responding to my question about their leadership styles, Danka describes herself as a democratic and collaborative leader. This is clearly a feminist leadership style because, as Decosterd explains, "feminist leaders do not want to reproduce oppressive hierarchies by exerting command-and-control leadership over subordinate groups. Therefore, democratic, web like, collaborative relationships seem more attractive than autocratic, hierarchical relationships."[26] Danka mentioned that her colleagues expect her to make final decisions so she tends to consult others: "I want to hear other opinions, and for me it is important to make just and good decision, and to be sure that we will have benefits from that decision." She believes that leaders are made, not born. In the context of Bosnia and Herzegovina, leadership traditionally connotes patriarchy and male-led dictatorships. Danka suggests that women should develop counter-spheres of power and leadership:

> Women in leadership positions have to find different ways of work …. Women do it differently … we engage in a kind of democratic leadership in which everybody is involved, where the majority makes decisions and the leader on the top is there to give some guidelines and to enable all opinions and voices to be heard.

Danka attributes some of the reasons why women tend to be more collaborative, open, and focused on communication and networking to a feminine disdain for the trappings of wealth and power. She says: "A woman does not value economic power as the most important thing in her life, but rather peace, love, respect and appreciation. If a woman wanted something else, she would probably struggle to get paid for jobs she does in her home." Danka tends to essentialize some of these qualities based on the innate biological characteristics of women because, as she explains, some of the psychological and neuro-scientific research confirms that women use the left and right parts of the brain simultaneously. Therefore, as she explains, they are better at multi-tasking in communication than their male counterparts. Furthermore, Danka believes that these neural differences only underscore the different ways that men and women are socialized within patriarchy. Women are taught to take care of the family and men are taught to be leaders and to prove themselves in front of other men and women: "Men do not deal so much with problems as women do. Men are preoccupied with goals and results and to promote their work, while women first and foremost think about needs and how to help somebody." All of these factors, according to Danka, make women subtler and more oriented to the needs of people than to acquiring power.

Similarly, Sehija essentializes female qualities and differentiates women from men in their approaches to life, war, stability, and peace: "They [men] react faster and in a hurry, and do not take consequences into account. A woman cares much more about everything that comes after an action, because war will stop one day and life will start from the beginning." For Sehija, women are more instinctually driven than men, especially toward safety, which may be related to their role in child rearing. She also mentioned another important reason why women tend to work more for peace: women are often the first victims of war and conflict, often in circumstance which they had no hand in creating and no power in choosing. For Sehija, this suffering makes woman more inclined to peace and more focused on life-affirming activities and ideas. She expressed that women, perhaps more than men, are aware that war causes suffering and pain, loss and fear, and they know that war can cripple future generations. Men, on the other hand, she thinks, seem to care much less about the pain and suffering that their actions will inflict upon often innocent bodies. Instead, they tend to concern themselves with "big goals," "strategies," and winning against all odds. Sehija concluded by saying she would rather have a female leader in situations at the edge of conflict: "I would rather choose a woman, because she will try all recipes before war and to prevent war." But, as mentioned earlier, leadership is situational and contextual, and while a woman might want to try all other solutions before war, her decision may depend on what the majority around her say, and the majority in leadership are males.

Amra joins these two in essentializing gender differences. Her criticism of men, however, is even more trenchant. She is particularly bitter about those men who have a moral double standard: in public they claim to be egalitarian and inclusive, but reinforce patriarchal familial relations in their homes.

> I have not seen this same inconsistency in women. If she is a 'bitch' and does not have family and children and decides to dedicate herself to a career to be the manager of a big company, she is fully into that, and you know what to expect from her. There is no hypocrisy and boxes in which she functions, adjusting herself to situations.

However, Amra is also aware that the hardships of being a woman in a man's world can make women cruel. She thinks that women work hard to succeed in a world where the deck is stacked against them, and the emotionally exhausting struggle can drain women of their compassion and empathy. This emotional exhaustion is one of the reasons that Amra is ambivalent about expanding the role of women in leadership position in politics: in the greedy and exploitative current system (created by men and for men) it is not fair that women should suffer all of the burdens of both power and powerlessness, and at the same time share none of the rewards.

Conclusion

Amra, Sehija, and Danka are the faces of a new type of female (and occasionally feminist) leadership, particularly in the arena of peacebuilding. Informed by their similar goals, occupations, and cultural and historical contexts, each woman nevertheless has a unique understanding of her own relationship to leadership and femininity. All three are religious women and follow the ethics and dictates of their faith, but their religiosity in peacebuilding is reflected in different ways, either as the key argument for peace (Amra), or one of the arguments (Danka), or without emphasis of religious identity as something separate from her life and work (Sehija).

Although all three peacebuilders exhibit a discomfort with the term "leader," given that it connotes patriarchy and dictatorship, each woman is unquestionably a leader in the post-war Bosnia and Herzegovina peace movement. Their femininities are inseparable parts of their leadership styles; for Amra, Sehija, and Danka, female leaders are more compassionate, group-oriented, better communicators, and are unwilling to sacrifice their moral principles for success. For these women, female leadership in post-war Bosnia and Herzegovina, but also in the world at large, offers a viable alternative to the patriarchies of the past, which have led us mostly into war and destruction.

The three peacebuilders rely on essentialist notions of gender in order to explain their understanding of female leadership: women are "naturally" more compassionate than men, women's brains are "naturally" better at multitasking, women are "naturally" more future-oriented than men. But in truth, women are as "naturally" capable of cruelty, small-mindedness, and warmongering as their male counterparts, and men are as capable of care and compassion as women. Compassion, care, a nurture-orientation, communicativeness—any leader, male or female who is able to harness these traits, will be effective and admirable. In other words, the future belongs to people, regardless of gender, who embrace this "feminine" style of leadership. Following in the footsteps of Amra, Sehija, and Danka, we need to continue moving in a direction that emboldens women to speak their truth to power in a world begging for a different kind of leadership.

Notes

*   This chapter is a slightly revised version of an article that initially appeared in 2014 in the e-journal of Ekumenska Inicijativa Žena (the Ecumenical Women's Initiative) in Croatia, http://www.eiz.hr/who-we-work-with/meet-the-local-partners/fellows/?lang=en/&lang=en

1   Elissa Helms, *Innocence and Victimhood, Gender, Nation, and Women's Activism in Postwar Bosnia-Herzegovina* (Madison: University of Wisconsin Press, 2013), 93–4.

2   Svetlana Slapšak, "The Use of Women and the Role of Women in the Yugoslav War," in *Gender, Peace and Conflict*, ed. Inger Skjelsbaek and Dan Smith (Thousand Oaks, CA: Sage, 2001), 161–83; Helms, *Innocence and Victimhood*.

3   Johan Galtung, "Violence, Peace and Peace Research," *Journal of Peace Research* 6, no. 3 (1969): 161–91.

4   Zilka Spahić Šiljak. *Shining Humanity. Life stories of women peacebuilders in Bosnia and Herzegovina* (New Castle, UK: Cambridge Scholars Publishing, 2014), 15; Ina Merdjanova and Patrice Brodeur, *Religion as a Conversation Starter: Interreligious Dialogue for Peacebuilding in the Balkans* (New York: Continuum, 2009), 108–24.

5   Zilka Spahić Šiljak, *Contesting Female, Feminist and Muslim Identities: Post-socialist Contexts of Bosnia and Herzegovina and Kosovo*. (Sarajevo: Center for Interdisciplinary Postgraduate Studies, University of Sarajevo, 2012); Julianne Funk, "Public Expressions of Bosnian Muslim Religiosity and Lived Faith: The Cases of Friday Prayer and Hijab," in *Negotiating Islam(s): State, Religion and Religiosity in the Contemporary Balkans*, ed. Arolda Elbasani and Olivier Roy (London: Palgrave, 2017); Julianne Funk, "Women and the Spirit of Suživot in Postwar Bosnia-Herzegovina," in *Spirituality of Balkan Women*, ed. Nadija Furlan Štante and Marjana Harcet (Slovenia: Univerzitetna Založba Annales, 2013).

6   Zilka Spahić Siljak, "Nation, Religion and Gender," in *Politicization of Religion: The Case of Ex-Yugoslavia and Its Successor States*, ed. Gorana Ognjenović and J. Jozelić (London: Palgrave Macmillan, 2014).

7   R. Scott Appleby, *The Ambivalence of the Sacred: Religion, Violence and Reconciliation* (Lanham, MD: Rowman and Littlefield, 2000).

8   Janine Natalya Clark, "Religion and Reconciliation in Bosnia & Herzegovina: Are Religious Actors Doing Enough?" *Europe-Asia Studies* 62, no. 4 (June 2010): 675.

9   Michael Sells, *The Bridge Betrayed: Religion and Genocide in Bosnia* (Berkeley: University of California Press, 1996); Neven Andjelic, *Bosnia and Herzegovina: The End of a Legacy* (London: Frank Cass, 2003); Paul Mojzes, *Balkan Genocides: Holocaust and Ethnic Cleansing in the Twentieth Century* (Lanham, MD: Rowman and Littlefield, 2011).

10   Mile Babić, *Nasilje idola* (Sarajevo: Did, 2000); Dino Abazović, *Za naciju i Boga* (Sarajevo: Magistrat Sarajevo, 2006); Ivan Cvitković, "Sociology of Religions and Challenges of Globalization," *Sociološki diskurs* 3 (2012): 19–22.

11   Clark, "Religion," 679.

12   Mitja Velikonja, *Religious Separation & Political Intolerance in Bosnia-Herzegovina*, trans. Rang'ichi Ng'inja (College Station: Texas A&M University Press, 2003), 290.

13   Clark, "Religion," 683.

14   Appleby, *The Ambivalence*, 283.

15   John Paul Lederach, *Building Peace: Sustainable Reconciliation in Divided Societies* (Washington, DC: United States Institute of Peace Press, 1997), 40.

16 Zilka Spahić-Šiljak, Aida Spahić, and Elmaja Bavčić, *Baseline Study: Women and Peacebuilding in BH* (Sarajevo: TPO Foundation, 2012).

17 Mojzes, *Balkan Genocides*, 97.

18 Šiljak, Shining Humanity, 198.

19 Lederach, *Building Peace*, 1–20.

20 Amina Wadud, *Qur'an and Woman—Rereading the Sacred Texts from a Woman's Perspective* (New York: Oxford University Press, 1999), 36–8.

21 Shining Humanity, 292.

22 Jean Lau Chin, Bernice Lott, Joy Rice, and Janis Sanchez-Hucles, eds., *Women and Leadership. Transforming Visions and Diverse Voices* (Hoboken: Wiley-Blackwell, 2007), 236–8.

23 Robert Coles, *Lives of Moral Leadership: Men and Women Who Have Made a Difference* (New York: Random House Publishing Group, 2000), 9–22.

24 Ibid.

25 Regine Birute, *Iron Butterflies: Women Transforming Themselves and the World* (New York: Prometheus Books, 2010), 264.

26 Mary Lou Decosterd, *How Women Are Transforming Leadership. Four Key Traits Powering Success* (Santa Barbara, CA: Praeger, 2013), 139–40.

11 MUSLIM AMERICAN ACTIVISM IN THE AGE OF TRUMP

Grace Yukich

In the wake of the 2016 election of Donald Trump as president of the United States, much attention has been paid to the role white evangelical Christians played in Trump's victory.* In part, this was due to surprise: surprise that Trump had won at all, and surprise that white evangelicals (unlike Latinx and black evangelicals) had supported a candidate like Trump in such high numbers, given the very public examples of his behavior that stood in stark contrast to commonly held evangelical moral standards. Many commentators were puzzled by the continued power of the religious right, which some had regarded as on the decline.

Those narratives of decline were not entirely wrong. White evangelical Protestantism is shrinking as a proportion of the United States; it simply has not disappeared as a political force quite as quickly as some observers expected.[1] If current demographic trends continue, white evangelical Christians will indeed lose much of the political power they once had, particularly if other forces rise to take their place.[2] Indeed, other religious actors have been seeking to fill that space, though with far less attention paid to their efforts. Much of this activism might be deemed "progressive," with the religious people involved seeking to directly counter the policies and messages of the religious right. While progressive religious activism is not new—indeed, some of the most important social movements in US history were led in part by religious groups and leaders typically considered progressive (e.g., the Civil Rights Movement)—the waning influence of the religious right warrants more focus on religious activism that is not associated with the religious right.

The campaign, election, and presidency of Donald Trump have roused progressive Americans of all stripes to become more involved in politics. Many are religious, though not all fit the typical definition of "progressive." Some agree with most of the key issues often emphasized by the Democratic Party and the Working Families Party: government programs to alleviate poverty and decrease economic inequality, immigrant-friendly policies, ecological sustainability, civil rights for LGBT people, and access to abortion services. Others, though, support the first three while leaning more conservative on the last two issues, particularly the issue of abortion rights.

Perhaps these complexities—the ways in which they challenge both standard notions of who counts as progressive or conservative and conservative/progressive categories themselves—have contributed, in part, to the relative lack of attention to progressive religion in the last few decades. But when we neglect religious activists who are not affiliated with the religious right, we miss a lot. For instance, while half of Muslim Americans agree with the white evangelicals who elected Trump about the dangers of homosexuality,[3] many had serious concerns about Trump's presidency, partly rooted in his anti-Muslim rhetoric, his so-called Muslim ban, and his proposal to create a Muslim registry. Substantial majorities of Muslim Americans disapproved of Trump's job performance (65 percent), said he makes them feel worried (68 percent), and saw him as unfriendly toward Muslims (74 percent).[4] Given the focus on Muslims in so much of Trump's campaign and early presidency, surely Muslim responses to Trump warrant some of the attention that white evangelicals received in 2017.

Much of the media coverage around Trump's anti-Muslim positions has focused on resistance to these policies from progressives in general. Instead, this chapter asks: how did Muslim Americans themselves respond to the Trump presidency, and what can this teach us about religious activism more generally? Using key Muslim websites, social media, and newspaper sources, I identify eight ways Muslims reacted to the Trump presidency: (1) educating non-Muslims about Islam; (2) resisting the role of "defender of Islam"; (3) advocating for progressive Islam within Muslim circles; (4) building solidarity between immigrant and African American Muslims; (5) strengthening interfaith bonds; (6) advocating for Muslim rights; (7) advocating for other forms of social change; and (8) embracing Trump's presidency. The diversity of their responses demonstrates the inadequacies of the typical conservative/progressive dichotomy in many studies of religious activism, showing the need for a fuller conception of how religious activists operate in the United States today.

Religious Activism in the United States

Throughout the course of 2017, newspaper articles appeared with headlines like: "Religious liberals sat out of politics for 40 years. Now they want in"[5] and "'Religious left' emerging as U.S. political force in Trump era."[6] As is often the case, these headlines, and the stories in the articles themselves, sought to make a rather old phenomenon seem new and exciting. As religion and politics scholars know well, religious liberals (or the term many prefer—"religious progressives") most certainly have not sat out of politics for forty years. Religious progressives have been involved in countless social movements during the last forty years, from the anti-war movement to the movement against nuclear proliferation to the 1980s Sanctuary Movement and New Sanctuary Movement and many, many more.[7] Some of this involvement has been "quiet,"[8] such as responsible investing efforts or environmental advocacy, but the power of religious progressives demonstrated in the Civil Rights Movement never fully disappeared.

However, both the media and scholars have often ignored religious progressives. They challenge the dominant media narrative that the major political division in the United States exists between the religious right and the secular left. Religious progressives muddy the waters, demonstrating that the narrative is not as simple as many would wish it to be. They challenge dominant definitions of "religion," as well as reigning notions of what it means to be politically progressive; as such, their existence forces scholars to rethink categories that often seem well-established.

"Progressive religion" could mean many things: it could refer to the types of religious beliefs people hold, their identities, the types of practices in which they engage, the denominations and congregations with which they are affiliated, or just the fact that a group is *not* part of the religious right.[9] Even using a broad definition that potentially encompasses all of these, progressive religious activism has received only limited scholarly attention in recent years, and most of the studies that do exist have focused on activism among Christian and Jewish groups. Indeed, sociology of religion more generally has been critiqued in this regard, since "for most scholars in the field, the default category reflects a broadly shared conception of American religion directly linked to Protestant American theological conceptions."[10]

However, though renewed attention to progressive religious activism is a welcome change, a very broad definition of progressive religion may not be the most useful way forward. While it is important to distinguish the types of activism associated with the religious right from other types of religious activism, the activism often deemed "religiously conservative" is relatively limited; among the plethora of other types of religious activism, some might be usefully categorized as progressive, while other types of activism may not easily fit into either a "conservative" or "progressive" category. The current religious conservative/ progressive polarity is also, in many ways, rooted in the cultural dominance of white evangelical Protestantism, with the definitions of these categories depending on issues like economics, gender, and sexuality being bundled in ways that are relevant to the concerns of white evangelical conservatives (and their detractors), but may be less pertinent to the concerns of religious others. In the past, the tendency has often been to ignore groups that do not easily fit these categorizations—immigrants, African American Christians, religious minorities— such that scholars do not have a good sense for whether the varieties of religious activism in the United States today really do primarily fall into "conservative" and "progressive" camps, or whether much of the empirical reality is too complex to be categorized in this way.

Religious activism occurring outside of the religious right has received more attention in the last few years due to an increase in research on faith-based community organizing.[11] Faith-based community organizing offers one example of activism that does not easily fit into conservative and progressive labels (though it is sometimes characterized as more progressive), but its focus on congregations (as opposed to individuals) and on political action (as opposed to other types of actions) means that the types of activism being observed will necessarily be limited. Furthermore, most of the groups involved in these organizations are Christian or Jewish.[12] so it reveals little about whether current understandings of religious activism are adequate for explaining the religious activism of other religious groups.

Though there are several exceptions to this general focus on Christian and Jewish activism, such as a limited number of studies examining Hindu activism in the United States,[13] studies of "socially engaged Buddhism,[14] and research on Muslim political engagement,[15] much of this research focuses on contexts outside of the United States and was conducted long enough ago that it is difficult to know whether the studies' findings are still relevant in the current context. For instance, some studies have examined Muslim activism in the United States,[16] but most were conducted or published before Trump became a serious presidential candidate—a development that may have shifted the activism of Muslims and other religious minorities in significant ways.

Much of the research on religious activism has adopted a "resource mobilization" approach by examining how existing organizations (e.g., congregations) and their resources make mobilization more possible and therefore more likely.[17] While some research indicates that non-Judeo-Christian groups adopt more congregational forms in the American context,[18] many remain less rooted in congregationalism, such that congregations may not serve the same mobilizing functions that they do for Christian and Jewish activists.[19]

Thus, focusing on non-Judeo-Christian traditions provides a way to move beyond the focus on conservative/progressive religion, on congregations, and on resource mobilization in religious activism, raising different sorts of questions. For instance, how does being a member of a religious minority, particularly one that faces high levels of discrimination, affect the types of activism in which a person engages? How does it influence their political positions? How does it impact the strategies and tactics they choose? Similarly, much social movement research has treated changing government policy as the primary goal of any serious movement, but more recent scholarship emphasizes that power and authority do not reside solely in the state, instead pointing attention toward other institutional contexts like religious organizations or the military.[20] How might being a member of a marginalized religious group shape the extent to which religious activism targets the state versus other sources of power and authority?

Members of marginalized religious communities may find it necessary to engage in activism that, elsewhere, I have called "multi-target social movement" activism: activism that challenges both government policy (for a variety of reasons, including potential discrimination against one's own religious group) and,[21] simultaneously, other targets such as their own religious institutions, as they battle over what the public face of those institutions should look like. Because of the explicit discrimination directed toward Muslims during the 2016 presidential campaign, for example, Muslims may feel pressure to ensure that the public image of American Islam, as well as local mosques, is one with which non-Muslim Americans feel comfortable. By examining activism among people who are on the religious margins, scholars may find that traditional notions of what counts as "activism" need to be expanded to more fully account for the varieties of religious activism occurring in the United States today.

Scholars are largely missing accounts of the ways that members of religious groups other than Christianity and Judaism—such as Buddhists, Hindus, and Muslims—are engaging in religious activism both generally and in this particular time and place. Because Trump's victory is at least partly due to his fear of and disdain for racial and religious minorities, feelings many of his supporters share, it is particularly important in this specific time period to understand how religio-racial minorities are working to challenge Trump's rhetoric and the right-wing policies of his administration. Furthermore, greater attention to non-Judeo-Christian religious activism will help scholars to develop a fuller understanding of what these phenomena look like in an increasingly diverse American religious landscape.

Muslim Activism in the United States

Recent years have been especially difficult ones for many American Muslims. While Muslims in American society have faced higher levels of discrimination since the attack on September 11, 2001,[22] anti-Muslim sentiment intensified following the rise of ISIS as a global force in 2014, arguably reaching its zenith (at least up to this point) during the 2016 presidential campaign of Donald Trump. Not only did Trump refuse to correct supporters at rallies who voiced anti-Muslim bigotry, but also the candidate himself proposed a ban on Muslims entering the United States, as well as a national registry for Muslims. After he became president, Trump followed through on one of those proposals, seeking to create a ban on refugees from seven Muslim-majority nations, a ban that later underwent revisions (some argue the purpose of these revisions was to make the ban appear less anti-Muslim) and received support from the US Supreme Court.

Muslims make up a small but growing part of the overall US population; 3.3 million Muslims reside in the United States, or 1 percent of the total US population, an almost 50 percent increase since 2007.[23] This means that they are currently the second largest religious minority in the United States (Jews make up the largest minority), but that is projected to change by 2050, by which time Muslims are expected to comprise the largest religious minority group due to factors like migration and fertility patterns.[24] Many American Muslims are recent immigrants: 76 percent are first- or second-generation immigrants, meaning they are likely to have ethnic and cultural ties to other countries.[25] Still, 82 percent of American Muslims are US citizens, suggesting that many immigrant Muslims seek to assimilate quickly, perhaps in part to avoid negative stereotypes.[26]

In addition, despite laws ostensibly protecting Muslims from religious discrimination, many Muslims report experiencing discrimination in their daily lives.[27] Most Muslim Americans say they are proud to be American (92 percent), demonstrating their commitment to being a part of American society, but about half say they have experienced religious discrimination during the past year.[28] About half say it has become more difficult to be Muslim in the United States in recent years, with 60 percent saying US media coverage of Islam and Muslims is generally unfair.[29] And between 2015 and 2016, hate crimes against Muslims in the United States rose significantly, surpassing even 2001 levels following the 9/11 attacks.[30]

In this context, one that was somewhat hostile for Muslim Americans even before the Trump campaign and presidency but has arguably grown even more challenging, it is especially important to understand how Muslim Americans are engaging with their surrounding communities. Doing so not only tells us more about Muslims themselves but also reveals something about the diversity of religious activism more generally.

The terms "progressive" and "conservative" are not necessarily common descriptors for different forms of Islam in much of the world, but some Muslim American scholars nonetheless argue that there is "a nascent community of Muslim activists and intellectuals" who identify as "progressive Muslims,"[31] with the "progressive Islam" label signifying a focus on issues like social justice, gender justice, and pluralism.[32] Though many Muslims are not progressive in many of their political positions, in this time period, simply being Muslim and not criticizing Islam might earn someone the label of "liberal" or "progressive," as being critical of Muslims has become a marker of conservatism in the United States.[33] Thus, while not all Muslims are progressive, in the Trump era, Muslim American activism—particularly activism defending Muslims from discrimination—might be deemed progressive. However, for some forms of Muslim activism, the terms "conservative" and "progressive" may be inadequate and even misleading descriptors of the types of actions taking place and the meanings associated with them.

In seeking to understand the variety of religious responses to the Trump presidency, focusing on Muslim American activism is key. Because we still know relatively little about the types of religious activism in which Muslims engage, this chapter seeks to identify the plethora of ways Muslim Americans are responding to the Trump presidency, some more progressive, some conservative; some focused on government policy, others focused on changing the beliefs and practices of individual Muslims and non-Muslims. To identify various forms of activism and responses to Trump, I gathered information from key websites, social media, and news sources. I examined the websites of several key Muslim organizations: the Council on American-Islamic Relations (CAIR), the Islamic Society of North America (ISNA), and the Muslim Students' Association (MSA). Examining these websites led me to multiple other sites of interest, such as LaunchGood and the Muslim-Jewish Advisory Council. I also examined social media, particularly Twitter, for examples of Muslim activism occurring there. Finally, I examined news coverage of Muslim activism, including but not limited to stories in the *New York Times*, the *Chicago Tribune*, and the *Washington Post*. The findings presented below demonstrate the diversity of Muslim Americans, of their responses to Trump, and of religious activism more generally, showing the importance of a research agenda on religious activism that incorporates more studies of non-Judeo-Christian activists.

Findings

Though there are almost certainly additional ways in which Muslims are responding to Trump, I identify eight main ways Muslims are reacting to the Trump presidency: (1) educating non-Muslims about Islam; (2) resisting the role of "defender of Islam"; (3) advocating for progressive Islam within Muslim circles; (4) building solidarity between immigrant and African American Muslims; (5) strengthening interfaith bonds; (6) advocating for Muslim rights; (7) advocating for other forms of social change; and (8) embracing Trump's presidency.

Educating Non-Muslims about Islam

The first two of these responses fall into the category of "Education." Some Muslims are working to educate non-Muslims about Islam, while others are resisting the role of "defender of Islam." Perhaps the most common way that Muslim Americans are responding to the Trump presidency is to fight back against the negative stereotypes and anti-Muslim sentiments expressed in public discourse by seeking to educate non-Muslims about Islam. In many ways, this is an uphill battle. Research has revealed the extensive networks of fringe anti-Muslim groups and their growth in public influence,[34] which likely impacted the mindsets of many Trump supporters and even Steve Bannon and Trump himself. While organizations like the Council on American-Islamic Relations (CAIR) and the Islamic Society of North America (ISNA) try to combat the images of Muslims produced by these fringe anti-Muslim groups, Trump's win as well as the opinions about Muslims expressed in national polls of Americans suggest that the fringe groups may be winning the public battle over the image of Islam in America—but only for Republicans.

Perhaps surprisingly, those polls show that, since 2015 when Trump announced his candidacy, Americans' views of Muslims and Islam have become *more* positive, not less, though the changes have almost all been due to increasingly positive views of Muslims among Democrats and independents, with Republican views remaining unchanged and largely negative.[35] In November 2015, Americans were split about evenly, with only 53 percent reporting favorable views of Muslims and less than 40 percent reporting favorable views of Islam. However, by October 2016, the percent of Americans reporting favorable views of Muslims had jumped to 70 percent, and about 50 percent reported favorable views of Islam. Thus, while Trump's anti-Muslim rhetoric may have stoked anti-Muslim views among Republicans, or even just reflected views that were already there, they may have backfired by increasing positive views of Muslims among non-Republicans, with shifts so large that they changed the breakdown of overall American views as well.[36]

However, the polls reveal less about Americans views during Trump's presidency. The heat of the presidential campaign and its associated partisanship, and dislike for Trump's policies and rhetoric regarding Muslims, may have produced a temporary shift in attitudes toward Muslims that did not last once the issue became less prevalent. Polls show that knowing a Muslim personally might create more positive attitudes toward Muslims and Islam,[37] perhaps with the potential to change views in the long term, but most Americans do not know any Muslims.[38] As such, many Muslims feel that the best way to combat Trump's anti-Muslim rhetoric and agenda, and anti-Muslim public sentiment, more broadly, is to create more opportunities for non-Muslims to get to know them.

These "getting to know you" campaigns often take the form of Islam 101 classes or lectures by Muslim speakers that are geared toward non-Muslims who want to be better informed about Islam. Some are sponsored by and held at local mosques; others are held at churches, synagogues, community centers, or other locations where groups of interested people typically gather. Some have been running for several years, while others started explicitly in response to Trump's campaign and presidency. For instance, Muslim couple Jenny Yanez and Anwer Bashi started an Islam 101 course at their New Orleans-area mosque, a free, six-week primer on the Muslim faith. While the course began as a way to teach new Muslims about Islam, the couple has seen more non-Muslims take the course recently. "People come because they have co-workers or family who have accepted Islam and they want to understand them better …. And some people come because they're afraid of Islam … I think those are very brave, brave people who come to the mosque," Ms. Yanez told a reporter.[39] The class provides students with the chance to read primary sources like the Quran for themselves, as well as the opportunity to hang out with Muslims. Ms. Yanez's husband added, "If every representation that they've seen is negative, it's not anybody's fault that when they think of Islam, immediately it starts from a negative place .... It [the course] really humanizes Muslims ... I mean it's almost sad that we have to say that, but Muslims have been pretty dehumanized."[40]

Another example is the practice of Muslim speakers giving talks about their faith to non-Muslims in non-Muslim spaces. For instance, Haroon Moghul, Muslim author of How to Be a Muslim: An American Story,[41] has given talks to non-Muslim groups about his book and his experiences as a Muslim, such as speaking at book club meetings, synagogues, and on National Public Radio.

While much of this work happens locally, there have been more national efforts to educate non-Muslims about Islam as well. Many Muslims write op-eds about Islam for newspapers and websites that are read widely by non-Muslims. For instance, Mansura Bashir Minhas, a Pakistani-American Muslim, wrote an op-ed in the Miami Herald titled "Get to know the 'True Islam,'" arguing that Muslim extremists "defy the norms of logic and distort its [Islam's] core message to pursue their depraved agendas."[42] She describes "True Islam," a campaign "to educate Americans on Islam's true teachings."[43] The website of "True Islam," hosted by the Ahmadiyya Muslim Community, "answers eleven misunderstood questions on Islam," offers chances to chat online with a Muslim, and hosts "Coffee, Cake, & True Islam" meetups around the country.[44] While Ahmadi Muslims are considered heterodox by many other Muslims, this op-ed and "True Islam's" efforts to educate non-Muslims about Islam are similar in many ways to education efforts by members of other sects of Islam, which attempt to demonstrate that Islam is not inherently violent by introducing non-Muslims to the main tenets of Islam and to the Quran itself.[45]

More specifically, many national efforts at educating non-Muslims about Islam are focused on combatting stereotypes of Muslims as terrorists or of Islam as an inherently violent religion. This has typically taken three forms: (1) public statements by imams condemning terrorist attacks perpetrated by Muslims; (2) marches or vigils held by Muslims to condemn terrorist attacks; and (3) the #NotInMyName campaign, which involves Muslims condemning terrorist attacks committed by Muslims.

Whenever a terrorist attack is perpetrated by a Muslim, whether in the United States or elsewhere, someone inevitably tweets something asking why Muslims are not condemning terrorism. Referencing this tendency and resisting it at the same time, twitter user and best-selling author Rabia Chaudry recently tweeted, "'Why don't Muslims condemn terrorism' Sorry, too busy dying from it," linking to a CNN story about twenty-six people being killed in a suicide bombing in Baghdad.[46] As Chaudry's tweet suggests, while some use the supposed silence of Muslims as evidence that Muslims approve of violence, even if they claim to believe in peace, in reality, Muslims frequently speak out against terrorist attacks committed by Muslims, making public statements condemning such actions as evil and contrary to Islam. In November 2016, nineteen-year-old University of Colorado student Heraa Hashmi tweeted "classmate: why don't muslims condemn things/me:*goes home makes 712 page long list of Muslims Condemning Things with sources*/me: fight me."[47] Indeed, she did make such a list, which went viral.[48] It also inspired the creation of the website Muslims Condemn, "a collection of all the cases where Muslims have condemned wrongdoings done falsely in the name of Islam."[49]

Similarly, marches and protests sponsored by Muslim organizations, held specifically to denounce terrorist attacks committed by Muslims, have been common in other countries, but have occurred in the United States as well. For instance, in the UK, thousands of Muslims marched against terrorism in the wake of terrorist attacks in the UK, with similar protests held by Muslims in Germany, Spain, the United States, and many other countries in recent years.[50] While this could also be seen as an example of what I call "working for religious change" or "activism for social change," these protests also provide a way for Muslims to educate non-Muslims about Islam, by demonstrating that most Muslims are law-abiding and peaceful, not terrorists or terrorist sympathizers.

Finally, the #NotInMyName twitter campaign began several years ago as a way for Muslims to speak out again terrorist attacks perpetrated by Muslims.[51] As with all social media, Twitter and Facebook posts are both ways to communicate content and ways to signal identity: in this case, Muslims are showing non-Muslims that Islam is diverse, and that while Muslim terrorists may get a lot of press, most Muslims do not support violence in the name of Islam. Indeed, they believe Islam condemns, rather than calls for, violence. Twitter users all over the world adopted the hashtag, sharing photos of themselves holding signs reading "#NotInMyName" or just using the hashtag and sharing tweets like, "Another disgusting threat from the un-Islamic State #NotInMyName."[52] Since Trump's election, this type of activism has continued as a way for Muslims to educate non-Muslims about Islam's teachings on violence.

By teaching Islam 101 courses to non-Muslims, giving lectures on Islam in non-Muslim spaces, publicly condemning terrorist attacks as antithetical to Islam, and speaking out against terrorism on social media, Muslims are seeking to educate non-Muslims about Islam. In doing so, they hope to change the stereotypes that have led to the anti-Muslim rhetoric and policies that have dominated Trump's campaign and presidency thus far.

Resistance to the Educator Role

While many Muslims have responded to Trump by trying to educate non-Muslims about Islam, others have resisted that role for reasons of principle and pragmatism, and as a form of resistance to what the general culture demands of them—in other words, that in order to be accepted, they must constantly apologize for other people who happen to have the same religious identity or ethnicity as them. Like people of color who argue that it is oppressive to have to educate white people about racism, some Muslims are tired of being told they must do the work of convincing bigoted Americans that they are not terrorists just because they are Muslim. Imam Johari Abdul-Malik, an imam at a DC-area mosque and leader in several national Muslim organizations, has said about Muslims issuing apologies for terrorism in an effort to educate non-Muslims that, "it sounded like they were apologizing for something they haven't done, like they were running for cover."[53] Sana Saeed, a producer at Al Jazeera channel AJ+, wrote in a blog post that she was "tired of people in my communities constantly partaking in and creating public campaigns to put up a good face of our religion …. When you ask Muslims to condemn or denounce heinous actions, ideologies or groups what you're saying is that you don't trust any Muslim."[54]

So, one response to Trump is to push back against the expectation that Muslims should be apologetic, docile, and uncritical of the United States in any way if they want to be truly accepted in American society. While many Muslims have decided that resisting the "defender" role is the appropriate response to the level of anti-Muslim sentiment that is now publicly and powerfully present in American society, different Muslims give different reasons for their resistance. For some, the resistance is related to the idea of oppression: that oppressed groups should not be responsible for convincing those in power that they should not be oppressed. Instead, bigoted people should take responsibility for their bigotry and educate themselves about groups they do not understand. Of course, those in the pro-education camp would point out that powerful people rarely do this, as the incentives to do so are not high. As Amanda Quraishi, a Muslim interfaith activist in Austin, Texas, told a reporter: "We are at a point in time where we have to bear the burden of wide-scale fear and misinformation about our faith and the cultures of many of the people who practice it … I quite literally view it as our jihad."[55] In other words, while it may indeed be unjust to ask marginalized people to do the work of educating those in power, that may be the only way to challenge prevailing stereotypes, as those who are marginalized may have the greater potential to benefit from changed stereotypes, and therefore the greater incentive to do the work of education.

Another reason some Muslims resist the educator role is that it runs the danger of affirming "violent Muslims" as the default, and of lending legitimacy to ridiculous arguments about Muslims by engaging with those arguments at all. Steve Bannon's role as Trump's campaign manager and, later, as a major player in his presidential administration, signaled that someone with a view of Islam as inherently dangerous and evil was shaping the policies of the US government. When that is the starting point of the conversation—your interlocutor believes you are evil simply because you are Muslim—it may seem not only pointless to engage but also damaging, as it suggests you consider the person and their views worthy of your time and your rebuttals. For instance, in explaining why it did not endorse a Muslim march against terrorism in Germany, a statement by the German Turkish-Islamic Union for Religious Affairs (Ditib) said, "Calls for 'Muslim' anti-terror demos fall short, stigmatise Muslims, and confine international terrorism to being just among them and within their communities and mosques."[56] Indeed, some argue that not only is it unfair to ask this of Muslims, but also it is not the most effective way for Muslims to change negative views about Islam. In a similar example, Dalia Mogahed, director of research at the Institute for Social Policy and Understanding, a research organization focused on Muslim empowerment, recently penned an op-ed titled "Don't ask Muslims to condemn terror: Our outrage at atrocities ought to be a given."[57] She argues that it is the "definition of biogtry" to suspect someone of supporting terrorism merely because of their ethnicity or religion, and that by condemning terrorism publicly, Muslims may inadvertently be reinforcing that bigotry rather than challenging it. She describes a research study that found that "people could reconsider Muslim collective guilt—not by Muslims condemning terrorism, but when they challenged the exclusive expectation to do so."[58]

In another example of this type of reaction, some Muslims, annoyed in part by the #NotInMyName campaign mentioned earlier, began using a different hashtag: #MuslimApologies.[59] The idea behind the use of this hashtag is to highlight the absurdity of asking all Muslims to constantly apologize for the actions of a few, something rarely asked of members of more powerful religious or ethnic groups in the West. Sometimes the hashtag is used to push back on expectations that Muslims should apologize for terrorism, like a tweet that shows an image of a t-shirt that reads "I'm Muslim and I'm sorry for everything" and then includes a tongue-in-cheek tweet that says, "I'm just going to wear this shirt every day from now on #MuslimApologies."[60] In many other examples, though, twitter users take it a step further, subverting expectations that Muslims apologize for terrorism by instead issuing sarcastic apologies for positive contributions Muslims have made to the world, making the campaign about educating non-Muslims to a certain extent. For instance, one user wrote, "I am sorry that Muslims invented algorithms and as a result you are able to view this tweet via your handheld device #Muslimapologies."[61]

Finally, some Muslims hesitate to participate in "educating non-Muslims about Islam" because these forms of education often involve simplifying a complex and diverse tradition to challenge prevailing negative stereotypes. For instance, public statements condemning terrorist attacks by Muslims, both from Muslims and non-Muslims such as past presidents Barack Obama and George W. Bush, often make arguments like "Islam is a religion of peace," and "these terrorists were not true Muslims." In seeking to defend Muslims and Islam from people who would paint all Muslims as violent because of the actions of a few, those "defenders" are painting with an equally broad brushstroke, by insisting that (1) there is only one valid way of practicing Islam and being Muslim, and (2) they know what the "true Islam" looks like. While many Muslims might appreciate the good intentions of those seeking to challenge negative stereotypes about Muslims as violent by emphasizing Islam's teachings about peace, they also want to be careful not to assert that there is only one valid version of Islam and want to be sure not to lend credence to the idea that non-Muslims, such as the US government, are the legitimate arbiters of what "true Islam" really is.

Working for Religious Change

The next three responses fall into the category of "Working for Religious Change." Some Muslims are discouraging the development of radicalism in their mosques through supporting progressive interpretations of Islam. Others are responding to anti-Muslim sentiment by strengthening bonds between immigrant and African American Muslims, who have often been divided in the past. Still, other Muslims are building ties with people of other faiths, hoping these bonds will increase goodwill and understanding.

Promoting Progressive Islam

For some Muslims, one of the ways to combat anti-Muslim sentiment during the Trump era was to promote more progressive forms of Islam in their own mosques and communities. Part of this effort may be to discourage radicalism, which can help ensure that broader stereotypes of Muslims as violent are not, in fact, true in American Muslim communities. More deeply, however, the injustices faced by many Muslims in contemporary American society serve as a reminder of the importance of pursuing justice in their own communities, leading many Muslims to challenge racism, sexism, and other problems that at times have plagued Muslim communities (and religious communities in the United States more generally).

For instance, Omid Safi, a professor at Duke University and columnist for *On Being*, the NPR show on religion and spirituality, has spent much of his career encouraging fellow Muslims to ask hard questions about racism and sexism in Muslim communities. His edited volume, *Progressive Muslims*, brings together a diverse set of Muslim scholars and community leaders to discuss and debate questions about race, gender, family, sexuality, and other topics with deep connections to Muslim faith and practice.[62]

Strengthening Bonds between Immigrant and African American Muslims

Both scholars of American Muslims and Muslim American communities themselves have highlighted the reality of divisions between immigrant Muslim and African American Muslim communities in the United States.[63] Sociologically, this division is perfectly understandable given institutional histories: African American Muslim communities have existed in sizeable numbers for decades due to the existence of the Nation of Islam,[64] while immigrant Muslim communities have been more in flux, as the national origins of immigrant Muslims changed over time. However, the divisions run deeper than this. Many of the divisions are cultural, racial, and theological; in particular, African American Muslims often report feeling treated by immigrant Muslims as "not really Muslim."[65] In an op-ed called "Islamophobia and Black American Muslims," activist Margari Hill discusses the challenges of combatting Islamophobia, writing, "The erasure of Black American Muslims undermines efforts towards developing a unified front in the face of our greatest threat."[66]

Though conversations about racial divides in American Muslim communities are not new, during a time when anti-Muslim rhetoric and policies have the public endorsement of the US president, many Muslims are feeling an even greater urgency to bridge the divide between immigrant and African American Muslims, to build solidarity based on their common religious identity. In November 2017, the Muslim Public Affairs Council held its seventeenth annual convention "Bridging the Divide: Religion, Race, and Politics," which focused in part on issues of race. The Muslim Anti-Racism Collaborative, an organization started in 2014 to combat all types of racism, including "intra-Muslim racism," released a video in 2017 that said, in part: "American Muslims are one of the most diverse faith groups in the United States. By successfully educating about racial inequities within the [Muslim] community, we can demonstrate a model for American society at a time when there is an even greater need for the work."[67]

When the Muslim Anti-Racism Collaborative launched during Black History Month in 2014, it used the twitter hashtag #BeingBlackAndMuslim to raise awareness about the marginalization of black Muslims within American Muslim circles as well as African American circles. It went viral, and since that time, many black Muslims have used the hashtag to assert both their Muslim-ness and blackness, in part as an attempt to create dialogue, greater acceptance, and cooperation with other Muslims during the Trump era. In April 2017, black Muslim artist Bobby Rogers used the hashtag to launch a photo series, which juxtaposed images of black Muslims with statements about what it means to be black and Muslim in the United States. For instance, in one post, an image of a young, black woman wearing hijab is set beside the words "#BeingBlackAndMuslim means you are the largest group of American-Muslims, but you are the last to be asked to speak on Islam."[68]

In another example, a group called "Townhall Dialogue," located in the Washington, DC area, has been working for several years to bring together Muslims from a variety of racial and ethnic backgrounds to discuss issues of pertinence to young Muslim Americans. The group holds dialogues on a variety of topics, with one recent dialogue called "Race in a Muslim Space." The webpage describing the event said the discussion was guided by questions like: "How has race played a role in your life as you navigate a [sic] Muslim spaces? Have you witnessed racial hierarchies in Muslim communities? Do you feel your religious community promotes a message of 'color blindness'? Is a message of 'color blindness' helpful (or harmful) in addressing the issue of racism in our religious communities?"[69]

Of course, even explicit efforts like this to bridge the divide often have limited success: the photos on the event's website suggest that few to none of the attendees were black Muslims. The organization seems to recognize this in text on the webpage that reads, "As a group, we discussed the inevitable self selection of attending even this event," perhaps referring to the fact that few of the organization's leaders appear to be black Muslims. Still, dialogues like this one demonstrate that many Muslims recognize the need to come together with their fellow Muslims across racial divides, because of the "religious message of equality" (see Townhall Dialogue website) but also to build stronger communities.

Building Interfaith Relationships

Muslim Americans have been deeply involved in interfaith work for years, partnering with Christians, Jews, and other people of faith to learn about each other's religions and to work on shared concerns in their communities.[70] Since Trump's election, many Muslims have sought to strengthen those relationships, calling on fellow people of faith to help defend Muslims' civil liberties, particularly their constitutional right to religious liberty. For instance, in the aftermath of the election, some mosques held interfaith events, where Christians, Jews, and Muslims came together to express grave concern about the results of the election and to commit to defending the rights of Muslims. In an event I attended at a New England mosque in the days following the election, which was packed full of people from multiple faith backgrounds (including none), some Christian and Jewish attendees, recalling the registering of Jewish people by the Nazi regime during the Holocaust, announced their intention to register as "Muslims" if Trump instituted a national Muslim registry. In the days following Trump's election, this was a frequent yet also criticized example of attempts to build interfaith solidarity in the Trump era.[71]

On a national level, some Muslims and Jews have strengthened their partnerships, recognizing their common position in the United States as religious minorities that have often faced marginalization, discrimination, and oppression, and seeking to support and defend each other from attempts to take away their rights. Just a few days after the presidential election in November 2016, the American Jewish Council (AJC) and the Islamic Society of North America (ISNA) partnered to create the "Muslim-Jewish Advisory Council." Though some Muslims voiced concerns about the partnership, worried that different positions on the Israel/Palestine conflict might make the partnership difficult,[72] the goal of the group is to strengthen interfaith bonds to enable better and quicker responses to growth in both anti-Muslim sentiment and anti-Semitism during Trump's campaign and the early days of his presidency. Specifically, the council's website says it has two policy objectives: "to combat the rise in hate crimes, and to promote the positive image of Muslim and Jewish citizens of the United States."[73]

Activism for Social Change

The following two responses fall into the category of "Activism for Social Change." Many Muslims fought the refugee ban passed by President Trump, which most saw as a rebranding of the "Muslim ban" he threatened on the campaign trail, attending rallies or calling their congressional representatives. Additionally, many Muslims are concerned about not only their own rights but also the wellbeing of immigrants and others endangered by Trump's election, such as a Texas imam who has called for mosques to offer sanctuary to undocumented immigrants.

Defending the Civil Rights of Muslims

One of the major ways that Muslim Americans are responding to the Trump administration is to defend their own civil rights, a practice that was common prior to the Trump era as well.[74] Because Muslims are a religious minority in the United States and have faced discrimination in the workplace and other realms for years, many organizations already existed that were engaged in this work: CAIR and the Arab American Anti-Discrimination Committee have been two of the main organizations doing this work.

Perhaps one of the most prominent examples was the mobilization of Muslim communities against Trump's Muslim ban. As is well known, during his campaign, Trump proposed a "total and complete shutdown of Muslims entering the United States until our country's representatives can figure out what the hell is going on."[75] To the horror of many Muslims and their allies, the proposed ban actually garnered a good deal of support from the American public (40 percent of

Americans supported the proposal), particularly among Republicans, 73 percent of whom said immigration from Muslim-majority countries was either too high or should be stopped altogether.[76] Still, many were shocked when the newly installed Trump administration moved forward with this proposal, couching it in different language in an attempt to curtail challenges asserting that it was unconstitutional.

In the early days of his presidency, Trump signed Executive Order 13769, which banned refugees from seven Muslim-majority nations (Iran, Iraq, Libya, Somalia, Sudan, Syria, and Yemen), explicitly prioritizing the acceptance of religious minorities (e.g., Christians) from those countries.[77] Detractors asserted that it was unconstitutional because it showed a religious preference for Christians and religious discrimination toward Muslims. In response, protests erupted around the United States, with Muslim Americans planning or involved in many of them. Some Muslims spoke at or attended protests at airports around the country, where even legal permanent residents from those countries were being detained by US Customs and Border Protection agents in the days following the executive order.[78] CAIR filed a federal suit challenging the constitutionality of the Muslim ban, as well as creating a Civil Rights app "to share critical 'know your rights' information and simplify the process to report hate crimes and bias incidents."[79]

Though the executive order has faced challenges in courts and has changed its content multiple times, as of this writing, the US Supreme Court allowed the Trump administration to implement a version of the ban while it faced challenges in lower courts. In light of this and other concerns about the rights of Muslim Americans in this era, it is likely that Muslim American activism around these issues will continue in the coming months and possibly years.

Working for a More Just Society

The Five Pillars are the center of Muslim practice. Several arguably focus primarily on one's relationship to Allah, but at least one, Zakah (religious tax), is also largely about one's relationship with other people—the collected money is partly used to feed those who are poor. Many also argue that Sawm (fasting during Ramadan) is partly about justice, as fasting reminds a person not only of their need for God but also of those among them who are always hungry and in need. At the end of Ramadan, Eid al Fitr, families often give the poor a sum of money equal to the amount of money they would have spent on the meals they skipped during Ramadan.[80] In addition to the Five Pillars, there are several other well-known teachings in Islam that highlight its emphasis on issues of social justice,[81] such as the prohibition on "riba," or usury, since it often has the effect of exploiting the poor.

Inspired and motivated by these and other religious teachings, Muslims have long been involved in various forms of social justice work, from organizations like the Muslim Coalition of Connecticut, which engages in various forms of community service and outreach, to more political organizations like Inner City Muslim Action Network (IMAN) in Chicago and Atlanta, which both provides community services and organizes for social change in issues like criminal justice, housing, immigration, and food access. An organization called LaunchGood describes itself as "a global crowdfunding platform to support Muslims Launching good all across the world by helping them raise funds for their campaigns"[82] and has raised more than 33 million dollars for over 3,000 campaigns, from building water wells in Rwanda to aid for refugees around the world to relief for homeless populations in Atlanta.

While many Muslim Americans have long been involved in social justice work in the United States, the Trump campaign's conservative positions on various issues, from immigration to health care, have provided new motivations to act for Muslims concerned about economic inequality and human rights. For instance, CAIR has provided alerts and calls to action for Muslims regarding the Trump administration's decision to end DACA, calling on fellow Muslims to support DREAMERs and the passage of legislation that would enable them to stay in the United States legally.[83] Although this may in part seem tied to Muslim self-interest, since many Muslims are immigrants, the vast majority of undocumented immigrants are from Mexico or other Latin American countries, so few are Muslim.

Similarly, some Muslims have joined the New Sanctuary Movement,[84] seeking to provide refuge to undocumented immigrants in danger of deportation and advocating on their behalf. In the days following Trump's inauguration, Imam Omar Suleiman of Dallas, Texas, called on mosques around the country to follow the example of a Cincinnati mosque by offering sanctuary to undocumented immigrants.[85] In an interview for a recent article, Suleiman said, "'Sanctuary' is as Islamic a concept as it is Judeo-Christian .... Four of the top five prophets in Islam ... were refugees, and were welcomed by another community .... Every human being is honored and dignified in the sight of God."[86] Suleiman and many other Muslims see helping undocumented immigrants, regardless of their religious or ethnic identity, as an example of enacting their belief in Allah's mercy.

Embracing Trump

Finally, some Muslims are "Embracing Trump": some estimates suggest approximately 13 percent of Muslims voted for him.[87] Some Muslims are conservative and support Trump because he is a Republican, while others like Trump because they see him as "tough on terrorism," and they fear Islamic terrorism more than anti-Muslim sentiment. Still others argue that despite his vulgar rhetoric, Trump's policies toward Muslim-majority nations are no more damaging to Muslims than those of Obama, Bush, and Clinton.

During the 2016 presidential election, a Muslim man named Sajid Tarar led a prayer at the Republican National Convention.[88] The founder and head of a group called "Muslims for Trump," Tarar began his prayer by saying: "Let's pray for a strong America, a safe America. And let's ask God to make us strong to fight terrorism all over the world." In prior conversations with reporters, Tarar, a Pakistani immigrant living in the Baltimore area, had insisted that Trump is not anti-Muslim: "When Donald Trump has said something about Muslims and Islam, he doesn't mean American Muslims, he's talking about terrorists."[89] Of course, many of Trump's comments have been directly about American Muslims (calling for surveillance in American mosques, to give just one example), so it is likely that people like Tarar have other reasons for supporting Trump. Indeed, according to one reporter, Tarar "calls Obama a socialist, thinks building a border wall is 'crucial,' and bemoans political correctness and the Black Lives Matter movement."[90] In other words, he is conservative, and his conservatism leads him to support Donald Trump despite the negative statements Trump has made about Muslims.

Similarly, during Trump's campaign, Saba Ahmed, the founder and leader of the Republican Muslim Coalition, overlooked his negative statements about Muslims and policy proposals designed to restrict their rights. She supported him in spite of his anti-Muslim statements because of his conservatism, particularly his economic policies.[91] Together, these examples serve as useful reminders that for at least some Muslims, Muslim identity politics were not the driving force in their vote; instead, other ideological positions and concerns, such as fiscal conservatism, led to their support of the Republican candidate over a more progressive candidate, even if that candidate was far more positive about Muslims.

While there may not have been much in the way of organized, vocal support of Trump from Muslims during his campaign, CAIR's estimate that 13 percent of Muslims voted for Trump demonstrates that his support among Muslims was not insignificant. Indeed, if that number is accurate, then up to 400,000 Muslims may have voted for Trump rather than Hillary Clinton. In Michigan, where the Muslim population is relatively high compared with most other states (2.75 percent of Michigan's 9.9 million people,[92] or about 272,000 Muslims), 13 percent of Michigan's Muslims would be 35,000 people—though some of these are children and nonvoters, the number far exceeds the margin of Trump's win in that state, which was less than 12,000 votes. In other words, Muslim support for Trump was more than just one or two people and was large enough that, if those Muslims had instead supported Clinton in key battleground states, she may have won the presidential election.

Having established that Muslim support for Trump is something to take seriously rather than to laugh off as unimportant or, indeed, impossible, the question remains as to why some Muslims supported Trump, both during the election and after Trump took office, despite his stoking of anti-Muslim sentiment. First, as the examples above suggest, many Muslims are conservative. More are social conservatives than fiscal conservatives. About half of Muslims believe homosexuality is morally wrong,[93] a position that aligns those Muslims more with the Republican party platform than the Democratic one. Muslims are less likely to agree with the Republican party's "small government" approach to fiscal policy (for instance, 67 percent of Muslims say they prefer bigger government that offers more services compared with 48 percent of the general American public), but 25 percent do prefer more conservative approaches to economics and government programs that align them more with Republicans.[94] Indeed, 13 percent of American Muslims identify as Republican, and 21 percent identify as conservative;[95] while these numbers are low compared with the general American public, they nonetheless demonstrate that a minority of Muslims identify with being Republican and conservative. Given the political polarization in the United States today,[96] it makes sense to expect that, like many non-Muslim Republicans who voted for Trump despite some concerns about him, many Muslim Republicans likely voted for Trump merely because he had an "R" beside his name—in other words, because the importance of their Republican identities and/or their support for Republican policies outweighed any concerns they had about Trump's attitudes and behaviors toward Muslims.

Furthermore, some Muslims voted for Trump not *in spite* of his pronouncements about Muslims and his emphasis on what he calls "radical Islamic terrorism," but, seemingly paradoxically, *because of* his views of Muslims as particularly dangerous and in need of greater regulation. In particular, some Muslims from countries where terrorist attacks are much more common than in the West—such as Iraq, Afghanistan, Pakistan, and Syria—may be especially likely to feel that, while not all Muslims are terrorists, Muslim terrorists are a danger to the United States and to ordinary people in many countries, and that a heavier hand is needed in dealing with them. For example, Asra Nomani, an Indian American journalist who has traveled in the Middle East as part of her work, wrote an op-ed arguing that as a Muslim woman, she voted for Trump in part because she "has experienced, first-hand, Islamic extremism in this world ... I have been opposed to the decision by President Obama and the Democratic Party to tap dance around the '*Islam*' in Islamic State."[97] Though this characterization of the Obama administration is arguably incorrect, for people in this category, Trump's tough talk during the campaign about "bombing the shit out of ISIS" and creating a Muslim registry was welcome rather than a cause for fear,[98] since they hoped this would help to protect everyone, including law-abiding Muslims, from terrorist acts committed by groups like ISIS.

Finally, still other Muslims may not have voted for Trump, but have nonetheless embraced him as president rather than resisting his authority. Part of this response may be due to general respect for authority or respect for the office of president, regardless of who holds it. But also, while some Muslims may not have been outright supporters of Trump, they did not fall into the anti-Trump camp either. Instead, during the election and after, they argued that despite Trump's pandering to anti-Muslim sentiment during his campaign, his proposed policies toward Muslim-majority nations were no less friendly to Muslims than the attacks perpetrated by the United States during Hillary Clinton's time as US Secretary of State. Of course, depending on how much emphasis these same Muslims place on Israel/Palestine issues, their support of him may have waned in the wake of his more recent, highly criticized decision to recognize Jerusalem as the Israeli capital in American foreign policy moving forward, a move interpreted by many as a show of support for Zionists and a slap in the face to Palestinians.

Discussion

Muslim Americans are on the front line battling anti-Muslim rhetoric and policy in the contemporary United States. While their engagement is not necessarily new—many activists have been engaged in this work for years—this chapter finds that many Muslims do indeed feel a new urgency to become active in opposing the anti-Muslim sentiments voiced by many Americans and given tacit (and sometimes explicit) approval by Trump and his administration. Muslim Americans are engaging in religious activism in many different forms, from seeking cultural change by educating non-Muslims about Islam, to working for change in their own religious institutions by making them more racially diverse or more progressive, to attempting to change government policy through protests, lawsuits, and other strategies and tactics.

The contemporary forms of Muslim American activism described in this chapter demonstrate the need for broader conceptions of what counts as "progressive religious activism." While raising awareness about one's religious tradition with outsiders has typically been considered proselytization, in the case of Muslims educating non-Muslims about Islam, an action that is not usually characterized as "activism" or as "progressive" might be fairly described as both. An expanded definition of "progressive religious activism" might include any public action from a marginalized group choosing to challenge its marginalization (such as attempts by Muslims to defend their civil rights during early days of the Trump administration) or could encompass efforts to build inter-ethnic and interfaith ties within religious communities themselves, since these attempts have the potential to further the cause of inclusion despite being aimed toward religious targets rather than political ones.

On the other hand, this chapter also challenges the dominant focus on conservative/progressive categorizations of religious activism, as well as the assumption that all Muslims are opposed to Trump, since some Muslims have responded to Trump not by engaging in resistance to Trump but instead by embracing his presidency. It is hard to imagine categorizing Muslim activism supporting Trump as "progressive," though it is not easily defined as an example of "conservative religious activism" either—if only because Muslims are involved, and the religious right has rarely included Muslims and, indeed, many of the religious right's leaders (such as Franklin Graham) are explicitly anti-Islam. In supporting Trump, some Muslims are challenging the conservative notion that all Muslims must believe or act the same way, troubling the waters of conservative/progressive categorizations; what Trump-supporting Muslims are doing is something in between conservative and progressive, or perhaps something best characterized as outside of the conservative–progressive continuum altogether.

The degree to which this type of action does not easily fit typical conservative/ progressive definitions is clearly related to Muslim marginalization, highlighting the ways that the actions of members of marginalized groups—immigrants, people of color, religious minorities—might be less likely to fit dominant categories of religious activism. Thus, while expanding definitions of and attention to progressive religious activism is important, this chapter also demonstrates the need to attend to and theorize a greater variety of types of religious activism, including (and perhaps especially) those types that do not easily adhere to conservative and progressive categorizations.

By providing examples of organizations and individuals engaged in a variety of responses to Trump, this chapter both sketches a picture of Muslim American activism in this era and creates an agenda for research on Muslim American activism in the coming years. In particular, some of the types of activism described here involve more risk than others. Because Muslims are already marginalized in US society, we might expect them to engage in less risky forms of activism. Indeed, the preferred form of activism does seem to be educating non-Muslims about Islam in relatively uncontentious ways. However, as this chapter has shown, some Muslims are engaging in forms of activism that carry greater risk. Specifically, the two activities that seem most likely to disrupt the societal status quo are (1) activism for social change and (2) resisting the role of defender of Islam. In the first case, the type of activism in which a person engages is related to the degree to which it is risky—more disruptive styles of protest often carry the highest risk. Thus, Muslims who sign a petition in support of the DREAM Act are facing lower levels of risk compared with Muslims who commit acts of civil disobedience in support of the DREAM Act, or who "come out" as undocumented immigrants as part of efforts to demonstrate the necessity of the DREAM Act's passage American Muslims who are not US citizens, whether they are legal permanent residents or undocumented immigrants, face especially high levels of risk when engaging in activities that might involve their arrest.[99] Thus, while it is possible that first-generation Muslim immigrants might engage in high-risk activism, it is reasonable to expect that many might restrict their responses to the Trump presidency to ones that avoid breaking the law.

Regarding the second, the decision to reject the "defender of Islam" role—to refuse to allow non-Muslims' desires and comforts to dictate how one depicts Muslims and Islam—likely involves some degree of privilege as well. Because of negative stereotypes about Muslims among the general US population and among the administration currently in power, Muslims seeking greater acceptance and social mobility may feel compelled to try to prove to people in positions of power that negative stereotypes about Muslims and Islam are not true. When a person does not feel compelled to do this—indeed, when they actively resist such a role— this likely signifies that the person has less need for the approval or acceptance of people in power; in other words, they may already have higher levels of education, decent paying work, and other economic and social resources that enable them to opt out of challenging negative stereotypes of Muslims.

Future research could examine these and other patterns to create greater understanding of whether different groups of Muslims—African American Muslims, immigrant Muslims, highly educated Muslims, etc.—are more or less likely to engage in certain kinds of activism due to their social locations. Because Muslim Americans are one of the most diverse religious groups in the United States, theologically and ethnically, studying that diversity can provide a way to understand the degree to which the choice of strategies and tactics by religious activists is shaped by theology and identity versus social location and its associated privileges.

The insights gleaned from studying Muslim activism in the United States—the varieties of religious activism, the multiple targets and tactics of religious activists, the need for a broader conception of "progressive" and "activism," the inadequacy of conservative/progressive categorizations—demonstrate the value in studying religious groups on the margins of US society. While religious and religio-racial minorities may make up smaller portions of the US population compared with white evangelicals, for instance, they often operate in ways that are different from dominant groups, yet nonetheless are relevant for understanding widespread patterns of religious action. For these and other reasons, future research on religious activism should prioritize studying groups on the religious margins.

Notes

*   This chapter originally appeared as Grace Yukich, "Muslim American Activism in the Age of Trump," *Sociology of Religion*, 79, no. 2 (Summer 2018): 220–47, https:// doi-org.proxy.lib.umich.edu/10.1093/socrel/sry004, with thanks to Oxford University Press for permission to reprint in this book. The author thanks three anonymous reviewers at *Sociology of Religion* for their helpful comments on this chapter.

1   Robert P. Jones, *The End of White Christian America* (New York: Simon and Schuster, 2016).
2   Grace Yukich, "Forum: Studying Religion in the Age of Trump," *Religion and American Culture* 27 (2017): 49–56.
3   Pew Research Center, "U.S. Muslims Concerned about Their Place in Society, but Continue to Believe in the American Dream" (Washington, DC: Pew Research Center, 2017).
4   Ibid.
5   Laurie Goodstein, "Religious Liberals Sat Out of Politics for 40 Years. Now They Want in the Game," *New York Times*, June 10, 2017, https://www.nytimes.com/2017/06/10/us/politics/politics-religion-liberal-william-barber.html. Accessed November 12, 2017.
6   Scott Malone, "'Religious Left' Emerging as U.S. Political Force in Trump Era," *Reuters*, March 27, 2017, https://www.reuters.com/article/us-usa-trump-religion/religious-left-emerging-as-u-s-political-force-in-trump-era-idUSKBN16Y114. Accessed November 12, 2017.
7   Ruth Braunstein, Todd Nicholas Fuist, and Rhys H. Williams, *Religion and Progressive Activism: New Stories About Faith and Politics* (New York: New York University Press, 2017); Sharon Erickson Nepstad, *Religion and War Resistance in the Plowshares Movement* (Cambridge: Cambridge University Press, 2008); Adam Smith, "Thousands of Muslims Protest against Isis and Terrorism in London," *Metro*, October 2, 2017, http://metro.co.uk/2017/10/02/thousands-of-muslims-protest-against-isis-and-terrorism-in-london-6971956. Accessed January 22, 2018; Robert Wuthnow and John H. Evans, eds., *The Quiet Hand of God: Faith-Based Activism and the Public Role of Mainline Protestantism* (Oakland: University of California Press, 2002); Grace Yukich, *One Family under God: Immigration Politics and Progressive Religion in America* (New York: Oxford University Press, 2013).
8   Wuthnow and Evans, eds., *The Quiet Hand of God*.
9   Grace Yukich, "Progressive Activism among Buddhists, Hindus, and Muslims in the U.S," in Branstein, et al., eds., *Religion and Progressive Activism*, 225–45, and other chapters in this volume.
10   Courtney Bender, Wendy Cadge, Peggy Levitt, and David Smilde, eds., *Religion on the Edge: De-centering and Re-centering the Sociology of Religion* (New York: Oxford University Press, 2012), 5.
11   Paul Lichterman, *Elusive Togetherness: Church Groups Trying to Bridge America's Divisions* (Princeton, NJ: Princeton University Press, 2005); Heidi Swarts, *Organizing Urban America: Secular and Faith-Based Progressive Movements* (Minneapolis, MN: University of Minnesota Press, 2008); Richard L. Wood, *Faith in Action: Religion, Race, and Democratic Organizing in America* (Chicago, IL: University of Chicago Press, 2002); Richard L. Wood, Brad Fulton, and Kathryn Partridge, *Building Bridges, Building Power: Developments in Institution-Based Community Organizing* (Longmont, CO: Interfaith Funders, 2012); Richard L. Wood and Brad R. Fulton, *A Shared Future: Faith-based Organizing for Racial Equity and Ethical Democracy* (Chicago, IL: University of Chicago Press, 2015).
12   Wood, et al., *Building Bridges*.
13   Prema Kurien, *A Place at the Multicultural Table:AU: The Development of an American Hinduism* (New Brunswick, NJ: Rutgers University Press, 2007); Vinay Lal, "The Politics of History on the Internet: Cyber-Diasporic Hinduism and the North American Hindu Diaspora," *Diaspora* 8 (1999): 137–72; Arvind Rajagopal, "Hindu

Nationalism in the United States: Changing Configurations of Political Practice,"
Ethnic and Racial Studies 23 (2000): 467–96.

14 Damien Keown, Charles S. Prebish, and Christopher Queen, eds., *Action Dharma: New Studies in Engaged Buddhism* (New York: Routledge, 2003); Sally B. King, *Socially Engaged Buddhism* (Honolulu: University of Hawaii Press, 2009); Christopher S. Queen, ed., *Engaged Buddhism in the West* (Somerville, MA: Wisdom Publications, 2000).

15 Karam Dana, Matt A. Barreto, and Kassra A. R. Oskooii, "Mosques as American Institutions: Mosque Attendance, Religiosity and Integration into the Political System among American," *Religions* 2 (2011): 504–24; Amaney Jamal, "The Political Participation and Engagement of Muslim Americans: Mosque Involvement and Group Consciousness," *American Politics Research* 33 (2005): 521–44; Pew Research Center, "U.S. Muslims."

16 Leila Ahmed, *A Quiet Revolution: The Veil's Resurgence, from the Middle East to America* (New Haven, CT: Yale University Press, 2011); Juliane Hammer, *American Muslim Women, Religious Authority, and Activism: More than a Prayer* (Austin: University of Texas Press, 2012); Pierrette Hondagneu-Sotelo, *God's Heart Has No Borders: How Religious Activists Are Working for Immigrant Rights* (Berkeley: University of California Press, 2008); Karen Leonard, "Finding Places in the Nation: Immigrant and Indigenous Muslims in America," in *Religion and Social Justice for Immigrants*, ed. Pierrette Hondagneu-Sotelo (New Brunswick, NJ: Rutgers University Press, 2007), 50–8; Erik Love, *Islamophobia and Racism in America* (New York: New York University Press, 2017).

17 Doug McAdam, *Political Process and the Development of Black Insurgency, 1930–1970* (Chicago, IL: University of Chicago Press, 1982); John D. McCarthy and Mayer N. Zald, "Resource Mobilization and Social Movements: A Partial Theory," *American Journal of Sociology* 82 (1977): 1212–41; Aldon D. Morris, *The Origins of the Civil Rights Movement: Black Communities Organizing for Change* (New York: Free Press, 1984); Christian Smith, *Resisting Reagan: The U.S. Central America Peace Movement* (Chicago, IL: University of Chicago Press, 1996); Swartz, *Organizing Urban America*; Wood, *Faith in Action*; Wuthnow and Evans, eds., *The Quiet Hand of God*.

18 Helen Rose Ebaugh and Janet Saltzman Chafetz, eds., *Religion and the New Immigrants: Continuities and Adaptations in Immigrant Congregations* (Walnut Creek, CA: Altamira Press, 2000); Kurien, *A Place at the Multicultural Table*; R. Stephen Warner and Judith G. Wittner, eds., *Gatherings in Diaspora: Religious Communities and the New Immigration* (Philadelphia, PA: Temple University Press, 1998).

19 Bender et al., *Religion on the Edge*; Hondagneu-Sotelo, *God's Heart Has No Borders*; Kurien, *A Place at the Multicultural Table*; Peggy Levitt, *God Needs No Passport: Immigrants and the Changing American Religious Landscape* (New York: New Press, 2007); Pyong Gap Min, *Preserving Ethnicity through Religion in America: Korean Protestants and Indian Hindus across Generations* (New York: New York University Press, 2010).

20 Elizabeth A. Armstrong and Mary Bernstein, "Culture, Power, and Institutions: A Multi-institutional Politics Approach to Social Movements," *Sociological Theory* 26 (2008): 74–99; Yukich, *One Family under God*.

21 Yukich, *One Family under God*.

22 Louise Cainkar, "No Longer Invisible: Arab and Muslim Exclusion after September 11," *Middle East Report* 224 (2002): 22–9; Richard Cimino, "'No God in Common': American Evangelical Discourse on Islam after 9/11," *Review of Religious Research*

47 (2005): 162–74; Lori Peek, *Behind the Backlash: Muslim Americans after 9/11* (Philadelphia, PA: Temple University Press, 2010).

23 Besheer Mohamed, *A New Estimate of the U.S. Muslim Population* (Washington, DC: Pew Research Center), http://www.pewresearch.org/fact-tank/2016/01/06/a-new-estimate-of-the-u-s-muslim-population/. Accessed May 19, 2016.

24 Pew Research Center, "The Future of World Religions: Population Growth Projections, 2010–2050," (Washington, DC: Pew Research Center, 2015).

25 Pew Research Center, "U.S. Muslims."

26 Peek, *Behind the Backlash*; Pew Research Center, "U.S. Muslims."

27 Steven Greenhouse, "Muslims Report Rising Discrimination at Work," *New York Times*, September 23, 2010, https://www.nytimes.com/2010/09/24/business/24muslim.html?pagewanted=all. Accessed March 28, 2018; Peek, *Behind the Backlash*; Pew Research Center, "U.S. Muslims."

28 Pew Research Center, "U.S. Muslims."

29 Ibid.

30 Katayoun Kishi, *Assaults against Muslims in U.S. Surpass 2001 Level* (Washington, DC: Pew Research Center).

31 Omid Safi ed., *Progressive Muslims: On Justice, Gender, and Pluralism* (Oxford: Oneworld, 2003), 3.

32 Yukich, "Progressive Activism among Buddhists, Hindus, and Muslims in the U.S." 225–45.

33 Shibley Telhami, *What Americans Really Think about Muslims and Islam* (Washington, DC: Brookings Institute, 2015), http://www.brookings.edu/blogs/markaz/posts/2015/12/09-what-americans-think-of-muslims-and-islam-telhami. Accessed May 19, 2016.

34 Christopher A. Bail, "The Fringe Effect: Civil Society Organizations and the Evolution of Media Discourse about Islam since the September 11th Attacks," *American Sociological Review* 77 (2012): 855–79.

35 Shibley Telhami, *How Trump Changed Americans' View of Islam—for the Better* (Washington, DC: Brookings Institute, 2017), https://www.brookings.edu/blog/markaz/2017/01/28/how-trump-changed-americans-view-of-islam-for-the-better/. Accessed January 20, 2018.

36 Telhami, *How Trump*.

37 Telhami, *What Americans*.

38 Michael Lipka, *How Many People of Different Faiths Do You Know?* (Washington, DC: Pew Research Center, 2014).

39 Nina Feldman, "Islam 101 Course Offers Primer for Non-Muslims," *WWNO/New Orleans Public Radio*, April 4, 2017.

40 Ibid.

41 Haroon Moghul, *How to Be a Muslim: An American Story* (Boston, MA: Beacon Press, 2017).

42 Mansura Bashir Minhas, "Get to Know the 'True Islam,'" *Miami Herald*, February 21, 2016, http://www.miamiherald.com/opinion/op-ed/article61687167.html. Accessed January 22, 2018.

43 Ibid.

44 www.trueislam.com.

45 BBC, "Who Are the Ahmadi?" May 28, 2010, http://news.bbc.co.uk.proxy.lib.umich.edu/2/hi/south_asia/8711026.stm Accessed January 22, 2018.

46 https://twitter.com/rabiasquared, January 15, 2018.

47   https://twitter.com/caveheraa, November 11, 2016.
48   Arwa Mahdawi, "The 712-Page Google Doc that Proves Muslims Do Condemn Terrorism," *The Guardian*, March 26, 2017, https://www.theguardian.com/world/shortcuts/2017/mar/26/muslims-condemn-terrorism-stats. Accessed January 22, 2018.
49   https://muslimscondemn.com.
50   The Independent, "Muslim Peace March: Hundreds Take to Cologne Streets to Protest Islamic Terrorism," *The Independent*, June 18, 2017, http://www.independent.co.uk/news/world/europe/muslim-peace-march-cologne-germany-islamist-not-with-us-isis-terror-attacks-love-for-all-hatred-for-a7795481.html. Accessed January 22, 2018; Bill Laitner, "Dearborn Rally Protests ISIS," *Detroit Free Press*, November 27, 2015, https://www.freep.com/story/news/local/michigan/wayne/2015/11/28/dearborn-muslims-against-isis/76466230/. Accessed January 22, 2018; Samuel Osborne, "Barcelona Attack: Thousands of Muslims March against Terrorism," *The Independent*, August 24, 2017, http://www.independent.co.uk/news/world/europe/barcelona-attack-muslims-march-terrrorism-protest-islamist-violence-las-ramblas-a7909611.html. Accessed January 22, 2018; Smith, "Thousands of Muslims."
51   Lorenzo Franceschi-Bicchierai, "Muslims Launch Powerful Social Media Campaign Against ISIS With #NotInMyName," *Mashable*, September 22, 2014, http://mashable.com/2014/09/22/notinmyname-muslims-anti-isis-social-media-campaign/#brLTqz5AiZq2. Accessed January 22, 2018.
52   Ibid.
53   Jaweed Kaleem, "Here's Why These Muslims Are Refusing to Criticize ISIS," *Huffington Post*, October 6, 2014, https://www.huffingtonpost.com/2014/10/06/muslims-condemn-isis-debate_n_5927772.html. Accessed January 22, 2018.
54   Ibid.
55   Kaleem, "Here's Why."
56   Chantal Da Silva, "Cologne Rally: As Many as 10,000 Muslims to Protest Islamic Extremism," *The Independent*, June 16, 2017, http://www.independent.co.uk/news/world/europe/cologne-rally-muslims-protest-islamic-extremism-germany-terror-attacks-uk-nichtmituns-not-with-us-a7792876.html. Accessed January 22, 2018.
57   Dalia Mogahed, "Don't Ask Muslims to Condemn Terror: Our Outrage at Atrocities Ought to Be a Given," *New York Daily News*, May 24, 2017, http://www.nydailynews.com/opinion/don-muslims-condemn-terror-article-1.3193126. Accessed January 22, 2018.
58   Ibid.
59   Antonia Blumberg, "#Muslim Apologies Highlights the Absurdity of Blaming an Entire Religion for Actions of Few," *Huffington Post*, September 24, 2014, https://www.huffingtonpost.com/2014/09/24/muslim-apologies-hashtag_n_5874840.html. Accessed January 22, 2018.
60   Ibid.
61   Ibid.
62   Safi ed., *Progressive Muslim*.
63   Ihsan Bagby, *The American Mosque 2011* (Washington, DC: Council on American-Islamic Relations, 2012).
64   Dawn-Marie Gibson, *A History of the Nation of Islam: Race, Islam, and the Quest for Freedom* (Santa Barbara, CA: Praeger, 2012).
65   Zeba Khan, "American Muslims have a Race Problem," *Aljazeera America*, June 16, 2015, http://america.aljazeera.com/opinions/2015/6/american-muslims-have-a-race-problem.html. Accessed January 22, 2018.

66 Margari Hill, "Islamophobia and Black American Muslims," *Huffington Post*, December 15, 2015, https://www.huffingtonpost.com/margari-hill/islamophobia-and-black-am_b_8785814.html. Accessed January 22, 2018.

67 http://www.muslimarc.org/about/. Accessed January 23, 2018.

68 Bloomberg, "#Muslim Apologies."

69 http://www.townhalldialogue.com/race-in-a-muslim-space.html. Accessed January 22, 2018.

70 For interfaith dialogue, see Kate McCarthy, *Interfaith Encounters in America* (New Brunswick, NJ: Rutgers University Press, 2007). For interfaith organizing, see Wood and Fulton, *Building Bridges*; Grace Yukich and Ruth Braunstein, "Encounters at the Religious Edge: Variation in Religious Expression across Interfaith Advocacy and Social Movement Settings," *Journal for the Scientific Study of Religion* 53 (2014): 791–807.

71 Heidi Stevens, "Non-Muslims Vow to Add Their Names to a Muslim Registry. Would That Help or Harm?" *Chicago Tribune*, November 22, 2016, http://www.chicagotribune.com.proxy.lib.umich.edu/lifestyles/stevens/ct-ways-to-combat-islamophobia-balancing-1122-20161122-column.html. Accessed January 22, 2018.

72 Islamic Society of North America (ISNA), "Clarification: ISNA and the Muslim-Jewish Advisory Council," November 18, 2016, http://www.isna.net/clarification-isna-and-the-muslim-jewish-advisory-council/. Accessed January 22, 2018.

73 http://www.muslimjewishadvocacy.org/about-us/. Accessed January 22, 2018.

74 Love, *Islamophobia*.

75 Jose A. DelReal, "Trump Campaign Staff Deletes Mention of Muslim Ban from Website," *Chicago Tribune*, November 10, 2016, http://www.chicagotribune.com.proxy.lib.umich.edu/news/nationworld/politics/ct-trump-muslim-ban-20161110-story.html. Accessed January 22, 2018.

76 Robert P. Jones, Daniel Cox, E. J. Dionne, Jr., William A. Galston, Betsy Cooper, and Rachel Lienesch. *How Immigration and Concerns about Cultural Changes Are Shaping the 2016 Election* (Washington, DC: PRRI/Brookings, 2016).

77 Presidential Documents, "Executive Order 13769 of January 27, 2017," *Federal Register* 82 (2017): 8977–82.

78 Theo Ellin Ballew, "The Man Trying to Turn Mosques into Places of Sanctuary," *Ozy*, February 7, 2017, http://www.ozy.com/rising-stars/the-man-trying-to-turn-mosques-into-places-of-sanctuary/75559. Accessed January 22, 2018; Lauren Gambino, Sabrina Siddiqui, Paul Owen, and Edward Helmore, "Thousands Protest against Trump Travel Ban in Cities and Airports Nationwide," *The Guardian*, January 29, 2017, https://www.theguardian.com/us-news/2017/jan/29/protest-trump-travel-ban-muslims-airports. Accessed January 22, 2018.

79 http://cair.com/press-center/press-releases/14647-cair-says-trump-s-new-muslim-ban-order-is-part-of-ugly-white-supremacist-agenda.html. Accessed January 22, 2018.

80 Seyyed Hossein Nasr, *Islam: Religion, History, and Civilization* (New York: HarperOne, 2003).

81 Nancy J Davis and Robert V. Robinson, *Claiming Society for God: Religious Movements & Social Welfare* (Bloomington: Indiana University Press, 2012).

82 https://www.launchgood.com/about-us#!/. Accessed January 22, 2018.

83 https://www.cair.com/press-center/action-alerts/14561-cair-action-alert-call-white-house-today-protect-daca-support-dreamers.html. Accessed January 22, 2018.

84 Yukich, *One Family under God*.

85 Ballew, "The Man."

86 Ibid.

87 Council on American-Islamic Relations (CAIR), "For the Record: CAIR Releases Results of Presidential Election Exit Poll," 2016, https://www.cair.com/press-center/press-releases/13909-for-the-record-cair-releases-results-of-presidential-election-exit-poll.html. Accessed March 28, 2018.

88 Abigail Hauslohner, "Meet the Muslim Guy Who Took the Convention Stage and Prayed for Trump," *Washington Post*, July 19, 2016, https://www-washingtonpost-com.proxy.lib.umich.edu/news/post-politics/wp/2016/07/19/meet-the-muslim-with-an-unusual-record-praying-in-arabic-at-the-rnc-tonight/?utm_term=.e839e49ac714. Accessed January 19, 2018.

89 Casey Tolan, "Meet the Muslims Who Are Supporting Donald Trump," *Splinter*, April 12, 2016, https://splinternews.com/meet-the-muslims-who-are-supporting-donald-trump-1793856118. Accessed January 19, 2018.

90 Ibid.

91 Manya Brachear Pashman, "Muslims for Trump Speak Up amid Criticism," *Chicago Tribune*, July 20, 2016, http://www.chicagotribune.com.proxy.lib.umich.edu/news/ct-illinois-muslims-for-trump-met-20160720-story.html. Accessed January 19, 2018.

92 Rebecca A. Karam, *Muslims for American Progress* (Washington, DC: Institute for Social Policy and Understanding, 2017).

93 Pew Research Center, "U.S. Muslims."

94 Ibid.

95 Ibid.

96 Jacob Westfall, Leaf Van Boven, John R. Chambers, and Charles M. Judd, "Perceiving Political Polarization in the United States: Party Identity Strength and Attitude Extremity Exacerbate the Perceived Partisan Divide," *Perspectives on Psychological Science* 10 (2015): 145–58.

97 Asra Q. Nomani, "I'm a Muslim, a Woman and an Immigrant. I Voted for Trump," *Washington Post*, November 10, 2016, https://www-washingtonpost-com.proxy.lib.umich.edu/news/global-opinions/wp/2016/11/10/im-a-muslim-a-woman-and-an-immigrant-i-voted-for-trump/?utm_term=.36ea02c9e80e. Accessed January 22, 2018.

98 Jack Moore, "Trump Really Is 'Bombing the Shit' Out of ISIS Just Like He Promised," *Newsweek*, September 14, 2017. http://www.newsweek.com/trump-really-bombingshit-out-isis-just-he-promised-664844. Accessed January 19, 2017.

99 William A Gamson, *The Strategy of Social Protest* (Homewood, IL: Dorsey Press, 1975); McAdam, *Political Process*.

CONTRIBUTORS

Asma Afsaruddin is Professor in the of Middle Eastern Languages and Cultures Department in the Hamilton Lugar School of Global and International Studies at Indiana University, Bloomington. She is author most recently of *Contemporary Issues in Islam* (Edinburgh University Press, 2015) and *Striving in the Path of God: Jihad and Martyrdom in Islamic Thought* (Oxford University Press, 2013).

Juan Cole is the Richard P. Mitchell Collegiate Professor of History at the University of Michigan. Among his recent books are *The Ruba`iyat of Omar Khayyam: A New Translation from the Persian* (IB Tauris, 2020), *Muhammad: Prophet of Peace amid the Clash of Empires* (Bold Type, 2018), and *The New Arabs: How the Millennial Generation Is Changing the Middle East* (Simon and Schuster, 2014).

Sherman Jackson is King Faisal Chair in Islamic Thought and Culture, Distinguished Professor of Religion and Professor of American Studies and Ethnicity at the University of Southern California. Among his recent books are *Sufism for Non-Sufis? Ibn 'Atâ' Allâh al-Sakandarî's Tâj al-'Arûs* (Oxford University Press, 2012), *Islam and the Problem of Black Suffering* (Oxford University Press, 2009), and *Initiative to Stop the Violence: Sadat's Assassins and the Renunciation of Political Violence* (Yale University Press, 2015).

Mohammad Hassan Khalil is Professor of Religious Studies, Director of the Muslim Studies Program, and Adjunct Professor in the College of Law at Michigan State University. He is the author of *Jihad, Radicalism, and the New Atheism* (Cambridge University Press, 2018) and *Islam and the Fate of Others: The Salvation Question* (Oxford University Press, 2012), and the editor of *Between Heaven and Hell: Islam, Salvation, and the Fate of Others* (Oxford University Press, 2013) and *Muslims and US Politics Today: A Defining Moment* (ILEX/Harvard University Press, 2019).

Alexander Knysh is Professor of Islamic Studies at the University of Michigan and Director of an Islamic studies program at the St. Petersburg State University, Russia. He has numerous publications in the field of Islamic studies, including twelve books. He serves as sectional editor for "Sufism" of the *Encyclopedia of*

Islam, Third Edition (Leiden and Boston: E.J. Brill) and is Executive Editor of the E.J. Brill *Handbooks of Islamic Mysticism* book series.

A. Rashied Omar is Research Scholar of Islamic Studies and Peacebuilding in the Keough School of Public Affairs at Notre Dame. He is co-author with David Chidester et al. of *Religion in Public Education: Options for a New South Africa* (UCT Press, 1994), a contributor to the *Oxford Handbook of Religion, Conflict and Peacebuilding* (Oxford University Press, 2015), and a contributor to the *Encyclopedia of Islam and the Muslim World* (Macmillan Reference USA, 2016).

James L. Rowell is Associate Professor of Religion in the Humanities Department at Flagler College. His interests lie at the cross-section of religion, politics, and morality. He has done work on religion and violence, inequality, science and religion, and many topics of religion, politics, and society. He also appreciates the connection of religion and creativity through film and fiction. He is author of *Making Sense of the Sacred* (Fortress Press, 2021), articles on religion, peace, and violence as well as *Gandhi and Bin Laden: Religion at the Extremes* (University Press of America, 2009).

Zilka Spahić Šiljak is Associate Professor on the Faculty of Philosophy at the University of Zenica in Bosnia and Herzegovina and also Associate Lecturer at the University of Roehampton in London. She serves as the program director of the Transcultural Psychosocial Educational (TPO) Foundation in Sarajevo. The author of numerous books published in Bosnia and Herzegovina, she holds a master's degree in human rights and democracy, jointly conferred by the University of Bologna and the University of Sarajevo, and a PhD in gender studies from the University of Novi Sad. As a research scholar and public intellectual, Šiljak also draws upon more than a decade of experience in the higher education and nongovernmental sectors in Bosnia and Herzegovina. Šiljak's research and activism focuses on the nexus of human rights, religion, politics, education, gender, and peacebuilding.

Elizabeth F. Thompson is Professor of History and Mohamed S. Farsi Chair of Islamic Peace, School of International Service, American University. She is author of *How the West Stole Democracy from the Arabs: The Syrian Arab Congress and the Destruction of Its Historic Liberal-Islamic Alliance* (Atlantic Monthly Press, 2020) and *Justice Interrupted: The Struggle for Constitutional Government in the Middle East* (Harvard University Press, 2013).

Rudolph Ware is Associate Professor of History at the University of California Santa Barbara and author of *The Walking Qur'an: Islamic Education, Embodied Knowledge, and History in West Africa* (University of North Carolina Press, 2014) and co-author of *Jihad of the Pen: The Sufi Literature of West Africa* (American University of Cairo Press, 2018).

Grace Yukich is Professor of Sociology at Quinnipiac University, with expertise in religion, immigration, race, social movements, and culture. Her most recent book, co-edited with Penny Edgell, is *Religion Is Raced: Understanding American Religion in the Twenty-First Century* (NYU Press, 2020). It calls on sociologists, religious studies scholars, pollsters, and journalists to recognize the inextricability of religion and race in the United States. Her first book, *One Family Under God: Immigration Politics and Progressive Religion in America* (Oxford, 2013), chronicles religious activists offering sanctuary in houses of worship, working both for immigration reform and for a more progressive, global vision of what it means to be religious in America.

SUBJECT INDEX

Abbasid caliphate 3, 25, 38, 41, 44 n.21, 143
'Abduh, Muhammad 7, 93, 105, 109, 113, 115 n.52
Abdul-Malik, Johari 181
Abi Rawwad, 'Abd al-'Aziz b. 51
abrogation (*naskh*) 44 n.21, 45 n.23
Abu 'Imran al-Juni. *See* Azdi, 'Abd al-Malik b. Habib al-
Abu-Nimer, Mohamed, *Nonviolence and Peacebuilding Islam* 18
Afghanistan 4, 119, 139, 190
Africa 6
    African American Muslims 10, 183–5, 193
    North Africa 75
    South Africa 1, 14, 76
    sub-Saharan 75
    West Africa 1, 75–7, 80, 83, 85, 87
Afsaruddin, Asma 3, 5, 25, 45 n.21
Ahmadiyya Muslim Community 179
Ahmadu Bamba Mbacke 5–6, 75–6, 80–1
    aphorism of Ibn Maslama 84
    Arabic Literature of Africa series 77
    commemoration of (in Touba) 78, 85
    imprisonment of 85
    and nonviolence 82
    poetry by 82
    and Prophet Muhammad 78–9, 81, 84–5
Ahmed, Saba 189
'A'isha 58
Alcmaeon of Croton 36
'Ali b. Abi Talib 50
Ali Haydar 92
Allah 25, 33, 94, 126–7, 187–8. *See also* God; Jesus
Ambrose of Milan 5, 43
American Jewish Council (AJC) 186

anti-colonial movements 16–17, 37
anti-Muslim 7, 172, 175, 177–8, 180–1, 183–4, 186, 189, 191–2
apartheid in South Africa 14
Appleby, R. Scott 15, 19, 156
    and peacebuilding 157
Arab American Anti-Discrimination Committee 186
'Arabi, Muhyi al-Din Ibn al- 5
Arab–Israeli conflict 4, 140
Arab Revolt 6, 94–5
Arberry, Arthur 31
archeology/excavation
    on churches 3
    in Tiberias 3
Arians 106, 113 n.10
Armenians 4, 89, 92–4
asceticism-mysticism 68–70
Athanasios of Alexandria 38, 43
'Attar, Farid al-Din 68
Augustine of Hippo 2, 5, 38, 43
authoritarian personality 146
autocracy 145–6
Awad, Mubarak 129
Azad, Abul Kalam 8
Azdi, 'Abd al-Malik b. Habib al- 61 n.18

Babou, Cheikh Anta, *Fighting the greater jihad: Amadu Bamba and the founding of the Muridiyya of Senegal, 1853–1913* 79–80
Badr 6, 78–9, 83
    Battle of Badr 6, 38, 79
    people of 78–9, 81–2, 84
Badshah Khan (King of Khans). *See* Ghaffar Khan, Abdul
Baghdadi, Abu Bakr al- 148
Balkan Wars (1912–13) 92

Banna, Hasan al- 100–1
Bannon, Steve 177, 181
Banu Hashim 35
Banu Muttalib 35
Bashi, Anwer 178–9
Basri, al-Hasan al- 50
The Bee group 9, 155
Berger, P. L., *The Sacred Canopy: Elements of a Sociological Theory of Religion* 151 n.28
Bernays, Edward 149 n.4
Bibliothèque Nationale (French national library) 79
bin Laden, Osama 19, 125, 130 n.44, 139
Bistami, Abu Yazid al- 65
Black Lives Matter movement 189
Bosnia and Herzegovina 9–10, 158–9, 163
    civil war in 8–9, 154
    interethnic/interreligious 153
    leadership 166
    post-war 153–4, 168
    women in (*see* women in peacebuilding)
Bridging the Divide: Religion, Race, and Politics convention 184
Britain/British 7, 80, 90, 94, 97–8, 101, 118
    British India 7, 56, 117
    and Ghaffar Khan 57–8
    Gandhi's boycott of 149 n.3
    racism 118, 125
    and Rida 95–6
Buddhism/Buddhist 20, 114 n.20, 174
    nirvana 65
Bukhari, al- 58, 61 n.36
Bush, George W. 10, 182, 189
Byzantium/Byzantines 143–4

Calvinism 69
Campos, Michelle, *Ottoman Brothers* 92
Chaudry, Rabia 179
Chidester, David 14
China 90, 139
Christian/Christianity 1–2, 5–7, 9, 20, 33, 35, 37, 40, 43, 45 n.24, 80, 92, 94–5, 97, 99–101, 105–6, 108, 111, 117, 119, 121, 125–7, 129, 151 n.28, 173–5, 185, 187
    African American 173
    archeology of churches 3

Armenian 92–3
The Bible 2, 44 n.13, 117, 149 n.6, 162
Byzantine 2, 103
Croat Catholics 9, 156
Didache/Didascalia Apostolorum 33, 42
European 91
fundamentalism 149 n.6
Gnostic 65
good deeds of 34
Hebrew Bible 31
Orthodox 156
peace studies 2
Syrian 93
and wars 4
white evangelical 171–3, 193
civilization 138
    and culture 144–5
    human 113, 143
Civil Rights Movement 171, 173
civil society organizations 9, 15, 153–5, 160. *See also specific organizations*
Clark, Janine Natalya 156
Clement of Alexandria 65
Clinton, Hillary 189, 191
coercion 133
Coles, Robert 164
Communism 9
compassion 14–17, 19–20, 22 nn.12–13, 24, 30, 156, 161, 167–8
Constantinople 92, 95
Cook, David, *Understanding Jihad* 61 n.22
Corrie, Rachel, killing of 129
corruption (*fisq*) 89, 111
Council on American-Islamic Relations (CAIR) 177, 186–7, 189
Crone, Patricia 46 n.37
Crossan, John Dominic 37, 40
Cytryn-Silverman, Katia 3

Damaghani, al- 66
Decosterd, Mary Lou 165–6
Dedović, Sehija 9, 155, 158–62, 164, 166–8
deeds (*a'mal*) 53. *See also specific deeds*
disorder, commission of (*fasad*) 30, 59
Donner, Fred 2, 34
Drame, Fode 83
DREAM Act 192

Easwaran, Eknath 118, 128
Egypt 90–1, 95, 98, 100, 137, 139, 141–2, 144
Wafd party (Cairo) 101
Egyptian Jihad Incorporated (*Tanzim al-Jihad al-Misri*) 136
Emerson, Steven, *American Jihad: The Terrorists among Us* 21 n.1
emigrant (*al-muhajir*) 54, 61 n.36
England 94
Esposito, John, *Unholy War: Terror in the Name of Islam* 19
ethnic (ethnicity)/national identity 40, 42, 153–6, 181–2, 185, 188
Europe/European(s) 2, 80, 90–3, 95–7, 99–100, 110, 113, 145, 154
European Council 9
and German 89
materialism 94, 97
slave-traders 5
war/warfare 4, 94
evil 54–5, 126, 152 n.53
evil deeds (*al-sayyi'a*) 5, 23, 32–4, 130 n.42 (*see also* good deeds (*al-hasana*))
evildoers 31, 33, 115 n.49
Hell (evil destination) 109, 112, 114 n.35
violence as 148
exegeses/exegetes 3, 33, 37, 45 n.23, 48
of *sabr* 48–50
extremism/extremists 1, 13, 18–20, 148–9, 156

Facebook 180. *See also* Twitter
faith (*al-iman*) 50, 53, 55, 57, 122, 127–8, 154–6, 160–3
altruism (*ihsan*) 87
complete (*al-iman al-kamil*) 111
faith-based organizations 9, 155, 158–9 (*see also specific organizations*)
liquid (*sa'il*) 86–7
solid (*sulb*) 86–7
true (*sidq al-iman*) 105
Faraj, Muhammad 'Abd al-Salam 136
al-Faridah al-gha'ibah (*The Neglected Duty*) 150 n.9
fatwa 92–3, 110, 148
feminism/femininity 158, 165. *See also* gender; women in peacebuilding
feminist leadership style 166, 168

fiqh al-waqi' (jurisprudence of factual reality) 137
First World War 6, 92, 99. *See also* Second World War
fitna 93, 96
Fodio, Usman Dan 79
France 6, 95, 97–8
French occupation 83
Great Powers at Paris 91, 96
Freedom of Religion and the Legal Position of Churches and Religious Communities (2004) 160–1
Fromkin, David 90–1
Frontier Gandhi. *See* Ghaffar Khan, Abdul
Fukuyama, Francis, *The End of History* 136
fundamentalism/fundamentalist 7–8, 134–6, 145–8
Christian 149 n.6
Muslim fundamentalist critique 136–40

Galtung, Johan 4, 9, 14, 21 n.6
Gama 'ah al-Islamiyya al-/Islamic Grouping 8, 140, 148, 150 n.7
assassination by (the attempt succeeded) 136
Correcting Misunderstandings (*Silsilat tashih al-mafahim*) 137
and Egyptian government 137
Initiative to Stop the Violence 137, 139–41, 147
Istratijiyah wa Tafj'irat al-Qa'idah: al-Akhta' wa al- Akhtar (*Al-Qa'idah's Strategy and Bombings: Mistakes and Dangers*) 139
and violence 137–9, 147
Gandhi, Mohandas K. 1, 7–8, 117–20, 122–5, 127, 129
ahimsa (nonviolence) 120, 123, 128 (*see also* nonviolence)
assassination of 124, 128
boycott of British cotton 149 n.3
and Ghaffar Khan 117–21, 124–6, 128
King Jr. on 121
and Pathans 118, 123
and religion 120
gender 9, 40, 42, 154, 158, 163, 167–8, 173, 176, 183. *See also* sexism; women in peacebuilding

genocide 4, 92, 154
Gentile 33, 40–2
George, Lloyd 102 n.28
Germany/Germans 6, 94, 97, 180, 182
    Berlin 100
    and Europe 89
Ghaffar Khan, Abdul 7–8, 48, 56–7, 130
    n.44
    against *badal*/blood-feud honor code
        118–19
    biographies of 130 n.21
    against British racism 118
    dhimmi 117, 119, 121, 126
    early life 117
    and (inspiration by) Gandhi 117–21,
        124–6
    legacy of 128–9
    Nehru on 123
    and nonviolence 117–20, 123–5, 127–8
    Pathans
        conversion to nonviolence 122–4,
            128
        education for 118
    and Prophet Muhammad 117–18, 121,
        125
    and Qur'an 127
    and religion 120–2, 127
    and Reverend Wigram 118, 122
Ghazali, Abu Hamid al- 48, 53, 107, 115 n.45
    Faysal al-tafriqa 103
    Gospel (al-Injil) 55
    Ihya ulum al-din (The Revival of the
        Religious Sciences) 52
    al-Mustasfa 104
    on non-Muslims (fourth category)
        103–4, 107–8
    on patience 53–5
    vs. Rida 111–13
    way-stations (*maqam*) 53–4
Ghazzali, Muhammad al- 5, 7, 65, 68, 70–1
    "The Revivification of Religious
        Disciplines" (*Ihya' 'ulum al-din*) 64,
        68–9
God 2, 7, 16, 25–30, 32, 35–40, 42, 54, 79,
    103, 111–12, 113 n.10, 120, 125–7,
    138, 156, 158, 162. *See also* Allah;
    Jesus
    address to Muhammad 35
    al-islam 105–6

Allahu Akbar 33
believers of 26, 28, 30–4, 36, 39, 41, 51,
    58, 105, 161
    Creation 85
    desires of 65
    love of 85
    mercy of 103–5
    obey/obedience to 47, 49, 51, 66, 85
    and pagans 32
    rewards of patience 26, 32, 34, 47–51
    Rida and religion of 105–7
    and Sufism 64–5, 67–70
    tariq/tariqa 64
    trust in 38, 50, 64–5, 72 n.13
    against violence 59
    unbelievers 58, 104, 111, 114 n.35,
        126–7
good deeds (*al-hasana*) 33–5, 41–2, 49,
    126, 130 n.42. *See also* evil, evil
    deeds (*al-sayyi'a*)
Gospel of Matthew 42
Graham, Franklin 192
Gülen, Fethullah 71

Habib, Kamal al-Sa'id 136
hadarah islamiyah 144
hadith 16–17, 50–3, 59, 61 n.34, 61 n.36,
    65–6, 77, 83, 86, 162
    of Gabriel 86
Hanbal, Ahmad b. 58, 61 n.36
Hanifs 108
Hijaz, West Arabia 41–2, 95
Hill, Margari 184
Hindu/Hinduism 2, 20, 121, 127, 129,
    174
    Bhagavad-Gita 2
hizmet movement 71
holy war 38, 47, 92
hudud (prescribed punishments) 145
human beings 10, 14, 57, 75, 77, 85, 87,
    109–11, 121, 123, 148, 158, 160–2,
    165, 188
humanity 20, 48, 76, 80, 85–6, 96, 99–100,
    104, 111–12, 115 n.50, 120–1, 138
humility 28, 30, 50, 94
Huntington, Samuel P., *The Clash of
    Civilizations and the Remaking of
    the World* 136
Hussein, Sharif 6, 92, 94–5

Ibn ʿAbbas 33, 53, 61 n.34
Ibn Abi al-Dunya 48
    faḍaʾil al-sabr (virtues of patience) 51
    and patient forbearance 50–2
    al-Sabr wa-"l-thawab ʿalayhi (patience
    and the rewards for it) 50
Ibn ʿAjiba 70
Ibn ʿArabi, Muhyi al-Din 65–8, 79
Ibn Kathir 25
Ibn Khaldun 70, 138, 146
Ibn Zayd, ʿAbd al-Rahman 34
Ibrahim, Najih 141–8
IDEA-based leadership model 165–6
immigration/immigrants 10, 172–3,
    187–8, 192–3
    and African American Muslims 184–5
    American Muslims 176
imperialism 7, 95
India 90, 95, 98, 123–4, 128
    British India 7, 56, 117
    Hindu Vardhana dynasty of Harsha 2
    Indian National Congress 120
    The Islamic Association in 58
Inner City Muslim Action Network
    (IMAN) organization 188
international peace 7, 14, 97
Iraq 6, 92, 95, 187, 190
Isfahani, Imam al-Raghib al-, *Mufradat al-
    Qurʾan* (Vocabulary of the Qurʾan) 16
ISIS 175, 190
    critique of 140–9
Islamic Society of North America (ISNA)
    177, 186
Islamic *state*/Islamic *caliphate* 100, 136,
    142
Islamophobia 10, 13, 21 n.2
Israel 20, 128, 147, 191
Israel/Palestine conflict 186, 191

Jabhat al-Nusrah group 142
Jackson, Sherman A. 8
Jahiz, al- 104, 112
Jamaʿat al-Faydah (community of the
    flood) 76
Jamaat-i Islami (The Islamic Association)
    58
Jansen, J. J. G., *The Neglected Duty: The
    Creed of Sadat's Assassins and
    Islamic Resurgence in Egypt* 150 n.9

Jawziyya, Ibn Qayyim al- 15, 52
Jazaʾiri, Abdul-Qadir al- 79
Jerusalem 37, 92–3, 118, 191
Jesus 4, 24, 32, 34, 37, 40–1, 113 n.10, 162.
    See also Allah; God
    Sermon on the Mount 5, 23, 29, 31,
    34–5
Jesus of Nazareth 42
Jews/Jewish 2, 6–7, 20, 34, 37, 40, 43, 92,
    100, 105, 108, 111, 119, 121, 126–7,
    173–4, 176, 185–6
al-jihad al-akbar (greater struggle) 52
al-jihad al-asghar (lesser struggle) 52
al-jihad fi sabil allah (striving in the path
    of God) 47, 59
Jihad Inc. (*Tanzim al-Jihad*) 136, 151 n.27
jihad/jihadism 6, 61 n.17, 77, 83, 92, 94,
    125, 128, 130 n.44, 137–40. *See also*
    violence
    Afsaruddin's studies on 5
    greater/lesser 16
    justice 17
    as nonviolence 52–6, 58–60
        in modern period 55–6
        in pre-modern period 52–5
    personal 16
    and Qurʾan 126–8
    and *sabr* 47–8, 52
    Salif Tal on 87
Judaism 20, 106, 175
Judgment Day 107, 111–12
justice/social justice 4, 14–17, 19, 54, 93,
    96, 105, 134, 156, 176
    and peace 90–1, 97, 99
    Sawm (fasting during Ramadan) 187

Kamara, Shaykh Musa 76
    devotional poem to people of Badr
    82–3
    on jihad 83
Kane, Abdul-Qadir 80
Khalidi, ʿAbd Allah al- 61 n.34, 61 n.36
Khalil, Mohammad Hassan 7
Khan, Syed ʿAbd al-Ghaffar. *See* Ghaffar
    Khan, Abdul
Khan, Wahid al-Din 5
Khudai Khidmatgar (servants of God)
    organization 8, 56, 119, 122–5, 128
    pledges for members of 57

kindness (*ihsan*) 27, 35–7, 54, 65, 161–2
King, Martin Luther, Jr. 125, 129
    on Gandhi 121
    on nonviolence 123–4
knowledge (*ma'arif*) 40, 42, 53, 67, 160
Knysh, Alexander D. 5
Kuyumcuyan, Ohannès Pasha 93

LaunchGood organization 177, 188
Lederach, John Paul 15
legitimacy/legitimate 7, 16–17, 19–20, 24,
    43, 117, 134–5, 146, 149 n.6, 181,
    183
liberals/liberalism 7, 90–1, 93, 97–101,
    133, 148, 172, 176
Lincoln, Bruce 19
love 6, 16, 23, 57, 76–7, 85–6, 120, 122,
    126
    and human being 77
    love of enemies 23, 27, 30, 33–4, 39
    and truth 87

Mahatma Gandhi. *See* Gandhi, Mohandas
    K.
Manela, Erez 91, 96
    The Wilsonian Moment 90
Mawdudi, Abul Alaa 58
Maximos the Confessor 42
    Four Centuries on Love 35
Mbacke, Mayumuna Kabira 81
Mbacke, Sokhna Muslimatu 81
McEvoy-Levy, Siobhan 21 n.5
Mecca/Meccan period 2, 23–5, 29, 32,
    34–5, 38–9, 42–3, 46 n.37, 49, 58–9,
    94, 106, 109, 111
    nonviolence 40–1
Medina/Medina period 4, 6, 23, 31, 37–40,
    43, 44 n.9, 49, 59, 109
    just war policy 23, 38, 43
Mehmed V, Sultan 92
The Middle East 6, 20, 90–1, 100
militant Islam 2
Milosevic, Slobodan 9, 154
Minhas, Mansura Bashir, "Get to know
    the 'True Islam'" 179
minority groups 9–10, 92, 98, 115 n.49,
    134, 140, 145, 165, 173, 176, 186,
    193
modern state (*dawlah 'asriyah*) 145

Mogahed, Dalia 182
Moghul, Haroon, *How To Be a Muslim: An
    American Story* 179
monotheism/monotheist 23, 34, 37,
    45 n.24, 58, 108, 110. *See also*
    polytheism/polytheist
Mount Lebanon 92–3
Muhammad (Prophet) 2, 4, 6–8, 16–17,
    23–8, 32, 34–5, 37–8, 41–3, 53, 57,
    70, 75, 83, 86, 103–7, 109–13, 127,
    139, 144, 146–7
    address by God 35
    and Ahmadu Bamba 78–9, 81, 84–5
    and believers 2, 4, 23, 26, 28, 31–2,
    35–9, 42–3, 49
    emigration to Yathrib 37–8
    and Ghaffar Khan 117–18, 121, 125
    hadith 51, 54–5, 58, 162
    on paradise 49
    and peaceful struggle 58–9
    rahmatan lil 'alamin 16
    Treaty of al-Hudaybiyya 59
Muhasibi, al-Harith al- 63
multi-target social movement activism
    175
Muqatil ibn Sulayman 49
Muslim Anti-Racism Collaborative
    organization 184
Muslim Brotherhood 7, 89, 141
Muslim Coalition of Connecticut
    organization 188
Muslim-Jewish Advisory Council 177, 186
Muslims 1–3, 16, 47, 50, 59, 68, 80, 83,
    90–2, 94–5, 97, 99–101, 107, 127,
    129, 144, 146–7, 158, 185–6
    activism in the U.S. 174–7, 191–3
    in Africa 75, 80
    African-American Muslims 10, 184–5,
    193
    Ahmadiyya Muslim Community 179
    American Muslims/Muslim Americans
    9–10, 21 n.1, 148, 172, 175–7, 183,
    185–6, 188–9, 191
    apologize for terrorism 181–2
    Arab Muslims 2–3, 6, 147
    black Muslims 184–5
    Bosnian 9, 160
    civil rights of 186–7
    crimes against Muslims in the U.S. 176

Five Pillars 187
fundamentalism/fundamentalist
    135–40, 145
genocide 154
"getting to know you" campaigns 178
homosexuality 172, 190
mosques 3, 162, 175, 178, 183, 185, 188
organizations (websites) 177, 180
peacebuilding, proposals for 17–20
progressive 176, 183
Qur'an (*see* Qur'an/Qur'anic verses)
Shiite 142, 148
sovereignty 4, 43, 94, 99–100
Sunni 69, 148
Syrian 92–3
and Trump's presidency (*see* Trump,
    Donald, presidency of)
tweets about terrorism by 179–80
ummah 136, 140–2, 144
violent 181
and wars 3–4
in the West 141
women (*see* Women, peace (in
    peacebuilding))
Muslims Condemn website 180
Muslims for Trump group 189
mystic/mystical path 5, 16, 64

Nahla organization 155, 160, 164
Najjar, Hisham al- 141–8
    Da'ish al-Sikkin Allati Tadhbah al-Islam
    (*ISIS: The Knife That Slaughters
    Islam*) 141
Naqshband, Baha' al-Din 70
nationalism 93
Nazi Germany 128–9, 185
Near East 2–3, 41
negative peace 4, 14, 153. *See also* positive
    peace
Negus (al-Najashi) 106
Nehru, Jawaharlal 118, 122–4
New Sanctuary Movement 188
New Testament 3, 37, 41
    and Qur'an 4, 23–4, 36
Niasse, Shaykh al-Islam Ibrahim 76, 86
Nicephorus (al-Naqfur) 143
Niebuhr, Reinhold 134
    Moral Man and Immoral Society 133,
    151 n.20

Nixon, Richard, *Seize the Moment* 136
non-Judeo-Christian groups 174–5
non-Muslims 6–7, 9, 47–8, 59, 77, 92–4,
    97–9, 107, 109–13, 113 n.1, 115
    n.52, 129, 135, 139, 144, 146–7, 152
    n.53, 177, 190–3. *See also* Christian/
    Christianity; Hindu/Hinduism;
    Jews/Jewish; Judaism; Muslims
    Americans 175
    categories of 103–4, 107–8
    educating Islam (Islam 101 courses) to
        177–80, 182–3
    kuffar 114 n.35
Nonnosos 41
nonviolence 7–8, 18, 23–4, 35, 59, 75, 80,
    117, 122, 125–6, 128–9. *See also*
    Gandhi, Mohandas K.; violence
    'adam tashaddud (Abdul Ghaffar
        Khan) 56–7
    Bamba's 82
    and Ghaffar Khan 117–20, 123–4, 127–8
    jihad as 52–6, 58–60
    King Jr. on 123–4
    Meccan 40–1, 58–9
    in Muridiyya 81–2
    satyagraha 57, 125, 129

Obama, Barack 143–4, 182, 189
    kalb al-rum 142–3
Omar, Rashied 4, 30
Orientalists 1, 47, 52, 60 n.1
Ottoman Empire 6, 89, 91–6

pacifism/pacifists 2, 5, 43, 75–6, 79, 87
    human liberty 6, 76, 80
    Pathan 8
    principles of 76, 78
paganism/pagans 6, 23–6, 28, 32, 34–7,
    41–2, 44 n.21
Pakistan 18, 56–7, 117, 119, 124, 128, 190
Palestine/Palestinian 42, 92, 128–9, 191
Pandžo, Amra 9, 155, 158–62, 164, 166–8
Paris Peace Conference (1919) 6, 89–91,
    95, 99–100
Pathan/Pakhtun/Pashtun 7–8, 56, 117
    badal/blood-feud honor code 118, 122
    conversion to nonviolence 122–4, 128
    culture of 119, 122–3
    and Gandhi 118, 123

patience/forbearance (*sabr/sabara*) 5, 25, 31–3, 59–60
    Ghazali on 53–5
    human attribute (*khassiyat al-ins*) 53
    Ibn Abi al-Dunya and 50–2
    rewards of 48–50
Paul, Pope John 158
peacebuilding 13, 155
    and Appleby 157
    definition of 14–15
    just peace 15, 20
    organization (*see specific organizations*)
    peacebuilders 8, 18, 20, 157–9, 164–5, 168 (*see also specific peacebuilders*)
    peacemaking 5, 38, 60, 90
    proposals for Muslim 17–20
    and reconciliation 154, 156–7, 159–60
    religion in 154–7
    religious women and 157–63
    women in (*see* women in peacebuilding)
Peace Studies 4
    peace and peacebuilding 14–15
    religion 2
    in the United States 1
People of the Book 28, 34, 105–6, 110–11, 117, 119, 121, 126
People of the Gap 108, 110
Photios 41
Pipes, Daniel, *Militant Islam Reaches America* 21 n.1
pluralism 7, 45 n.21, 100, 176
polytheism/polytheist 28, 36, 41–2, 58. *See also* monotheism/monotheist
Pope Benedict XV 94
Pope Paul VI 16
Pope Urban II 3
positive peace 4, 9, 14–17, 153. *See also* negative peace
power 26, 42, 84, 96, 98, 138–40, 142, 145–6, 151 n.20, 166–7, 174, 193
Prince Faisal 89, 95, 98–9
progressive religious activism 171, 173, 191–2
    religious progressives 10, 172–3

al-Qa'idah 139–40
Qaradawi, Yusuf al- 140
Quraishi, Amanda 181

Qur'an/Qur'anic verses 2–5, 7–8, 10, 15, 34, 37–8, 42, 43 n.1, 47, 66, 78, 94, 103–4, 117, 126, 137, 178
    beatitudes 29–30
    bismillahir rahmanir rahim 16
    Compassionate One (*al-Rahman*) 16
    to deny (*kadhdhaba*) 25
    on dominant culture 134
    excellences of patient forbearance (*fada'il al-sabr*) 48, 53
    fighting (*qital*) 47, 52, 58
    forgive (*ighfir*) 28
    hawnan 29–30
    healing and embrace (*ta'aruf*) 20
    jabbar 28
    and jihad 126–8
    justice (*qist* and *'adl*) 15
    kindness (*ma'ruf*) 36
    lex talionis 29–32, 42
    and New Testament 4, 23–4, 36
    paradise (*al-janna*) 26, 32, 49
    to pardon (*safaha*) 28
    patience/forbearance (*see* patience/ forbearance (*sabr/sabara*))
    people of patient forbearance (*ahl al-sabr*) 49
    preachings of 23
    rahma/rahm 16
    al-sabirun 49–50
    Sitz-im-Leben 41

racism 14, 118, 181, 183–5
    American 125
    intra-Muslim 184
Rashid, Harun al- 143
Rashid Rida, Muhammad 6–7, 89, 91, 94, 103–4, 114 n.24, 115 n.45
    and 'Abduh 105
    "The Abolition of Foreign Privileges and Threat of Civil Strife" 93
    constitutionalism 99–100
    diversity (Islamic revelation of individuals) 109–11
    early life 93
    "The Future of Syria and Other Arab Countries" 97
    letter to King Farouk 100
    al-Manar magazine 89–91, 93, 95–7, 99–100, 105, 108, 110

perfect believers (*almu'minun al-kamilun*) 115 n.50

"Principles of the Great Social Revolution and Freedom of Nations" 96

public interest (*al-maslaha al-'amma*) 98

and religion of God 105–7

on Resurrection Day 89

sovereignty 90

Syrian Arab Congress 90, 97–9

Syrian Arab Kingdom 90, 98–9

Tafsir 113 n.10

Tafsir al-Manar 115 n.45

vs. Ghazali 111–13

al-Wahy al-Muhammadi (The Revelation of Muhammad) 100

"War and Peace" 94

and Wilson 90–1, 95–7

Razi, al- 49

reconciliation 4, 8, 23, 36, 38–9, 45 n.21, 154, 156–7, 159–60, 165

Red Shirts. *See* Khudai Khidmatgar (servants of God) organization

refugees 9, 94, 165, 175, 186–8

religion(s) (*al-din*) 39, 133. *See also specific religions*

conservative 25, 98, 100, 105, 172–4, 176, 190–1

discrimination 174–6, 186–7

and Gandhi 120

and Ghaffar Khan 121, 127

in peacebuilding 154–7, 160–3

religious women and 157–60

and peace studies 2

progressive 10, 148, 171–4, 176, 191

religious activism in the U.S. 171–5, 191–2

religious autocracy 146

religious duties (*al-tā'at*) 54

religious right 171–4, 192

religious seminaries 19

Rida and religion of God 105–7

sociology of (Weber) 5

and victory of Trump 171

resource mobilization approach 174

Resurrection Day 27–8

Rida on 89

Ritter, Hellmut 63

Rogers, Bobby 184

Romans 2–3, 31, 38, 40–2, 45 n.33

Rowell, James L. 7–8, 117

Rumi, Jalal al-Din 16

Russia 89, 94, 139

sacred (service of peace) 19, 41, 83, 96, 98

Sadat, Anwar al-, assassination of 136, 150 n.9

Safi, Omid, *Progressive Muslims* 183

salafism 100

Salif Tal, Tierno Bokar 76, 86–7

on jihad 87

salvation 7, 70–1, 100, 103–5, 107, 109, 111–12, 122

San Remo accord 98

Sarraj, Abu Nasr al- 5, 64, 68

"Book of the Essentials of Sufism" 66

on spiritual state of tranquility 67

satisfaction/contentment (*al-rida*) 54, 64, 67

Schmitt, Carl 7

scholarship 19, 76–7, 84, 128, 156, 174

female 80

Second World War 100, 136, 153–4, 156. *See also* First World War

self-defense (fighting) 24, 38, 47, 83, 94

sentiments 4, 27–8, 35, 38, 40, 42, 122, 144

anti-Muslim 175, 177–8, 181, 183, 186, 189–91

Serbia/Serbs/Serbians 9, 92, 165

sexism 183. *See also* gender

shari'ah (Islamic law) 135–7, 140, 145, 148

Siddiqui, Abdul Hamid, Sahih Muslim 22 n.15

Sikhs 57, 118, 121, 127

Šiljak, Zilka Spahić 8–9

sin/sinfulness 63, 111, 115 n.49, 143, 162

Sisi, 'Abd al-Fattah al- 141

slave trade, abolition of 76, 80

Small Steps organization 9, 155, 159

social media 172, 177, 180. *See also* Facebook; Twitter

social movements 2, 14, 172–4

multi-target 175

soul, human (*nafs*) 53–4, 63, 68–9

sovereignty 4, 43, 90–1, 93–5, 99–100

spiritual retreat (*khalwa*) 69, 78, 81

spiritual state (*hal*/*ahwal*) 53, 64–5, 67–8, 72 n.13

spiritual struggle (*jihad al-nafs*) 5, 16
  in pre-modern/modern periods 52–6
striver (*al-mujahid*) 55, 61 n.36
struggle, strenuous (*illa bi-juhd jahid*) 54
Sufis/Sufism 1, 10, 25, 63–6, 76, 79, 162
  asceticism-mysticism 68–71
  cultural transfers 66, 72 n.20
  Fayda Tijaniyya movement 5, 85
  internal peace 64–5, 70–1
  Murids/Muridiyya 5–6, 75, 78, 80–2
  quietude 64–5, 67, 69
  stations (*maqamat*) 64–5
  sulh-i-kul 16
  Tijani 79
  tranquility (*itmi'nan*) 64–7, 69–71
    al-'amma 66
    al-khusus 66
    khusus al-khusus 67
    al-Sarraj on spiritual state of 67
  true realities (*haqa'iq*) 68
  Truth/Ultimate Reality (*al-haqiqa/al-haqq*) 64
  and Weber 69
Suleiman, Omar 188
sultah (political power) 145
sunna 48, 59, 66, 137
Sykes, Mark 95
Sykes–Picot agreement 95
Syria 6, 90, 95, 100, 190
  Dabiq 146
  Greater Syria 92–3
  independence of 98–9
  Syrian Arab Congress 97–9
  Syrian-Arab regime 9, 89, 93, 95, 98
  Syrian Christians 93
  Syrian Muslims 92–3

Tabari, Muhammad ibn Jarir 25, 30, 32–4, 44–5 n.21, 45 n.23, 49
  on Qatada b. Di'ama 44 n.9
Taliban movement 1, 119
Tamari, Salim, *Year of the Locust* 92
Tarar, Sajid 189
tasabbur 54
terrorism/terrorists 8, 20, 21 n.1, 134, 139, 179. *See also* violence
  9/11 attacks 128, 176
  Muslim march against (Germany) 182
  Muslims apologize for 181–2

radical Islamic 190
  Trump against 188–9
  tweets about 179–80
Theissen, Gerd 23, 25–6, 40–3, 44 n.13
Thompson, Elizabeth F. 6–7
Tijani, Ahmad al- 85
tolerance 7, 75–6, 80, 87, 98
Townhall Dialogue group, Race in a Muslim Space 185
Transjordan 3
Treaty of Versailles 6, 99–100
true Islam 98, 100, 179, 183
Trump, Donald, presidency of 9–10, 192–3
  discrimination against Muslims 174–6
  Muslim ban 172, 175, 186
  Muslim's reaction to 172, 177
    civil rights of Muslims 186–7
    educating Islam to non-Muslims 177–80
    immigrant and African American Muslims 184–5
    interfaith relationships 185–6
    Muslim support for Trump 188–91
    promoting progressive Islam 183
    resistance to educator 180–3
    social justice work 187–8
  signing of Executive Order 13769 187
  white evangelical Christians in victory of 171–2
truth 51, 58–9, 61 n.36, 77, 86–7, 94, 97, 103–4, 111, 114 n.20, 125
  and God 120
  of Islam 103–4, 109–10
  truth-seekers 107–8, 110, 112
  and women 168
Turjman, Ihsan 92–3
Turks/Turkish 4, 71, 89, 92–3, 95, 97, 103
Tusi, Abu Nasr al-Sarraj al-, "Book of the Essentials of Sufism" (*Kitab al-luma' fi 'l-tasawwuf*) 64
Twitter 180. *See also* Facebook
  #BeingBlackAndMuslim 184
  #MuslimApologies 182
  #NotInMyName campaign 179–80, 182

UG Grahovo association 155
'ulama (Muslim religious scholars) 18
'Umar Tal, Al-Hajj 79

The United States 94, 139, 145, 147,
    180–1
  African-American Muslims 10, 184–5,
    193
  American Muslims/Muslim Americans
    9–10, 21 n.1, 148, 172, 175–7, 183,
    185–6, 188–9, 191
  crimes against Muslims in 176
  foreign policy 20, 191
  Muslim activism in 174–7, 191–3
  Peace Studies in academy 1
  population of Muslims in 175–6, 189
  presidency of Trump (see Trump,
    Donald, presidency of)
  religious activism in 172–5

violence 1, 4, 13, 18–19, 21 n.1, 37, 41, 47,
    59, 91, 100, 121, 127–8, 133–40,
    144–9, 179. See also jihad/jihadism;
    nonviolence; terrorism/terrorists;
    wars/warfare
  cultural 21 n.6
  direct 21 n.6
  and Gama `ah al-Islamiyya 137–40,
    147
  hate crimes 13, 176, 186–7
  of ISIS 141–2, 148
  legitimization of 20
  political 91
  structural 14–15, 21 n.6
  wanton 17, 134, 139, 141

Wahiduddin Khan, Mawlana 18, 48, 56–9
  The True Jihad: The Concept of Peace,
    Tolerance and Non-Violence 58
Ware, Rudolph T. 5–6
  The Walking Qur'an: Islamic Education,
    Embodied Knowledge and History in
    West Africa 75, 80
war on terrorism 20
Wars of Religion 138
wars/warfare 4–5, 8, 24, 38, 43, 58–9, 153.
    See also violence
  aggressive 47
  civil war 9, 154
  and women 158

Weber, Max 5
  Sociology of Religion 69
West Africa
  abolition of slave trade 76, 80
  Islamic thought of 83
  Jakhanke community 77, 80, 84
    components of 83
  Jama'at al-Faydah community in 76
  Qur'an schooling in 75
Western media 47, 60
white supremacy 85
Wilson, Woodrow 94–5, 99
  address/speech by 96, 98, 102 n.20
  Fourteen Points 6, 91, 96
  League of Nations 7, 90–1, 96, 98
  and Rashid Rida 90–1, 95–7
Wolof language 79, 81–2
Women, peace (in peacebuilding) 9,
    57, 80, 95, 140, 146, 154. See also
    feminism/femininity
  Dedović 9, 155, 158–62, 164, 166–8
  equality of 119
  and hijab 155, 160, 184
  leadership/leadership skills 163–8
  Nahla organization 155, 160, 164
  Pandžo 9, 155, 158–62, 164, 166–8
  psycho-social therapy 158
  religious 157–63
  Small Steps organization 9, 155
  Zelić 9, 155, 159–60, 162–3, 165–8

Yanez, Jenny 178–9
Ya'qubi, Shaykh Muhammad 148
The Young Turks 4, 92–3
Yugoslavia 8, 153, 156
Yukich, Grace B. 9–10

Zakah (religious tax) 187
al-Zamakhshari 49
zealots/Zealot revolution 24, 47
Zelić, Danka 9, 155, 159–60, 162–3,
    165–8
Zen Buddhism, satori/kenshō 65
Zoroastrian 2, 110, 114 n.20
Zuhdi, Karam 136, 141
Zumar, Tariq al- 151 n.27